United States C
Peacekeepers in

MW00357122

# United States Cavalry Peacekeepers in Bosnia

*An Inside Account of Operation Joint Endeavor, 1996*

MARK A. VINEY

*Foreword by* MAJOR GENERAL JOHN R. S. BATISTE,
UNITED STATES ARMY (RET.)

McFarland & Company, Inc., Publishers
*Jefferson, North Carolina, and London*

LIBRARY OF CONGRESS CATALOGUING-IN-PUBLICATION DATA

Viney, Mark A., 1968–
    United States Cavalry peacekeepers in Bosnia : an inside
account of Operation Joint Endeavor, 1996 / Mark A. Viney ;
foreword by John R. S. Batiste.
        p.      cm.
    Includes bibliographical references and index.

    ISBN 978-0-7864-6340-4
    softcover : acid free paper ∞

    1. Operation Joint Endeavor, 1995–1996.
    2. Yugoslav War, 1991–1995 — Bosnia and Hercegovina.
    3. Peacekeeping forces — Bosnia and Hercegovina.
    4. United States. Army. Cavalry, 4th Squadron, 1st.
    5. IFOR (Organization)    I. Title.
    DR1313.3.V56 2012
    949.703 — dc23                              2011051925

BRITISH LIBRARY CATALOGUING DATA ARE AVAILABLE

Front cover: Quarterhorse scout in his Bradley at Alcatraz OP,
summer 1996 (1st Infantry Division Public Affairs Office)

Front cover design by David K. Landis (Shake It Loose Graphics)

Manufactured in the United States of America

*McFarland & Company, Inc., Publishers*
   *Box 611, Jefferson, North Carolina 28640*
   *www.mcfarlandpub.com*

# TABLE OF CONTENTS

# FOREWORD

Mark Viney's account of the 1st Squadron, 4th U.S. Cavalry's experience in Bosnia in support of the IFOR mission captures the very essence of an Army in transition and the challenges of the peace enforcement mission. The squadron was an integral component of the 1st Armored Division's 2nd Brigade Combat Team in the year-long mission to enforce the terms of the Dayton Accords in a very complex region with sectarian agendas that few Americans appreciate. The soldiers of the squadron served with honor, and along with the entire Task Force Eagle team, can justifiably take credit for the success of the mission.

In reading this account, I am reminded of the American military's competence and versatility. The lessons learned during the IFOR mission would continue to serve us well during the follow-on mission in Kosovo. Perhaps most importantly, the Balkans experience reminds us all of the value of a comprehensive national strategy, and that we walk away from our military doctrine and principles of war at our own peril. Mark Viney's cavalry squadron did it right. It was an honor to serve with these great soldiers and their magnificent families.

*John R. S. Batiste, Major General, U.S. Army (Ret.), served a distinguished 31-year career in the U.S. Army. As the Senior Military Assistant to the Deputy Secretary of Defense in 2001–02, he was involved in the early planning stages of the wars in Afghanistan and Iraq. Retired in 2005, he is now president and CEO of Klein Steel in Rochester, New York.*

# PREFACE

"I don't think we could have done what we are doing in Iraq and
Afghanistan without having done what we did in Bosnia first." —
General George Casey, Chief of Staff of the Army, 2009

The United States Army released *Field Manual 3-07, Stability Operations*,
in October 2008. In its foreword, Lieutenant General William B. Caldwell
IV characterizes the current era of uncertainty and persistent conflict as a time
in which the lines separating war and peace, friend and foe, have blurred and
no longer conform to the clear delineations that we once understood. Military
success alone will no longer suffice to prevail in today's environment. The
challenges before us require strengthening the capacity of other elements of
national power, leveraging the full potential of our interagency partners.

In today's complicated global security climate, the achievement of victory
will assume new dimensions as the United States strengthens its ability to
generate "soft" power to promote participation in government, spur economic
development, and address the root causes of conflict among disenfranchised
populations of the world. At the heart of this effort is a comprehensive
approach to stability operations that integrates the tools of statecraft with our
military forces, international partners, humanitarian organizations, and the
private sector.

This comprehensive approach postures the U.S. military to perform a
role common throughout our history, that of ensuring the safety and security
of local populations, assisting reconstruction, and providing basic sustenance
and public services. Of equal importance, it defines the role of military forces
in support of civilian agencies charged with leading these complex endeavors.

*FM 3-07* further points out that during America's relatively short history,
our military forces have engaged in only eleven wars considered conventional.

1

Spanning from the American Revolution through Operation Iraqi Freedom, these wars constituted significant or perceived threats to our national security interests, where the political risk to our nation was always gravest. These were the wars for which our military forces traditionally prepared to fight. These were the wars that endangered our American way of life. Of the hundreds of other military operations conducted in the intervening years, most are now categorized as stability operations, in which the preponderance of effort was toward stability tasks. Contrary to popular conception, the military history of the United States is characterized by stability operations punctuated by distinct episodes of major combat.

Following the end of the Cold War, the U.S. Army began to reduce its force structure with the expectation of reaping the benefits of a new era of peace. However, this "peace dividend" was not to be realized. The strategic environment evolved from one characterized by the bipolar nature of the relationship between the world's dominant powers to one of shared responsibility across the international community. In the decade following the fall of the Berlin Wall, the U.S. Army participated in more than 15 stability operations in such places as Haiti, Liberia, Somalia, Macedonia, Bosnia, and Kosovo. Many of these operations continued into the 21st century. Together with more recent military operations in Afghanistan and Iraq, they revealed a disturbing trend throughout the world: the collapse of established governments, the rise of international terrorist and criminal networks, an apparently limitless array of humanitarian crises, and crushing poverty. The global implications of such destabilizing factors have proven monumental.

As a keystone doctrinal publication, *FM 3-07* institutionalizes the hard-won lessons of the past while charting a path for tomorrow. One of the more recent stability operations that informed this publication was Operation Joint Endeavor, conducted in Bosnia-Herzegovina in 1996.

General overviews of the decade-long American experience in Bosnia are found in such books as *Armed Peacekeepers in Bosnia* by the Combat Studies Institute and *Bosnia-Herzegovina: The U.S. Army's Role in Peace Enforcement Operations, 1995–2004* by the Center of Military History. These works are surveys focused at the strategic and operational levels on the whole of our stability operations there. What has been missing from the historical record up to this point is a tactical view of a specific Balkan stability operation.

This book answers this call as a muddy-boots perspective on the first, dramatic year of Bosnian peacekeeping. The experiences of the 1st Squadron, 4th U.S. Cavalry (Quarterhorse) in Operation Joint Endeavor are a perfect case study of how modern tactical units of the U.S. Army prepare for, conduct, and then recover from stability operations.

The unit history of this elite cavalry squadron is a reflection of our Army's experience with stability operations. Quarterhorse cavalrymen performed many stability tasks in Bosnia that would have been recognizable to their predecessors in "Bleeding Kansas," during Reconstruction, the Indian Wars, the Philippine Insurrection, during the occupation of Germany following World War II, and in Vietnam.

As the first-ever ground operation conducted by NATO and the largest military operation in Europe since World War II, Operation Joint Endeavor sought to implement a peace agreement concluding a bloody, ethnically motivated civil war in Bosnia. The operation commenced in December 1995 and was concluded twelve months later, followed immediately by Operation Joint Guard. The 900 cavalrymen of Quarterhorse and its attached units were a small but prominent portion of the international task force in Bosnia that numbered at its height over 57,000 NATO soldiers.

Quarterhorse was one of the first combat units of NATO's Implementation Force (IFOR) to enter Bosnia in early 1996. It played a pivotal role in the international effort to mend that nation still smoldering from three and a half years of brutal civil war. Despite the mountainous terrain, bad weather, tens of thousands of land mines, and the periodic threat of terrorist attack, Quarterhorse upheld the peace in one of the most challenging parts of the American sector. For its achievements, the squadron was awarded the Army Superior Unit Award. Five Quarterhorse cavalrymen further distinguished themselves through individual acts of gallantry, for which they were awarded the Soldiers Medal. I was honored to serve among such fine men.

This account is a perspective of stability operations from the battalion level within the context of the entire year of Operation Joint Endeavor. The strategic and operational threads of the operation are interwoven with the tactical to convey the multifaceted, complex nature of modern stability operations.

At the strategic level, this book outlines the Dayton Peace Accord and NATO's original intent for how IFOR would implement the military provisions of the agreement. It highlights the reluctant and problematic expansion of IFOR's mission toward providing security and logistical support to the various international and nongovernmental organizations striving towards political and humanitarian objectives in Bosnia, often with inadequate infrastructure. Also discussed are American political influences that shaped the course of Operation Joint Endeavor, namely the presidential election of 1996 and tepid public support for the operation.

At the operational level, this book illustrates how IFOR separated and contained the military forces of the Former Warring Factions (FWF), and how it secured, marked, and then guaranteed freedom of movement across the Zone of Separation surrounding the Inter-Entity Boundary Line. It also explains how IFOR deterred aggression by FWF forces; how it supported the national and municipal elections; and how IFOR assisted the training and arming of Federation military forces.

Primarily focused at the tactical level, this is a candid, balanced history of my Quarterhorse comrades in action before, during, and after our tour in Bosnia. Painting a human face on stability operations, it is organized in a generally chronological order and addresses every aspect of our experience in Bosnia, including training, sustainment activities, living conditions, and morale issues. Drawn from interviews, firsthand experiences, and contemporary media, this primary account conveys what we saw, heard, thought, and felt in 1996. History is an interpretation of events, and this is the history of Operation Joint Endeavor as we interpreted it at our squadron and troop level. The views expressed herein are those of the author and do not necessarily reflect the views of the Department of Defense or any of its agencies.

That nearly 900 Quarterhorse cavalrymen deployed to Bosnia served with such distinction for nearly a year, and returned from that hostile environment without losing a single life was truly a blessing. This book is dedicated with gratitude to the Lord.

It would never have come into being without the encouragement and assistance of my fellow Quarterhorse cavalrymen who shared my appreciation for the history we were making in Bosnia. I hope the final product lives up to their expectations. In particular, I wish to thank Captain (now Lieutenant Colonel) Scott Downey and former Staff Sergeant Thomas Daniels, both of whom served in our Squadron Intelligence Section. Both reviewed drafts of the text for accuracy and operational security, offered invaluable suggestions, and shared their photos. I am grateful to the many Quarterhorse officers and noncommissioned officers who sat for interviews. Some also provided documents that were tremendously helpful. Special thanks to Bravo Troop's Captain (now Lieutenant Colonel [Ret.]) Bob Ivy and First Lieutenant (now Lieutenant Colonel) Pat Michaelis. Both sat for several interviews and were very enthusiastic about this project. Their input was invaluable. Thanks also to CW5 (Ret.) Phil Nusbaum for his photos, plus CW5 John Roberts, and former Captain Devin Weil.

I am also grateful to Major General (Ret.) William L. Nash and Colonel (Ret.) Edward Skender for their review and comments of the draft text. Dr. Stephen A. Bourque of the Command and General Staff College was a much-valued resource and inspiration with his book, *Road to Safwan: The 1st Squadron, 4th Cavalry in the 1991 Persian Gulf War*.

Special thanks to Mr. Randy Rakers for his operational security review of the text, to Mr. Frank Martini for the maps, to Major Earl Mitchell for his legal review, and also to Captain (now Lieutenant Colonel) Rob Vasquez for his legal advice. The following members of the staff and faculty of the U.S. Army War College provided much-appreciated encouragement, advice, and technical assistance: Colonel (Ret.) Rob Dalessandro, Dr. Con Crane, Colonel (Ret.) John Agoglia, Mr. Michael Lynch, Colonel (Ret.) Kevin Weddle, Dr. Antulio Echevarria, Dr. Clayton Chun, Colonel Greg Cantwell, Major Lisa Bloom, Mrs. Louise Arnold-Friend, Ms. Kathleen Gildersleeve, Mrs. Christine Shoffner, Ms. Jeanette Moyer, Mr. Scott Finger, and Mr. John Murray.

I am especially grateful for the support of Major General (Ret.) John R.S. Batiste, one of the finest officers I have ever had the pleasure to serve with.

I cannot express thanks enough to my wife Michele for her love and patience. She and our children are my greatest pride and joy.

# 1

# THE STAGE
# FOR INTERVENTION

## *Grim Discovery*

The pair of Kiowa Warrior armed scout helicopters wove around the lush, green mountains and over the cultivated valleys east of the Bosnian city of Vlasenica. These OH-58Ds were an aerial weapons team (AWT) from the 1st Squadron, 4th U.S. Cavalry (Quarterhorse) on an aerial reconnaissance of the 2nd Brigade Combat Team sector. It was a hot day in May 1996, and the air was thick with humidity. Chief Warrant Officer Three John Roberts and his three fellow pilots from the squadron's Echo Troop had taken the doors off their aircraft so the rushing wind would keep them cool.

The Kiowa Warrior was a much-improved version of the scout helicopter flown by Quarterhorse five years earlier in Operation Desert Storm. With its advanced optics and a variety of onboard weapons, the "Fifty-eight Delta" could identify and destroy targets over eight kilometers away. On this day, however, the pilots relied upon naked eyesight to detect any signs of military violations of the Dayton agreement.

The mountains in this area were tall and densely wooded. The Kiowas flew low, only a couple of hundred feet or less above the undulating forest. A particular hilltop that looked to have been clear-cut caught the pilots' attention. CW3 Roberts banked his aircraft around for a closer look. The Kiowas made a slow pass over what appeared to be a pile of cut lumber, haphazardly strewn along a line several hundred meters long. Shuddering with the realization of what they were actually looking at, the Quarterhorse pilots brought their aircraft to a hover and grimly switched on their integrated video cameras. The debris field wasn't lumber at all, but the sun-bleached bones, clothing, and baggage of a column of 300 to 600 civilians, apparently Muslims slaugh-

7

Evidence of war crimes discovered in May 1996 near Vlasenica: a trail of bones pictured between the .50 cal machine gun and skid of an Echo Troop Kiowa Warrior (photograph: Phil Nusbaum).

tered in flight from vengeful Bosnian Serbs. Quarterhorse had made an important discovery of yet another act of ethnic cleansing that marked the brutal three-and-a-half-year Bosnian civil war.[1]

Almost seven years earlier, Communism died in several nations of the Warsaw Pact. In 1992, the ethnically diverse Socialist Federal Republic of Yugoslavia disintegrated into several hostile independent states. Macedonia, Bosnia-Herzegovina, and Croatia became their own nations. Serbia dominated the states of the rump Yugoslavia. Several republics succumbed to ethnically motivated civil war. Fighting centered in the republics of Bosnia-Herzegovina and Croatia. Serbia actively supported ethnic Serbs fighting in these republics, as well as in Slovenia. Fighting threatened to erupt in other Balkan states, and eventually did in Kosovo.

For over three years, dismayed Americans watched horrifying scenes from the Bosnian civil war on TV. Expectations were high for America, as the world's sole remaining superpower, to do something to end the carnage. Foreign policy makers struggled for the appropriate response. American interests were not readily apparent in this part of the world.

After the deadly Somalia peacekeeping debacle just two years before,

Bosnia and Herzegovina, 1995 (map: Department of History, United States Military Academy).

Americans were wary of committing troops to another forlorn nation. In that operation, the United States sent peacekeeping forces to a famine-stricken anarchist state, only to depart in haste after mission creep led to combat operations and the loss of eighteen Americans killed and nearly one hundred wounded.

Yet reports of the worst war crimes atrocities since World War II streamed out of Bosnia. The United States had to act. The United Nations had proven itself powerless to stop the Bosnians from massacring each other. European leadership proved incapable of presenting a unified, determined response. Only American diplomatic leadership and the U.S. military could mobilize NATO to stop the fighting in Bosnia.

Policymakers throughout Western Europe and the United States were well aware of the Balkans' reputation as a catalyst for major wars. The fact that a Serb assassin started the chain of events leading to the First World War did not go unnoticed. Some Western leaders voiced legitimate concern over the possibility that the Bosnian civil war could spill over into the neighboring republics of Kosovo and Macedonia. This, in turn, could provoke military conflict between other Balkan nations like Albania, Greece, Bulgaria, Romania, and Turkey. Ancient hatred and mistrust lingered just under the surface in these ethnically mixed populations. Both Ukraine and Russia held historic ties to the Serbs.

Political debate raged in Washington for many months over the proper course that American Balkan policy should take. Although senior political and military leaders eventually sanctioned the use of American aircraft over Bosnia, they remained averse to committing ground troops to the Bosnian war zone itself. Instead, America slid its foot in along the fringe by participating in the United Nations peacekeeping mission in Macedonia.

## Orders for Macedonia

Our squadron's commitment to the Balkans began in the summer of 1995, when the squadron (then designated the 3rd Squadron, 4th Cavalry, or 3-4 CAV) received orders to prepare for deployment to Macedonia in March 1996.[2] We planned to send about 300 cavalrymen to form the bulk of a 550-man task force. Our Squadron Commander, Lieutenant Colonel Constantine "Gus" Chamales, would command Task Force Able Sentry during our eight-month deployment. We would serve as part of the United Nations Preventive Deployment Force (UNPREDEP), which had been established in Macedonia back in December 1992.

"The goal of UNPREDEP is to ease tensions before they erupt into conflicts," said an officer at UNPREDEP headquarters in the Macedonian capital of Skopje. "Because there isn't a defined border between Macedonia and Serbia, UN peacekeepers ease tensions before they escalate into conflicts."[3]

Some American political leaders considered Macedonia relevant to U.S. interests because of its central location at the regional juncture of Europe,

Asia, and Africa. The precedent of spiraling Balkan war also justified the introduction of American troops to the region.

In November 1992, the president of Macedonia requested a deployment of UN peacekeepers to bolster his fledging, newly independent state. Internal tensions ran high between Albanian-Macedonians and Serbian-Macedonians. Demonstrations, although peaceful, had been accompanied by foreign intrusions along the disputed borders.[4]

Macedonia also felt tension along its southern border with Greece, which accused the new nation of stealing the name of its northern province. The nation's official name was the Former Yugoslav Republic of Macedonia, or FYROM.

Militarily, Macedonia was left almost unprotected when Yugoslavia broke up. With only 20,000 soldiers, four tanks, four airplanes, and five helicopters, Macedonia urgently needed foreign protection to emerge as its own nation.[5]

More than 40 countries participated in the UNPREDEP mission. The United States, Finland, Norway, and Indonesia provided the bulk of military manpower. Assisting this force were twenty-six civilian policemen and 131 civilian UN employees providing administrative, informational, political, and humanitarian services.

UN officials in Macedonia advised local governments on how to run democratic systems, explained foreign policy, and promoted good relations with Serbian and Bulgarian neighbors. The UN also monitored elections and collected census data from the populace.[6]

American soldiers participating in the UNPREDEP mission alternately spent twenty-one days at a time patrolling and observing a sixty-five-mile stretch of border between Macedonia, Serbia, and Bulgaria. From ten small compounds painted white with large black UN letters, Americans reported the movements of residents and potentially hostile elements.

Located about thirty miles behind the border patrol line was a command post named Uniform 60. Approximately sixty American soldiers worked there. Accessible only by helicopter and difficult mountain roads, the camp was the forward hub of American observers headquartered further back at Camp Able Sentry near Skopje.

Under LTC Chamales's command, our cavalrymen looked forward to taking our turn among other 3rd Infantry Division units already rotating through Macedonia. Our normal training for high-intensity warfare was interwoven with additional instruction in peacekeeping. One officer who had served in our squadron for three years said he'd never seen a busier time than the first half of 1995.[7]

But our orders for Macedonia were unexpectedly countermanded in late

September. Instead, we were to prepare for immediate deployment to Bosnia-Herzegovina as part of a multinational peace enforcement task force. We would deploy sometime soon after the former warring factions (FWF) concluded a peace agreement.[8] That looked to be soon, and we were thrown for a loop.

## Organization and Equipment

Operation Desert Storm demonstrated the need to make heavy division cavalry squadrons more lethal and agile. Over the ensuing four years, tanks were incorporated into the ground cavalry troops for organic lethality. A third ground troop was added for flexibility and to enable the squadron to cover larger zones more effectively. OH-58Ds were provided to the air cavalry troops as a replacement for the Vietnam-era hunter-killer teams of OH-58Cs and AH-1 Cobras.

In terms of organization and equipment, the Quarterhorse squadron of 1996 was much better suited for combat than it had been in Operation Desert Storm. It would also prove well-suited to stability operations. As the eyes and ears of the 3rd Infantry Division (later 1st Infantry Division), our cavalry squadron was institutionally geared toward fighting in unfamiliar territory and gathering intelligence. Comprising three ground cavalry troops and two air cavalry troops, the squadron was organized, equipped, and trained to operate over extended distances in order to protect our parent division. A headquarters troop and aviation support troop sustained our ability to fight.

The three ground cavalry troops — Alpha, Bravo, and Charlie Troop — were each organized with two scout platoons, two tank platoons, a heavy mortar section, a troop headquarters section, maintenance section, and a troop trains element. Our ground cavalry troops were largely self-sufficient and were capable of semi-independent operations over long distances. They were also the most heavily armed company-sized units in the U.S. Army.[9] Each was equipped with thirteen M3A2 Bradley Cavalry Fighting Vehicles (CFVs), nine M1A1 Abrams main battle tanks, two M106A2 heavy mortar carriers, and twelve various wheeled and tracked support vehicles.

The armored threat that IFOR expected to encounter in Bosnia was low, so Quarterhorse left one tank platoon from each of our ground cavalry troops at our home station in Schweinfurt, Germany, for the duration of our deployment. Small Unit Snow Vehicles (SUSVs) were issued to the ground cavalry troops for winter movement through the Bosnian mountains.

The M3A2 CFV and the infantry's BFV variant were commonly referred to as the "Bradley." This family of vehicles was named after Omar N. Bradley, the American general of World War II fame. Our CFV versions were armed with a TOW antitank missile launcher with twelve missiles, a 25mm automatic cannon, and a coaxial mounted 7.62mm machine gun. They had five-man crews. Three soldiers manned the vehicle while two scouts rode in back. When dismounted, the scouts' job was to survey and gather intelligence.

The Bradley's high profile and billowing plumes of diesel exhaust made it highly conspicuous. Our cavalrymen hated them as scout vehicles. They were too big, too loud, and their smoke signature made them too easy to detect.

Six months into our tour in Bosnia, our ground cavalry troops were issued several of the newly developed XM114 Up-Armored High Mobility Multi-Purpose Wheeled Vehicles (HMMWV). These "up-armored Humvees" were standard utility Humvees transformed into armored cars by adding an armored cab and upgraded suspensions and transmissions. The up-armored Humvee was quiet and highly mobile, so it was a step in the right direction in terms of what we wanted for our scout platoons. It had its drawbacks, though.

For one thing, the version we employed could only mount one weapon, either a .50 caliber machine gun, M60 machine gun, or Mk-19 automatic grenade launcher. The weapon was mounted above an open ring in the roof. A cavalryman manning the weapon station had to stand half exposed out of the top of the vehicle. There was no armored protection for the gunner eight feet off the ground.

The seriousness of this deficiency had already been clearly demonstrated in Somalia, where Humvee crews suffered heavy casualties as soldier after soldier was killed or wounded while manning the exposed weapon station. But it was not until after the Global War on Terrorism commenced in 2001 that armored gun shields became standard features on up-armored Humvees.

This development mirrored the initiative our predecessors had taken over thirty years earlier when Quarterhorse deployed its M113 armored personnel carriers (APCs) to Vietnam. One of its first orders of business was to jerry-rig armored shields around its vehicles' .50 caliber and 7.62mm machine guns. In Bosnia, Captain Mark Viney, the Squadron Maintenance Officer and Command Historian, suggested that we do the same thing for our up-armored Humvees. Such a task would have been easy for our mechanics. However no American IFOR soldier had yet been killed while manning a Humvee-mounted weapon, so none of our leaders had been personally confronted with the issue. CPT Viney was incredulous that his suggestion was dismissed by the Quarterhorse leadership and our ground troop commanders.

One ground troop commander replied that we had less than six months of the operation to go, and he really didn't think that the threat of ambush was very high. Considering it unwise to discount enemy intentions or capabilities, CPT Viney would have erred on the side of caution. Not all of our officers shared his concern. Some admitted that they were primarily concerned with keeping the Humvees in good condition for eventual turn-in upon our redeployment home.

(Unfortunately, CPT Viney's concern was borne out when Quarterhorse returned to the Balkans in early 1999 to patrol the Macedonia-Serbia border during Operation Allied Forge. Three cavalrymen from Bravo Troop were captured by Serbs in an ambush. When they came under heavy direct fire in their lone Humvee, the gunner did not man his machine gun. Instead of exposing himself to the enemy fire, he dropped down into the relative protection of the vehicle.[10])

Another complaint many of us had about the up-armored Humvee was its tiny side windows, which forced passengers into contortions in order to see above the horizon. We didn't complain too much, though. The Humvees were far easier to maintain than our Bradleys, and they rode much better. Senior officers liked the fact that Humvees did a lot less damage to the already poor Bosnian roads.

The M1A1 Abrams main battle tank was regarded at the time as the best tank in the world. Named for General Creighton Abrams of World War II and Vietnam War fame, it boasted superior crew protection and survivability features. The "M1," as we referred to it, mounted a 120mm smoothbore gun, coaxial mounted 7.62mm machine gun, commander's independent .50 caliber machine gun, and loader's externally mounted 7.62mm machine gun. Thus, each tank had more firepower than a light infantry company.

Our M1s contributed mightily to "force presence" in Bosnia. Their chief drawback was their requirement for constant maintenance to remain in operational condition. Tank crews spent a major portion of the operation just pulling maintenance. After the first three months, we seldom rolled the nearly 70-ton tanks out of the motor pool. They really did tear up the roads. As a result, our tankers took turns on dismounted and Humvee-mounted patrols, and also manned checkpoints and observation posts (OPs).

The M106A2-mounted M30 4.2-inch heavy mortar had been in the Quarterhorse inventory for over thirty-five years. A design first adopted in the 1950s, the "Four-Deuce" was capable of firing high explosive, white phosphorous, or illumination rounds. Our tracked mortar carriers were old and the guns themselves were even older, but the system was adequate despite being beyond its own lifetime. Our ground troop commanders enjoyed the confidence of knowing that their two organic mortars were ready to provide immediate fire support.

As Quarterhorse staged in Hungary prior to entering Bosnia, the Army threw Small Unit Snow Vehicles (SUSVs), all sorts of generators, lighting sets, and other equipment at us. Most of this stuff came without manuals, repair parts, operator training, or logistical support. Not surprisingly, most of this equipment was broken and unusable within a few months, despite the best efforts of our maintenance personnel. It remained unserviceable until we finally turned it all back in during our redeployment. That said, our ground cavalry troops enjoyed using their SUSVs while they ran. They had great mobility in the mountains during even the worst conditions of snow, mud, and ice.

Our two air cavalry troops provided depth and mobility to our operations. Delta and Echo Troop each had two aeroscout platoons. Each air cavalry troop had eight of the Army's latest armed scout helicopters, the OH-58D(I) Kiowa Warrior.[11]

Our "Kiowas" or "Fifty-eight Deltas" usually operated in pairs as aerial weapons teams (AWTs). Each air cavalry troop typically kept three teams operational at a time. Our aviators preferred night operations since darkness increased their survivability and maximized the effectiveness of the Kiowa's systems.

Quarterhorse OH-58D(I) Kiowa Warriors undergoing maintenance, Schweinfurt, Germany, fall 1995 (photograph: DoD Joint Combat Camera Center).

The Kiowa mounted two universal weapons pylons, one on each side. These pylons mounted a variety of weapons to support unique mission requirements. Available armament included a .50 caliber machine gun, a seven-shot 2.75-inch rocket pod, two Hellfire antitank missiles, and/or two Stinger air-to-air missiles.[12]

On top of the aircraft was a ball-shaped protuberance with large lenses on the front. This was the mast-mounted sight (MMS), which enabled the Kiowa to hover behind hills and trees for protection while exposing only the sight to the enemy. The MMS featured a thermal imaging sight (TIS), low-light television sensor (TVS), laser range finder/designator (LRF/D), and an 8mm videotape recorder. The mast could rotate 360 degrees.[13] The unique features of our Kiowa Warriors, helicopters far more advanced than what our squadron fielded during Operation Desert Storm, gave us an intelligence gathering capacity unavailable to any other IFOR unit.

## Preparations for Bosnia

Much was required to prepare Quarterhorse for deployment in a very short time. In early October 1995, we began an intensive sixty-nine-day training and preparation period. During the first three weeks, our ground cavalry troops practiced tactical maneuvers on Simulation Network (SIMNET), an interactive computer simulation in which units of up to troop size fight a programmed enemy. Individual tank and Bradley crews honed their gunnery skills on Unit Conduct of Fire Trainer (U/COFT) simulators. Our cavalrymen also conducted classes on mine awareness and basic individual skills.

We recognized that Quarterhorse would have to conduct a long tactical road march from Hungary into Bosnia. Every vehicle would have to make it on its own power, so our mechanics worked feverishly to bring our 219 vehicles up to operational condition. At the same time, communications personnel installed the Army's latest, most sophisticated Single Channel Ground Airborne Radios (SINCGARS) in them.

On October 20, we departed our home station in Schweinfurt for the Grafenwoehr Training Area (GTA) near the Czech border. Before training began, an informal squadron change of command ceremony was held.[14]

Despite the fact that Quarterhorse was only weeks away from deploying on a "real world" operation that entailed the very real possibility of combat, the U.S. Army decreed nonetheless that it was still time for Lieutenant Colonel Chamales to relinquish command. Squadron command was strictly a two-year assignment. In the post–Cold War era, the Army's Officer Personnel

Management System never skipped a beat, not even on the eve of the Persian Gulf War. Continuity of command was not an overriding concern.

Our squadron's collective personality reflected LTC Chamales's own: proud, loud, and aggressive. We were confident in Chamales's tactical abilities, having been led by him to "victory" over the opposing force (OPFOR) at the Hohenfels Training Area (HTA). Our cavalrymen knew what to expect from LTC Chamales and would have felt more secure following him into harm's way than some other officer whom they knew nothing about.

Replacing Chamales as Squadron Commander (SCO) was Lieutenant Colonel Anthony W. Harriman, a quirky, quiet, unassuming scholar. LTC Harriman had taught English at West Point. He was also a tactically proficient cavalry officer and would soon prove himself an effective arbitrator and negotiator.

Individual and unit peace enforcement exercises occupied most of our squadron's first week of training at GTA. During six days of intensive situational training exercises (STXs), Quarterhorse practiced checkpoint operations, patrolling procedures, and how to deal with mines.[15]

On October 28, we transitioned to our next phase of training. Our three ground cavalry troops conducted independent tactical road marches to Hohenfels. This 85-kilometer movement gave them practice with the sort of driving conditions that we expected to face upon entering Bosnia. Brigadier General James P. O'Neal, the 1st Armored Division's Assistant Division Commander for Support, observed our movement and praised Charlie Troop's road march as the best he'd ever seen.

Upon arrival at Hohenfels, training began immediately. The ground cavalry troops conducted more checkpoint and mine awareness lanes. We were taught how to deal with the press and local nationals. We also rehearsed procedures for establishing lodgment areas. Quarterhorse then moved "into the box" for tactical maneuver training. The stability tasks that we would conduct in Bosnia were interwoven with simulated combat operations against enemy motorized rifle battalions (MRBs) replicated by the OPFOR. Several American reporters used footage of our training in their stories of American preparations for the imminent Bosnian operation.[16]

Quarterhorse then returned to Grafenwoehr, where our tank and Bradley crews fired gunnery qualification tables. We arrived back in Schweinfurt just in time to spend Thanksgiving Day with our families.

A week then followed during which we cleaned and repaired our vehicles and equipment. We continued our individual skills training while vehicles were prepared for rail movement. We were issued cold weather clothing, and loaded shipping containers with gear.[17] It was tedious, non-stop work preparing the squadron for deployment.

Meanwhile, back in the States, our three detached air cavalry troops concluded an accelerated fielding program with their new OH-58D(I) Kiowa Warrior scout helicopters. They had been detached from the squadron back on April 28, and were temporarily based at Fort Hood, Texas.

Between November 15 and December 2, our air cavalry troops moved en masse to Schweinfurt. Delta, Echo, and Fox Troops brought all of their equipment and 40 percent of Headquarters Troop with them. In all, the move involved nearly 400 cavalrymen and 250 family members.

Since our air cavalry troops would soon deploy to Bosnia with the rest of the squadron, prior arrangements had been made to reserve housing for their families to occupy upon arrival. We completed many administrative matters en masse, such as issuing German driver's licenses to spouses, as well. Our air cavalrymen had very little time to get their families settled in before the year-long operation began. Needless to say, the stress level in these families ran very high, especially for the younger and newly-married enlisted wives.

While our air cavalry troops were at Fort Hood, they were designated as the 1st Squadron, 4th U.S. Cavalry in anticipation of a series of unit redesignations that would occur throughout the Army over the upcoming months. The senior aviator, Major Robert Elias, was appointed as the Squadron Commander. This created a dilemma once the air cavalry troops returned to Germany, since the "real" squadron already had its authorization of two majors. With MAJ Elias's arrival, we now had an extra. Elias was simply "demoted" to Deputy Squadron Commander. This was an unauthorized position, but it allowed us to retain his considerable flying experience.

Despite the physical reunification of our air and ground elements, Quarterhorse continued to exist in spirit as two separate units for several months. A clearly noticeable rift remained between the air and ground cavalry troops. This rift was nowhere more apparent than among the officers' wives. Air and ground cliques formed around the two most senior wives.[18] Eventually, the shared tribulations of our year-long operation in Bosnia helped to unite the squadron.

## The Dayton Peace Accord

On November 1, 1995, U.S.-sponsored peace negotiations commenced between the three warring factions. Practically held captive at Wright-Patterson

*Opposite:* Major General Montgomery Meigs (left), commanding general of the 3rd Infantry Division (Mechanized), faces Lieutenant Colonel Anthony W. Harriman during Harriman's assumption of command of 3-4 CAV (later redesignated 1-4 CAV), Grafenwoehr Training Area, Germany, October 1995 (photograph: DoD Joint Combat Camera Center).

Air Force Base near Dayton, Ohio, were the presidents of Croatia, Bosnia, and Serbia. On November 21, the leaders reached an agreement on a comprehensive settlement to the 43-month Bosnian civil war. The presidents later signed a formal peace treaty in Paris on December 14. The agreements reached during these negotiations were alternatively referred to as the Dayton Peace Agreement, the Dayton Accord, or officially the General Framework Agreement for Peace (GFAP).[19]

The civilian, humanitarian, and political portions of the agreement comprised an inch-thick document of sixty-seven pages. Their aim was to put the three factions back together as peaceful partners, not simply as foes who merely stopped fighting each other.

The three presidents agreed upon a very broad and deep commitment, which actually amounted to the complete, systematic restructuring of Bosnian society. The accord provided for a new constitution, a constitutional court, a central bank, a human rights commission, and a high representative appointed by the UN. This last provision caused some fears in the West that Bosnia would become a United Nations protectorate.

The military portion of the agreement was twenty-four pages long. It involved the separation of warring factional forces and the establishment of a 600-mile-long demilitarized zone between the two entities of Bosnia-Herzegovina (BiH) and Republika Srpska (RS).

Western professors and politicians wrangled over how to guarantee the agreement's success. Some aspects were given, based on hard lessons learned in Somalia and Haiti. The GFAP had to be implemented full-time without exceptions. Military and civilian tasks had to be synchronized and mutually supporting. The factions had to reduce their military presence. The peace implementation force had to retain continuity of leadership and clear lines of command and control. Most importantly, America had to provide overall leadership.[20]

## The Implementation Force

On December 1, NATO authorized the deployment of 60,000 soldiers to Bosnia to execute the military provisions of the Dayton Accord. This force was under the command of U.S. Navy Admiral Leighton W. Smith, Jr., the commander of NATO's southern theater. Nineteen days later, NATO assumed command of the Bosnian peacekeeping mission from the United Nations Protection Force (UNPROFOR).[21]

The mission in Bosnia was forecasted as a likely paradigm for future military operations. It entailed deploying a multinational peacekeeping force into an environment that was neither benign nor wholly hostile, and under circumstances in which vital American interests were peripheral at best.[22]

Tactical commanders were expected to retain their units' prowess for the type of high-intensity combat seen during Operation Desert Storm. But they also had to become masters of negotiation, arbitration, bluff, and restraint. These were new skill requirements at the time, and the Army had no solid program for developing them.[23]

Lieutenant General John N. Abrams, the Commander of the Fifth U.S. Corps in Germany, said, "The Lieutenants and Sergeants and Captains and young Majors are going to learn a great deal in Bosnia. They're going to develop competence and confidence that will be very important for the Army. In that regard it's like Vietnam, where we had to make good decisions as Platoon Leaders in a Platoon Leader's war. And if you made bad decisions, you got fired."[24]

For nearly three years, the U.S. Army's 1st Armored Division had been on stand-by for eventual deployment to Bosnia. With the signing of the Dayton Peace Agreement, America (or at least President Bill Clinton) finally secured favorable conditions for the commitment of ground forces. After standing on the sidelines of this European conflict for so long, the Clinton administration was ready to restore America's unquestioned leadership in world affairs.

For service in Operation Joint Endeavor, Quarterhorse was detached from the 3rd Infantry Division and attached to the 2nd Brigade Combat Team (2 BCT), 1st Armored Division. The 1st AD already had its own division cavalry squadron — the 1st Squadron, 1st U.S. Cavalry — but senior planners felt that the American force would benefit from the capabilities of two cavalry squadrons, since each provided extra combat power and intelligence-gathering capabilities. The inherent mobility and flexibility of cavalry squadrons were also important assets for the implementation force.

On December 2, President Clinton visited the assembled units of Task Force Eagle, as the American contingent was to be known. Quarterhorse sent several cavalrymen per troop over to Baumholder to hear the president's address. He told them:

> For three years I refused to send our American forces into Bosnia where they could have been pulled into war, but I do want you to go there on a mission of peace.... Without you, the door will close, the peace will collapse, the war will return, the atrocities will begin again. The conflict could then spread throughout the region, weaken our partnership with Europe and undermine our leadership in other areas [that are] critical to our security. I know you will not let that happen.[25]

The president promised our soldiers that the mission would end in less than one year. Many of our young cavalrymen were unenthusiastic about his speech. They sensed that President Clinton hadn't come to motivate them for the mission at hand, but rather to use them as a photo backdrop to sell his agenda to the American people.[26]

Clinton had quite a pitch to sell. Americans never really warmed up to the idea of sending U.S. forces to yet another region that arguably had nothing to do with American interests. After America's humiliating retreat from Somalia two years earlier, the public was in no mood to see more dead American soldiers on the evening news. Officials worried over the "mother test"—a euphemism for the number of American casualties that public opinion could withstand before support crumbled for the operation.[27] (This is an enduring concern in all contemporary American military operations.) Thus, the task of protecting the force was paramount in Bosnia.

President Clinton addressed the concern. "America's role will not be about fighting a war. Our mission will be limited, focused, and under the command of an American General."[28]

Secretary of Defense William J. Perry announced five main tasks for the multinational peace Implementation Force (IFOR):

1. Protect the force, and ensure self-defense and freedom of movement for the IFOR.
2. Enforce the required withdrawal of forces to their respective territories.
3. Establish and patrol a Zone of Separation.
4. Enforce the cessation of hostilities.
5. Provide a secure environment that permits the conduct of civil peace implementation functions. (These were humanitarian, nation-building, and political components of the Dayton Peace Agreement, and were handled by international nongovernmental agencies.)[29]

These were humanitarian, nation-building, and political components of the Dayton Peace Agreement, and were handled by international nongovernmental agencies. Shortly thereafter, the Department of Defense (DOD) assigned two additional tasks for IFOR:

6. Supervise the marking of a cease-fire boundary between the two sides and establish the Zone of Separation (two kilometers on either side of the actual demarcation line).
7. Monitor, and if necessary, enforce the withdrawal of forces to their respective territories within the agreed time period.[30]

The DOD's task list mirrored the provisions of the GFAP. The two entities had agreed to withdraw from the zone of separation within thirty days of the accord's signing. Furthermore, they had agreed that forces in areas that were to be transferred from one side to another were to depart within forty-five days. IFOR would then guarantee that no more forces were reintroduced into these vacated areas for another forty-five days.[31] IFOR began the enforcement of the zone of separation on January 19, 1996.

Additional requirements of the Dayton Peace Agreement included the removal of all obstacles and mines by the former warring factions (FWFs) within thirty days. (This process would not be completed during the year that Quarterhorse served in Bosnia.) All armored vehicles, artillery, and other heavy weapons had to be moved to cantonment areas within 120 days of the signing. IFOR was authorized to use force if necessary to compel the factions to comply with these requirements.[32]

The 900 cavalrymen and attached soldiers of Quarterhorse were a small but prominent part of an international task force that numbered at its peak over 57,000 NATO troops. Operation Joint Endeavor was the largest military operation in Europe since the end of World War II. It was also the first-ever ground operation conducted by NATO.[33]

For the operation, NATO divided Bosnia-Herzegovina into three IFOR areas of operation. American Major General William L. Nash, the Commander of the 1st Armored Division, commanded "Sector North" from Tuzla airfield. Great Britain's 3rd Division operated in "Sector West" with its headquarters in Banja Luka. The French 6th Division operated in "Sector Sarajevo." These divisions fell under the control of the Allied Rapid Reaction Corps (ARRC) commanded by British Lieutenant General Sir Michael Walker in Kiseljak.[34]

The American sector covered 144,000 square miles of territory.[35] Colonel Gregory Fontenot commanded the 1st AD's 1st Brigade Combat Team (1 BCT) up north, while Colonel John R.S. Batiste commanded 2 BCT in the more rugged south. Our squadron was attached to COL Batiste's 2 BCT in November 1995.

The American sector also included several allied units. There was a mixed Nordic brigade from several Scandinavian countries, a Polish battalion, a Turkish brigade, and a Russian airborne brigade. Smaller elements from Lithuania, Latvia, and Estonia also served in the American sector. The Scandinavians and Poles occupied the northwest sub-sector near Doboj. The Turks occupied the southwest near Zenica, while the Russians covered the volatile northeast near Brcko.[36] German forces entered the 2 BCT sector in the summer.

The 1st Armored Division's mission statement read, "On order, Task Force Eagle deploys to AOR TUZLA, Bosnia-Herzegovina and conducts

**Bosnia and Herzegovina, IFOR Sectors, December 1995 (map: Department of History, United States Military Academy).**

peace enforcement operations to implement military provisions of the Peace Accord; ensures force protection."[37]

The Quarterhorse mission statement followed closely: "To deploy to area of responsibility TUZLA, Bosnia-Herzegovina, and conduct peace enforcement operations in sector to implement the Dayton Peace Accord; protect the force. Upon release to 1st Infantry Division, train to fight as the division's cavalry squadron."[38]

The American decision to deploy heavy armored forces to the mountainous Balkan region was criticized from many corners. Some argued for a lighter, more flexible and maneuverable force. Others chastised the Army for being overly cautious.

In the summer of 1996, German combat forces occupied a portion of the muddy Thunderdome next to Workhorse Troop. Quarterhorse cavalrymen listened with envy to the sounds of their nightly beer drinking (photograph: Mark Viney).

But it was a prudent decision and a hard lesson learned from the decisive firefight in Mogadishu in October 1993. In that battle, nearly one hundred American soldiers were either killed or wounded, in part because no American armored vehicles were present to assist the lightly armed raiding force. Then–Secretary of Defense Les Aspin was roundly derided for his political decision to withhold the previously requested armor. The U.S. Army would not enter Bosnia with one hand tied behind its back. (The same could not be said in 1999, however, when Quarterhorse assumed a dangerous screen mission in Macedonia without its armored vehicles and helicopters. The consequence of that unfortunate decision was the much publicized and humiliating capture of three Bravo Troop cavalrymen by Serb forces who had easily penetrated the squadron's ineffective screen line.[39])

A staff officer in Germany said, "We don't think there are going to be tanks attacking us [in Bosnia], but a tank sitting there is pretty good deterrent. It has great capabilities as far as sighting and precision fire, and just its presence sometimes keeps people from doing things they would have done if it hadn't been sitting there."[40]

In mid–December 1995, American defense officials categorized land mines and treacherous roads as the most likely threats to American forces in Bosnia.[41]

The 2 BCT headquarters warned us about the potential for undetectable NBC agents and terrorist attacks. It was also assumed that local Bosnian "civil authorities could not maintain effective administration of law and order within the brigade sector."[42]

The primary forces IFOR expected to encounter were the militaries of the three former warring factions (FWFs). These included on one side the Bosnian Serb Army (VRS), made up of ethnic Serbs in Bosnia-Herzegovina, and the Chetniks or Serbian irregulars, operating throughout the former Yugoslavia. On another side were the Croatian Defense Forces (HVO), controlled from Croatia but operating in BiH, and Bosnian Croatian forces, nominally under the control of either Croatian leaders or the BiH government. One the third side of the military triangle were Muslim forces (ABiH), generally under the control of local commanders. Various local civilian militias were employed by all three sides.

A huge disparity existed among these factional forces. The Muslim-dominated ABiH numbered 110,000 troops plus reserves. However, it only had twenty obsolete tanks, thirty armored personnel carriers, and a few artillery pieces. Assisting the ABiH were nearly 1,000 Islamic foreign nationals known as mujahadeen. The Croat militia totaled 50,000 troops, fifty tanks, and 500 artillery pieces. Opposing them with the bulk of the former Yugoslav Army's materiel was the Bosnian Serb Army, with 80,000 troops, 330 tanks, 400 armored personnel carriers (APCs), 800 artillery pieces, surface-to-air missiles, five MIG fighters, and thirty other aircraft.[43]

American forces took no chances. We entered Croatia and Bosnia in full battle array. The Task Force Eagle Chief of Staff, Colonel John M. Brown, stated that his planners recognized the need for "a very aggressive force protection program to ensure we never risked a small unit defeat, minimize the opportunity for ambush, and eliminate the opportunity for hostage taking."[44]

While some of our cavalrymen echoed other U.S. soldiers' complaints about having to wear helmets and heavy, stifling flak vests for an entire year, a majority seemed to appreciate that our battle attire enhanced our appearance of combat readiness. Lieutenant Colonel Harriman later wrote,

> Think about it from the perspective of a Bosnian or VRS soldier for a minute. Wherever we go, five Soldiers, ten Soldiers, 110 Soldiers, we all have the same stuff on — the same helmet, the same flak vest, the same LBE, the same stuff on the LBE in the same place. The Bosnian or VRS soldier looks left and right and sees Joe Shit the Ragman. That look left and right must do wonders for his morale and for his will to fight. Uniforms and uniformity. Ain't nothin' we do here that doesn't contribute directly to keeping this peace peaceful.[45]

Another rule in effect from the start was the stipulation that American vehicles would only travel in convoys of at least four vehicles. Convoys had to have at least one crew-served weapon and combat lifesaver equipment for specially trained soldiers to use.

Most of us bought the official line that these and other "force protection" measures sent an effective psychological message to the Bosnians that American soldiers were professional, well-armed, well-disciplined, and present in force.[46] However, there were other, more cynical voices who were convinced that our flagrant obsession with not letting anyone get hurt was actually a dangerous thing. It was America's Achilles heel, not only in Bosnia, but in all other U.S. military operations in the post–Cold War era. Critics argued that an astute aggressor would recognize our fixation with avoiding casualties and capitalize on it. All it would take to send us home was a finite number of dead American soldiers. Such had been the case in Lebanon and Somalia, where U.S. resolve and public support had been minimal at best. Public support for Operation Joint Endeavor wasn't a whole lot higher.

We were sent to Bosnia to enforce the peace, but were prepared to respond with maximum force against anyone who dared threaten us. We would not let the factions brush aside IFOR as they had done with impunity to the weak and ineffective UNPROFOR during the civil war.

# 2

# THE DEPLOYMENT

President Clinton's mildly received visit to Baumholder on December 2 was only a brief interruption to our harried preparations. From mid–October through the end of December, the relentless pace prevented most of our cavalrymen from taking any time off whatsoever to spend with their families. Christmas Day was the sole exception. Lieutenant Colonel Harriman approved only three leave requests during this 69-day period, and those were only granted for extreme situations.

By December 9, we still did not have a departure date. LTC Harriman estimated that we would leave before the middle of January, but sometime after Christmas.

We were equally uncertain about when the German flatcars would arrive to pick up our vehicles. We hung in limbo with our families over the holiday season. If a train had arrived on Christmas Day, then we would have loaded it. Fortunately, none did.

On December 11, a mobile training team from the Vermont Army National Guard's Mountain Warfare School began a series of cold-weather operations classes for our squadron. The Vermonters' expertise proved useful in the first phase of the operation when our cavalrymen lived out of their vehicles in below-freezing conditions for weeks.

On December 19, Quarterhorse began a five-day air-ground coordination exercise to improve command and control of our maneuver elements. This event included most of the squadron leadership — commanders, platoon leaders, platoon sergeants, helicopter crews, Troop Tactical Operations Centers (TOCs), the Squadron TOC, the Squadron Tactical Command Post (TAC), and the Squadron Field Trains.

Meanwhile, down in Bosnia, Brigadier General Stanley F. Cherrie led an advance party into Tuzla. BG Cherrie was the 1st Armored Division's Assistant Division Commander for Maneuver (ADC-M). His party established the forward division headquarters at a former Yugoslav air base ten miles south of Tuzla. This headquarters became known as "Eagle Base."

A huge camp quickly sprang up at the airfield. "Tuzla Base," as it was alternately known, was the U.S. military's sole aerial port of debarkation into Bosnia. Logistics packages, replacement soldiers, mail, and (months later) personnel departing Bosnia on R&R leave, all passed through the base. Its most famous landmark, second only to the antenna-studded and concertina-draped "White House" headquarters building, was the post exchange (PX), the largest in all of Bosnia. Interestingly, allied soldiers from other NATO countries were some of its best and most frequent customers.

Sadness abounded around the squadron when our final departure dates were announced on the day after Christmas. LTC Harriman justified our having to depart before the New Year:

> Why leave before the New Year? (1) Power Vacuum. We leave the 29th to get us into sector before the Pakbat (Pakistani Battalion) leaves. I believe that allowing a gap to form between the departure of the Pakbat and our arrival isn't good. (2) COL Batiste may get lonely. COL Batiste flies to Belgrade soon with the 2nd Bde assault CP. He then drives into sector to Lodgment Area (LA) BRIGHT from the Serb side. I expect him to arrive in sector on the 30th or 31st. His S3 will provide security using his 9mm main gun (pistol) until we arrive. COL Batiste's early arrival will do lots for us. He will have time to quiz the Pakbat for lessons learned. He will have time to get intelligence on the conditions of lodgment areas.[1]

On December 27 and again the following day, LTC Harriman briefed our families on the latest information about our departure.

The deployment order called for Quarterhorse to move our vehicles from Germany to Hungary by rail. Unforeseen delays resulted from a French rail strike and sovereignty issues with Austria, the Czech Republic, and Hungary.[2]

Prior to our departure, LTC Harriman disseminated ten rules of conduct he'd received from Colonel Batiste:

**Lieutenant Colonel Anthony Harriman addresses Quarterhorse families on impending deployment, December 27, 1995 (photograph: 1st Infantry Division Public Affairs Office).**

- The Sergeant is in charge with iron discipline.
- Use the Buddy system.
- PMCS (Preventive Maintenance Checks and Services) to standard every day.
- Clean weapons and boresight daily.
- Drink plenty of water.
- Never allow an atrocity to happen.
- Know and live by the ROE (Rules of Engagement).
- When in doubt, dig or berm — use the dirt.
- Combat power never below the platoon level — no exceptions to the four vehicle escort.
- Change and clean socks daily.[3]

COL Batiste also wanted us to rehearse the deployment order, understand the ROE, and to certify our rear detachment.

We rail-loaded our vehicles at Conn Barracks in Schweinfurt on December 29 and 30. The train pulled out at 1:00 A.M. on the 31st. At 9:30 A.M. on January 1, 1996, the bulk of our cavalrymen boarded buses and departed for Hungary.

Meanwhile, on December 31, our air cavalry troops flew their sixteen helicopters to Rhein-Main Air Force Base, the aerial port of embarkation (APOE). There, they were loaded onto the Air Force's brand-new C-17 cargo planes. The planes departed for Hungary on January 3.[4]

As Quarterhorse elements departed Schweinfurt, Captain Dave Brown, the squadron chaplain, offered prayers for good fortune and decent weather.

We linked back up with our vehicles and aircraft at the Intermediate Staging Base (ISB) in Taszar, Hungary. Captain Bob Ivy, the Bravo Troop commander, described the scene there as "a mess with units arriving, supplies arriving, and the base trying to get set up." Deploying units' vehicles completely covered the entire flightline and runway.[5]

In the ISB, our cavalrymen configured their equipment for combat. Extra gear was issued. Crews boresighted weapons, and units continued rehearsals. Vehicles were lined up in convoy march orders and tracked vehicles were loaded onto Heavy Equipment Trailers (HETs) for the movement south. It was in the ISB that we enjoyed our last warm showers and hot chow for many weeks to come.[6]

On January 2, LTC Harriman, CPT Ivy, and a large contingent from Alpha Troop ventured south into Croatia on a leaders' recon. They surveyed the Sava River crossing sites near Zupanja. The Sava formed the border between Croatia and Bosnia-Herzegovina.

While readying their Kiowa Warriors in Taszar, Quarterhorse pilots befriended several Hungarian Air Force fighter pilots. The Hungarians staged an aerial demonstration of the three types of Soviet-made fighters in their

Quarterhorse Kiowa Warriors prepared for loading into U.S. Air Force C-17 cargo planes, Rhein-Main Air Force Base, January 1996 (photograph: DoD Joint Combat Camera Center).

service. Some of our pilots enjoyed the rare opportunity of sitting in the cockpit of a MIG fighter plane. We reciprocated by demonstrating the capabilities of our helicopters. This was perhaps the first of many professional development exchanges that Quarterhorse enjoyed with allied IFOR units. Such experiences provided some of our best memories and greatest stories.

On the day that our air cavalry troops departed Taszar for Bosnia, a Hungarian sergeant gave Chief Warrant Officer Three (CW3) Cook a foil-wrapped sandwich that his wife had made. CW3 Cook ate half of it during the flight and shoved the rest behind the instrument panel. The half-eaten sandwich festered there for many months. The ground crew and every pilot who flew that aircraft was disgusted by the smelly, fuzzy sandwich, but it had become something of an icon. Someone dubbed it "Mister Cook's lucky sandwich."

It is debatable whether the sandwich helped our air cavalry troops fly several hundred combat flight hours without accident, which they did. But on the day that some NCO finally removed it, an odd thing happened. As the aircraft sat inside Fox Troop's portable clamshell hangar undergoing maintenance, a shackle fell from the ceiling and smashed its windshield. Perhaps Mister Cook's sandwich had been lucky after all.

Our ground elements rumbled out of Taszar in multiple, troop-sized convoys along Route Arizona. They traveled to Staging Area Harmon at the bridgehead on the Sava River. There was a danger of mines even in Croatia, so our vehicles had to stay on the road. Typical for this movement, Bravo Troop's convoy took nineteen and a half hours to reach the staging area.

Task Force Eagle's crossing of the Sava River was the largest American river crossing since World War II. Bad weather, flooding, and misrouted bridging equipment had delayed completion of the pontoon bridge by several days. Our cavalrymen put this extra time to good use.

Some western commentators complained that the American deployment was less than the swift show of force promised by the Pentagon when the Dayton Agreement was signed. Some thought the U.S. Army had reason to be embarrassed. But such suggestions were erroneous.[7]

From the start of the deployment, Major General Nash insisted that the buildup of the 20,000-man 1st Armored Division would proceed at a "deliberate pace." Senior leaders wanted to avoid casualty-causing accidents as much as possible. "I have no deadline to meet," said MG Nash. "We're not in a rush."[8]

Colonel Stephen Hawkins, commander of the division's engineer brigade, said, "It's very coordinated, very deliberate. If we've got bad weather, we're not going to cross. There's no need to rush."[9]

The first Quarterhorse element to cross into Bosnia-Herzegovina was Alpha Troop on January 3. Bravo Troop and its attachments crossed two days later. Its seventy-seven vehicles formed a column two kilometers long. Charlie Troop crossed the next day.

Colonel Batiste expected all elements of his 2nd Brigade Combat Team to move tactically and deliberately along designated routes into sector and to inspire respect and credibility.[10] The plan called for Quarterhorse to lead the way. After completing a forward passage of lines through the 1st Squadron, 1st Cavalry (1-1 CAV), we would occupy a buffer zone near Tuzla. From there, our squadron would deliberately occupy and clear the rest of the 2 BCT sector.[11]

COL Batiste expected us to treat all factions evenhandedly. No one would tell IFOR that we couldn't move through our sector. Force protection, strict discipline, and synchronization of combat power were all critical, we were told. Once the sector had been occupied, Quarterhorse would reposition "to establish long term capability to monitor and compel compliance with the peace accord." Initially, no operations would be undertaken with forces smaller than platoons.[12]

The route to our sector was narrow, hazardous, and mine-laden. It stretched nearly 120 miles. Terrain and weather proved every bit as challenging as we'd expected. Insufficient sleep was a problem, too. Two accidents occurred en route, resulting in heavy damage to four Quarterhorse trucks. No one was hurt, though. It took Bravo Troop twenty-three hours to reach Tuzla, including a seven-hour halt for rest and maintenance.[13]

Sergeant John Bales of Alpha Troop later recalled the Bosnian people who greeted our cavalrymen from porches, yards, and roadsides. He said, "There was a good cause for coming here."[14]

The scale of destruction that the Bosnians had inflicted upon their fellow countrymen was immense. Entire villages lay in rubble. Houses still standing were mostly vacant, gutted, pocked by bullets, and spray-painted with ethnic graffiti.

Another NCO from Alpha Troop, Staff Sergeant Wilfredo Comse, said, "We didn't really understand why the U.S. Army was here until we saw a little girl [in a village near Olovo] with a heart with IFOR on it. There were older people crying. They couldn't believe it. Most of the old people threw kisses. It was breathtaking."[15] "They knew peace was here," added Staff Sergeant Anderson, Alpha Troop's Mortar Section Sergeant.[16]

Bravo Troop rolled into Tuzla West Airfield, located three kilometers southwest of Eagle Base. There, it established a perimeter on the expansive cement airstrip. The troop set up concertina wire obstacles to defend itself from Bosnian children who attempted to steal anything not guarded or tied down.[17]

The remainder of Task Force Eagle followed Quarterhorse into Bosnia during the first six weeks of 1996. The IFOR buildup continued at a steady pace. Forty-five days after UN forces turned over control to IFOR, 15,000 of the 20,000 American troops had arrived. Immediately, U.S. forces established twenty-three pre-planned base camps (or lodgment areas).[18]

At the same time, allied IFOR units also occupied their respective sectors within the American zone. The deployment of the Russian airborne brigade was delayed several times, causing some concern at NATO headquarters. The Russian Army had recently taken a mauling by separatist guerrillas in Chechnya. It seemed that the once most feared army in the world was now something of a decrepit paper tiger. Some of our cavalrymen wondered aloud whether the Russians "could fight their way out of a wet paper bag."[19]

## Occupying the Sector

From Tuzla, our ground cavalry troops split up to occupy the entire 2 BCT sector, an area of more than 4,300 square kilometers. The Quarterhorse

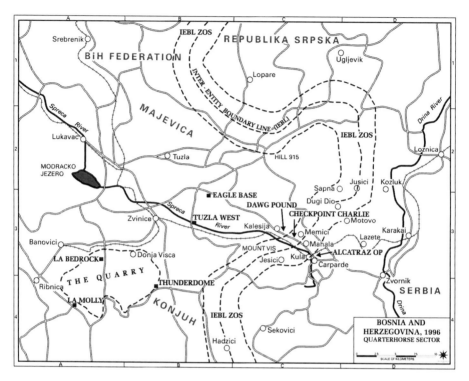

Bosnia and Herzegovina, Quarterhorse Sector, 1996 (map: Department of History, United States Military Academy).

sector comprised the northernmost part of the brigade sector and extended along the Tuzla valley. The relatively flat and open valley was marked on its northern edge by a line of low hills, while tall, heavily forested mountains stretching all the way to Sarajevo ran along its southern edge. The squadron's 750-square-kilometer sector stretched from Banovice, BiH, in the west to Zvornik, Republika Srpska, in the east. It included the other major population centers of Zvinice and Kalesija. In terms of sheer size and local activity, the Quarterhorse sector was the most challenging portion of the entire American zone.

To our Kiowa Warrior pilots in the air, the dense Bosnian forests, rolling hills, and red-tiled roofs reminded them of our home station in Bavaria. But upon closer inspection, shattered, bullet-ridden walls supported these red roofs. Fields were fallow and covered with trench lines and minefields. Concertina wire replaced humble wooden fences. Everything was broken, blackened, or shot-up. Snow, dirty slush, or mud covered everything.

Quarterhorse immediately began daily reconnaissance patrols to create

**Russian armored personnel carriers accompany Quarterhorse Bradleys and Humvees during one of the first combined operations between Russian and American forces since World War II, February 29, 1996 (photograph: DoD Joint Combat Camera Center).**

a force presence and to compel the Former Warring Factions (FWFs) to comply with the GFAP provisions. Significantly, some of our patrols were among the first combined operations between American and Russian forces since World War II.

Another mission we began immediately was to locate and ensure the withdrawal of factional military forces out of the field and into registered cantonment areas. Our squadron focused its reconnaissance and surveillance activities to find these sites. A true team effort enabled Quarterhorse to report mission completion by late March.

The burden of enforcing the GFAP provisions was not the exclusive purview of our scouts and tankers. Support cavalrymen played major roles as well. Our air and ground cavalry troops' actions were complemented by a supporting engineer company, civil affairs teams, a counterintelligence team, and a psychological operations team.

In late March, one Quarterhorse element discovered ten VRS T-34 tanks within the 10-kilometer exclusion zone for heavy weapons. Some of the tanks were inoperable and could not be moved under their own power. A crew from our Squadron Maintenance Section used its M88 recovery vehicle to tow the tanks to a cantonment area.

Soon thereafter, an HHT mechanic used his welding set to cut up and remove a destroyed bus blocking a major road through Kalesija.

From Tuzla Air Base, Captain Semuel Shaw moved his Alpha Troop south into the mountains to link up with French peacekeeping forces. As the troop ventured the high, winding road towards Olovo, it opened Route Mississippi from Kladanj to Vlasenica.[20] Alpha Troop used its M88 recovery vehicle to clear rock obstacles blocking the narrow road. This was not an approved use for the vehicle's blade, but it was a necessary and successful expedient.

After newly arrived engineer support linked up with Alpha Troop, CPT Shaw's cavalrymen opened Routes Skoda and Python. Once cleared of abattis, mines, and craters, this route provided IFOR with a direct line of communication from Tuzla to Sarajevo.[21]

In Olovo, which was known to local Bosnians as the "Valley of Mines," Alpha Troop cleared and established LA Linda in a destroyed transportation facility.[22] Eventually, the troop separated ABiH and VRS forces in the area. It also cleared the Zone of Separation (ZOS) running through Task Force 2-68 Armor's entire sector.[23]

This sector of steep mountains and dense forest was home to the VRS Drina Corps. Nearby was the volatile town of Han Pijesak, home of the VRS General Staff headquarters, where the indicted war criminal General Ratko Mladic hung his hat.

Meanwhile, back in the Tuzla valley, Captain Ivy took his Bravo Troop officers to visit the NORDBAT 2 compound. The Swedish mechanized infantry battalion that had been garrisoned there as part of UNPROFOR was now a member of IFOR. The Swedes had only just removed their distinctive blue UNPROFOR headgear and were preparing to move to a new sector. CPT Ivy's group toured the Swedish compound and coordinated for future combined patrols. The first such patrol was conducted on January 10, when the Swedes took Bravo Troop's platoon leaders and platoon sergeants on a 48-hour orientation patrol of our new sector.[24]

At the same time, Captain Jeff Erron's Charlie Troop departed Tuzla, moved east beyond Bravo Troop, and assumed control of a Swedish checkpoint in the ZOS. CPT Erron's cavalrymen established a temporary perimeter in a bombed-out ice cream factory east of the devastated city of Kalesija.[25]

Meanwhile, Captain Joseph D. Wawro led his Headquarters Troop (HHT) south and established the Quarterhorse field trains in an abandoned strip mine south of Zvinice. Our Squadron TOC and the three air cavalry troops moved to the opposite end of the mine, nearly two miles west of HHT.

## The Dawg Pound

Bravo Troop remained at Tuzla West for only four days. When it departed on January 9, the troop moved east towards the Inter-Entity Boundary Line (IEBL), nearly fifteen kilometers away. A destroyed bridge east of Kalesija prevented Bravo Troop from reaching its objective, the village of Memici.

With early winter darkness falling, the troop needed a suitable place to pull off the road and form a temporary perimeter. First Lieutenant Pat Michaelis, the troop's executive officer, spied a suitably large open area south of the road. Six long, crumbled buildings marked the remains of a cattle yard.

1LT Michaelis dismounted with two senior NCOs and followed a Sagger anti-tank missile wire into the area. Three Muslim soldiers met them. Fortunately, one of the Muslims spoke some German, so our cavalrymen were able to communicate that they were looking for a place to circle up the vehicles for a few days. The Bosnians showed them around. The large amount of concrete pavement was appealing, since every yard of soil potentially hid a land mine.[26]

Bravo Troop moved its vehicles onto the concrete. The troop expected to receive orders to move out at any time, so its cavalrymen slept on or inside their vehicles for five days. On the sixth day, it appeared that the troop would remain for awhile. Tents were erected, while the troop's M88 recovery vehicle knocked down the remaining walls to make more room.

There was only one Porta-Potty for all 131 cavalrymen to share. Bravo Troop had clandestinely acquired it from Tuzla airfield. (Historically, cavalrymen have always been known as notorious foragers.) No one in the troop dared to dig a hole to crap in since mines were supposedly all around. The Porta-Potty was strapped down in the high bed of a cargo truck. Cavalrymen had to climb up to relieve themselves.

"The shitter got full pretty quickly," said 1LT Michaelis. The troop then pondered how to get the overflowing latrine down from its lofty perch. The solution involved paying out a considerable length of cable from the M88's winch, wrapping it around the Porta-Potty, and getting the hell out of the way! It made a huge mess.[27]

As Bravo Troop set about improving its temporary living space, its cavalrymen observed many Muslim soldiers traveling west towards Kalesija carrying armfuls of recovered mines. The tedious demining project was already underway.

Cavalrymen scrounged some paint and plywood and made a sign for their new lodgment area. They called it "The Dawg Pound" since Bravo Troop's radio call sign was Bull Dawg. The name stuck, although Task Force Eagle had officially designated it Lodgment Area Alicia.

No one in Quarterhorse knew why our three lodgment areas were named Molly, Alicia, and Angela. Most of us assumed that they were the names of some high-ranking officers' wives. Actually, they'd been chosen at random by 2 BCT plans officers.[28] For the most part, we disregarded our camps' official names. To us, they remained simply Molly, the Dawg Pound, and the Thunderdome.

The Dawg Pound grew quickly. Materials for more permanent living accommodations arrived in March. Assembling them was an Air Force Redhorse construction team.[29] Then Brown and Root contractors took up the task. By March 15 — two and half months after our arrival in Bosnia — all three ground cavalry troops were finally settled in relatively comfortable tents with wooden floors and walls. Trailers with showers and real toilets soon appeared as well. A huge, prefabricated mess hall seating nearly two hundred was erected in the middle of the camp.

The Quarterhorse mess hall in the Dawg Pound, which was staffed by squadron cooks and locally hired Bosnians, eventually won the Task Force Eagle Commanding General's Award for Excellence.[30] We weren't surprised. Our contracted French chef made homemade soups; poached, chocolate-covered pears in custard; and even swan-shaped crème puffs that were simply phenomenal. Of course, these luxuries did not appear until six months after Bravo Troop first set eyes on the place!

The Dawg Pound was a showcase for visiting dignitaries. The First Lady, the Secretary of Defense, the Secretary of the Army, the Secretary of Commerce, and many others came and marveled at our accommodations. Our other cavalrymen at Molly and the Thunderdome didn't have it so good and were extremely jealous.

## The Thunderdome

When HHT (also known as Workhorse Troop) departed Tuzla West in early January, it headed south toward the city of Zvinice. Captain Joe Wawro led the troop to a vast strip mine just south of the village of Donja Visca. This mine covered an 11-kilometer area, and had been very active in previous decades. Now, the mine was out of operation, whether because of the war or for want of serviceable equipment.

Amid towering slag heaps and wide pools of deep, sticky mud, Workhorse Troop halted for what was supposed to be an overnight stop. Despite the terrible mud, the place was expansive and isolated. Just as Bravo Troop's temporary halt established the permanent location of the Dawg Pound, so did

**Early view of the muddy Thunderdome, February 1996 (photograph: DoD Joint Combat Camera Center).**

Workhorse actually pick another. Many of us thought the barren, rocky wasteland resembled some post–Armageddon landscape. Someone dubbed it "The Thunderdome" after a location in the third Mad Max movie.

CPT Wawro chose the relatively driest spot in a kilometer-sized plain. At the base of a 100-foot slag heap, it was the driest spot, but certainly not dry. The clingy brown mud stuck to everything. It varied from ankle deep to seemingly bottomless. Rain and occasional thaws contributed to the morass.

A staff officer up in 1 BCT's sector made a comment about the Bosnian mud that we could all relate to. He said, "There is something about mud that is different from dirt or snow or anything else. It's demoralizing, it saps your soul, it sucks at your will to live. Even if you go to a clean place, it follows you and reminds you how miserable you are."[31]

No doubt, our cavalrymen in the Thunderdome occasionally shared these sentiments. We lived in the mud for nearly nine months. Only when summer heat temporarily dried all but the deepest bogs did we get any break from it. But then, for two months, heavy clouds of blowing dust coated everything.

The Thunderdome was home to our Squadron Field Trains, the HHT Command Post (CP), the Squadron Personnel Section, the Support Platoon, HHT Maintenance Section, Squadron Maintenance Headquarters, and our attached "Team Cav" Maintenance Support Team (MST). In all, about 300 Quarterhorse cavalrymen lived there.

About a month after HHT established its new home, the 47th Forward Support Battalion moved in next to us. The 47th FSB provided all classes of support to units of 2 BCT. We were eager for them to begin support operations for reasons to be covered later. However, we were unenthusiastic about their moving into such close proximity to us. HHT kept its motor pool and work areas under guard and surrounded by concertina wire. Around the same time, field trains elements from each of 2 BCT's other subordinate units also moved into the Thunderdome. With the arrival of these new units came the camp's official name: LA Angela. Others may have called it Angela, but it remained the Thunderdome to Quarterhorse.

## Mount Vis

A day after Bravo Troop moved into the area that eventually became known as the Dawg Pound, one of its scout platoons helped to secure Mount Vis from Bosnian Serb forces.[32]

Mount Vis was a prominent, volcano-shaped hill south of Kalesija. During the war, VRS forces seized this key terrain and used it as an observation post (OP) to direct heavy bombardments of Muslim positions in Kalesija and along supply routes leading to the embattled "Sapna Thumb." Muslim militia attempted many times during the three-and-a-half-year war to take Mount Vis, but they were repulsed each time. During the NATO airstrikes that forced Serbia to the negotiating table in Dayton, Mount Vis was pounded by cluster bombs that denuded the summit's foliage.

Quarterhorse recognized the need to occupy the promontory. Captain Ivy rightfully observed, "This is dominant terrain. Whoever owns this, owns the valley."[33]

On January 9, our squadron sent a small party of officers to the top of Mount Vis for a conference with the Bosnian Serb outpost commander. The manner in which these officers secured the hill was a classic example of tactful negotiation, an essential skill in stability operations.

Captain Ivy, Lieutenant Michaelis, a Bosnian Serb officer, and a reporter accompanied Major Bryan Roberts, our squadron operations officer (S3). The group rode in two Humvees, but left a section of Bradleys below for security. The reporter went along as a translator. For the first couple weeks of the operation, we were forced to rely on reporters to translate for us, since the U.S. Army had yet to provide us with any Serbo-Croatian linguists.

The party met with the VRS commander, an officer named Zorn. Adhering to local custom, our officers shared coffee and vodka with him before explaining the relevant GFAP provisions concerning the hill. As diplomatically as possible, they indicated that his forces would have to leave their precious hill. CPT Ivy took a long look around the summit and told Zorn he wanted a good place for his cavalrymen to stay. Zorn took the hint and offered the hilltop. He promised to move out the next day.[34]

Our officers had played to the Serbs' sense of honor. They categorized the move as a "relief in place." Not a shot was fired, and intimidation proved unnecessary.[35] MAJ Roberts and CPT Ivy pulled off quite a coup.

The following day, 1LT Michaelis watched VRS soldiers ceremoniously detonate some of their command-detonated mines. Some of the mines ringing the summit were PROM-1 anti-personnel mines. Others were massive, jerry-rigged contraptions consisting of a TMM-1 antitank mine stacked on top of three 60mm mortar shells, all linked to an MRUD — a Claymore-type antipersonnel mine. These explosives would surely have had a devastating effect on attacking Muslim infantry.[36]

Bravo Troop quickly moved its 3rd Platoon atop Mount Vis. While his scouts set up tents for shelter from the harsh winter elements, the platoon leader, First Lieutenant Jamie Wells, supervised more combined mine-clearing operations. An unexploded U.S. Air Force 2,000-pound bomb had to be dealt with as well. On January 12, 1LT Wells's scouts joined VRS soldiers in a pig roast to celebrate the relief-in-place.[37]

A few days later, a space heater in the platoon's NCO tent started a fire. The tent burned to the ground very quickly. The NCOs lost a lot of personal gear, as well some weapons and a radio. The accident reminded all of us in Quarterhorse to stay focused on safety.[38]

After the weather improved sufficiently in later months, Quarterhorse asked the opposing faction commanders tell us how they fought for Mount Vis. They were happy to oblige. We conducted separate battlefield staff rides that proved insightful and fascinating.

## The Zone of Separation

Our cavalry training and mindset were vital to the success of our small-unit activities in Bosnia. Each of our ground cavalry troops juggled several missions simultaneously. Bravo Troop's activities during the second week of January typified those conducted by all three ground cavalry troops.[39]

While part of Bravo Troop's 3rd Platoon monitored VRS mine clearing

Echo Troop aerial weapons team encircles Quarterhorse position atop Mount Vis, from which Bosnian Serb forces directed artillery onto the Muslim city of Kalesija in background, March 1996 (photograph: Phil Nusbaum).

on Mount Vis, a detachment on patrol seized three AK-47s and an SKS rifle from a Serb OP near the village of Citluk.

Second Lieutenant Liermann took his 2nd Platoon to LA Molly, where his four tanks secured the Quarterhorse airfield and provided an on-call Quick Reaction Force (QRF) for Task Force Eagle. 2LT Liermann's tankers stayed at Molly until February 17, when they returned to the Dawg Pound. The tankers then performed some mounted patrols, assisted mine-clearing and route-clearing actions, and also pulled radio retransmission duty.

Second Lieutenant Graham Parnell led Bravo Troop's 1st Platoon on daily patrols within the Zone of Separation (ZOS) and helped to mark its boundaries. His platoon also cleared routes and conducted reconnaissance on both sides of the Inter-Entity Boundary Line (IEBL).

The ZOS was delineated in the Dayton Agreement. The location of front lines where the fighting actually stopped was known as the Agreed Cease-Fire Line (ACFL). IFOR units first marked the ACFL, then a two-kilometer zone on each side of it. This four-kilometer zone was called the ACFL ZOS.[40]

The ZOS was a dynamic area whose dimensions varied according to the requirements and specified deadlines of the GFAP. Most deadlines proceeded from the date that authority was transferred from UNPROFOR to IFOR.

The former warring factions were required to withdraw all forces to their respective sides of the ACFL ZOS within thirty days. All mines, unexploded ordnance, explosive devices, wire obstacles, and fortifications were to be removed. (This second requirement proved unrealistic, as will be covered later.[41])

Quarterhorse succeeded in separating ABiH and VRS forces in our sector by February 10. ABiH forces moved west of the ACFL ZOS, while VRS forces repositioned east.

During the Bosnian Civil War, the factions fought a war of attrition from trenches and bunkers along battle lines that changed hands several times. Trench systems ran along either side of the ACFL ZOS. Between them were numerous minefields and destroyed villages. Roads running across the ZOS were blocked by minefields, craters, tank ditches, berms, and bunkers.[42]

The IEBL was the line that parties to the Dayton Accord agreed upon as the permanent boundary between the two entities of Bosnia-Herzegovina and Republika Srpska. In some places, the IEBL and the ACFL were the same.

Bradley crew from Bravo Troop pauses on patrol within Quarterhorse sector, February 29, 1996 (photograph: DoD Joint Combat Camera Center).

Areas where the ACFL and the IEBL did not match were called "areas of transfer." The IEBL went into effect forty-five days after UNPROFOR transferred authority to IFOR.

All FWF forces were required to completely vacate and clear the areas of transfer. Mines, demolitions, and unexploded ordnance had to be removed. Entities to which an area was to be transferred were forbidden from positioning forces there until ninety-one days after the transfer date, or whenever IFOR gave its approval.[43]

A 10-kilometer Exclusion Zone on both sides of the IEBL was established. IFOR required the FWFs to report all forces and equipment in the zone. The accuracy of the map overlays that they produced to show precise locations of all units, weapons, and equipment varied considerably from good to poor. Quarterhorse employed our air and ground assets to verify this information.

The FWFs were also required to notify local IFOR units whenever any personnel or equipment were to be moved. IFOR kept communications open with FWF military headquarters just for this purpose. Ultimately, the factions provided liaison officers at the headquarters of IFOR brigades to facilitate communications.[44]

## Checkpoint Charlie

IFOR's first priority was to provide freedom of movement. Not just our own, but to help the entities restore normal commercial and civilian traffic along main highways.[45] This required a concentrated effort among all Quarterhorse elements.

The focus of 2 BCT's initial effort was to clear routes within the ZOS. IFOR and the FWFs accomplished this by "punching holes" through the zone. That is, we immediately cleared major routes, then turned our attention to separating forces and other GFAP requirements.

Freedom of movement through the ZOS was specified under the GFAP. The locations of FWF forces became an immediate issue since they influenced that freedom. Faction forces were mostly concerned with the security of their villages in or near the ACFL, and sought to affect the positioning of arriving IFOR units. IFOR repeatedly emphasized that its commanders, not the factions, would dictate the locations of our units.[46]

The key for IFOR was visibility. Our cavalrymen conducted day and night patrols along all cleared routes and areas. To sustain freedom of movement once it was established, Quarterhorse, like other IFOR units, manned checkpoints along primary commercial routes. We secured and retained control of key intersections, interchanges, and bridges within our sector.[47]

From its temporary camp in the destroyed ice cream factory east of Kalesija, Charlie Troop sent its 1st Platoon farther east on January 9 to coordinate with Swedish infantrymen manning an observation post near Memici. These Swedes were from the 8th Mechanized Infantry Battalion.[48]

Charlie Troop then sent one of its scout platoons on a combined patrol with the Swedes over most of the Republika Srpska territory east of our segment of the IEBL. Soon afterwards, both of the troop's scout platoons conducted combined patrols with the Swedes through Muslim territory. From these initial contacts, a good working relationship blossomed between Quarterhorse and our Swedish allies. Captain Erron eventually pushed his 2nd Platoon's tanks into Zvornik. This was the farthest move east by our tanks up to that time.

Charlie Troop began intensive patrolling in mid–January. Its scouts identified ABiH and VRS positions, cleared routes through the squadron sector, and generally checked up on FWF forces on a daily basis.[49]

At the end of January, Lieutenant Colonel Harriman instructed, "If you see an AK-47 in the ZOS, then confiscate it. Where I come from cops don't carry AK-47s. We won't let the cops carry them in the ZOS either. What the factions don't know about American ATF agents won't hurt them."[50]

On January 12, a platoon from Charlie Troop relieved the Swedes at Checkpoint A0. The troop later moved the checkpoint a couple of times to more effectively control lines of communication through the area. The first move shifted the checkpoint south along the ACFL to cover a portable bridge spanning the Spreca River.[51]

Eleven days later, the checkpoint was moved again about a kilometer east to a four-way intersection in Memici. This destroyed village about four miles east of Kalesija was a perfect location for a checkpoint. Quarterhorse remained in Memici until late August, when we moved our checkpoint again eastward toward the village of Carparde.

Charlie Troop cavalrymen dubbed their post "Checkpoint Charlie" since Bravo Troop had already named the Dawg Pound in its own honor. As checkpoints went, Checkpoint Charlie wasn't much to look at besides sandbagged emplacements, tents, lots of concertina wire, guard shacks, and the imposing barrels of our M1A1 tanks covering the approaches.[52]

Checkpoint Charlie helped Quarterhorse prevent unauthorized shipments of arms in the ZOS. It provided freedom of movement for both entities across the IEBL. Without the post, we could not have controlled all trans–IEBL traffic along Route Hawk nearly as well as we did.

*Top:* Checkpoint Charlie in Memici ensured freedom of movement across the IEBL along Route Hawk between Kalesija and Zvornik, March 1996 (photograph: Phil Nusbaum). *Bottom:* M1A1 Abrams tank from Charlie Troop guards entrance of Checkpoint Charlie as HHT convoy passes through, May 1996 (photograph: Mark Viney).

**Bosnian civilians and a convoy of Quarterhorse Humvees make way for NORD-POL vehicles along the narrow and heavily-trafficked Route Hawk near Eagle Base, June 1996 (photograph: Mark Viney).**

Route Hawk ran east-west and connected the medium-sized cities of Zvornik and Kalesija. By Bosnian standards, it was a major highway. We saw it as an unmarked strip of narrow, broken, potholed pavement. What made it even more treacherous for Quarterhorse convoys was that we constantly had to compete for road space with pedestrians, herds of farm animals, tractors, large trucks, horse carts, tiny run-down cars, bicycles, and many other IFOR convoys.

In late February, LTC Harriman observed that our vehicles braked for people in the road. He said that the locals noticed and appreciated it, too. There were no sidewalks and often no shoulder, so pedestrians walked right in the lanes of traffic. LTC Harriman suggested that just the way we drove alone made IFOR seem twenty times better than UNPROFOR in local eyes. He was talking about restraint and consideration for others. It made sense. "Every person we don't splash with mud is another person on our side. Keep driving safely. Keep considering the mothers, children, men, and women who walk on the edges of the roads."[53]

At any given time, one of our ground cavalry troops manned Checkpoint Charlie with a scout platoon, a mortar section, and a tank section. Our cavalrymen lived and worked at the checkpoint for up to thirty days at a time.

When Alpha Troop rotated through checkpoint duty, it gave the place another name, Avenger Alley. Since Quarterhorse elements continued to use our own names for our positions simultaneously with their official designations, newcomers to the squadron found it all very confusing.[54]

Whichever ground cavalry troop manned the checkpoint also ran daily mounted patrols throughout the Quarterhorse sector to maintain force presence. These patrols also attempted to convince local civilians that it was all right to cross the IEBL.

"We spread the word that they can cross the IEBL, and they can go anywhere they want, and nobody will stop them," said Sergeant First Class Leon Snyder of Alpha Troop. "Some will come to the checkpoint, stop, and ask if they can stay here and wait for their family to come up. There's still a lot of hate and fear to overcome."[55] Checkpoint Charlie provided a neutral zone for Bosnians to reunite with old friends and family from the other side of the IEBL.

Alpha Troop continued its searches for illegal weapons in vehicles. It monitored the movement of persons from one side of the ZOS to the other. It also completed several upgrades to the checkpoint, among which was the addition of a 20-foot observation tower.

Quarterhorse manned Checkpoint Charlie continuously until relieved of our sector on October 28 by Task Force 1-26 Infantry (TF 1-26 IN).

## Command and Control

Stability tasks in Operation Joint Endeavor necessitated decentralized planning and execution from squadron down to platoon level. Assisting the squadron commander and our seven cavalry troops were the Squadron Tactical Operations Center (TOC) and the Tactical Command Post (TAC).

The TOC and the Squadron Headquarters were collocated with our air cavalry troops at LA Molly. The TOC's primary function was to coordinate with and report to all higher echelon headquarters. Major Elias, our deputy squadron commander, normally remained in the TOC whenever he was not in a convoy bound for logistics meetings at distant base camps, which he attended regularly. Since MAJ Elias was the senior Quarterhorse aviator, the TOC assumed the major task of integrating our scout helicopters into squadron missions. A flight operations cell within the TOC planned air missions and debriefed returning pilots. The TOC also handled most of our administrative, day-to-day information, and focused on planning future operations.

The TAC monitored ongoing activities within the Quarterhorse sector. It was located at the Dawg Pound, and served as a forward command post. Whenever MAJ Roberts was not out on patrol helping LTC Harriman keep a handle on things, he was usually to be found in the TAC. The TAC was centrally located close to most of our action. After the second Mahala incident in late August, LTC Harriman spent most of his time operating out of the Dawg Pound. The TAC assumed much greater importance during his extended presence.

During large-scale incidents or events, the TOC and the TAC both tracked what was going on. Sometimes our TAC personnel spoke directly with 2 BCT headquarters, but usually we tried to consolidate all information at the TOC first before sending it higher. We kept intelligence officers in both the TOC and the TAC. Captain Scott Downey usually worked in the TOC with his NCOIC, while First Lieutenant Jordan Friedmann worked forward out of the TAC. CPT Downey hated this arrangement. He wished that he could have kept his section together in the Dawg Pound.[56]

To help 2 BCT headquarters keep track of our activities, we submitted daily reports of what Quarterhorse was doing down to the troop level for the next day's operations. While missions were ongoing, the TOC had to report all significant events or a negative report at least every two hours. When missions concluded, we sent a closing report up to brigade.

Our TOC and TAC kept very close track of all Quarterhorse elements outside the relative safety of our camps. Vehicle convoys had to report start times, end times, and checkpoints en route either by radio or Mobile Subscriber Radio Telephone (MSRT).[57]

In view of the accountability imposed by these reports, some junior officers maintained that our operations were not so decentralized at all. Rather, they suggested that we were being micromanaged to the point that little more was expected of junior leaders than to execute and report on their assigned missions in accordance with the very proscriptive Task Force Eagle standard operating procedure (SOP). This was an exaggerated view, but a good point to consider. How would the U.S. Army's emphasis on control, accountability, centralized decision-making, and the fear of incurring casualties in stability operations transcend to future battlefields? With all the information technology now available to senior commanders, would they become "Squad Leaders in the Sky," as sometimes occurred in Vietnam?

## Initial Air Operations

Our air cavalry troops performed valuable service during our movement into Bosnia. As our ground elements conducted tactical road marches, Quarterhorse aerial weapons teams (AWTs) provided security far to the front and

For the first three months of Operation Joint Endeavor, mud and snow were constant companions to all Quarterhorse elements, including this Kiowa Warrior from Echo Troop at LA Molly, February 1996 (photograph: Phil Nusbaum).

flanks and provided a general idea about the trafficability of our route. Our squadron intelligence and operations sections made extensive use of the videotapes recorded in flight by our aeroscouts.[58]

From Tuzla West, our three air cavalry troops moved to a flat, open hilltop on the southwestern edge of "the quarry." There, an airfield was established for them next to our Squadron TOC.

For the first three months of Operation Joint Endeavor, our air cavalry troops flew the same type of reconnaissance missions that they would perform in combat. There was so much terrain to survey that all sixteen flight crews, including the two troop commanders' crews, flew nearly continuous, 24-hour missions. Initially, Captain Brian MacFadden's Echo Troop flew missions between noon and midnight, while Captain Kerry Brunson's Delta Troop flew the other twelve-hour shift. The troops swapped shifts later on.[59]

Our air cavalry troops were tasked to locate faction vehicles and forces in the ZOS. What usually transpired was that an AWT located a rogue element in an unauthorized location, and then the Squadron TOC vectored ground cavalry patrols to intercept and escort them back to approved cantonment areas.

Our Kiowa Warrior helicopters were perfectly suited for this task. In contrast, the older OH-58C models flown by 1-1 CAV up in the 1 BCT sector lacked the sophisticated targeting capabilities of our "Fifty-Eight Deltas." As our predecessor Quarterhorse air cavalry troops had done in Operation Desert Storm, 1-1 CAV's aeroscouts relied on Global Positioning System (GPS) receivers and a little guesswork to determine grid locations of objects on the ground. This proved generally adequate, but our Kiowa Warriors' position and azimuth determining system was a tremendous improvement.

The "Slick Fifty-Eights" also lacked the super-zoom video recording capabilities that our aircraft possessed. This feature allowed us to conduct a more in-depth analysis of the ZOS, and to obtain more thorough mission debriefs from our air crews. Periodically, we dispatched some of our Kiowa Warriors up to the 1 BCT sector for missions requiring these capabilities.[60]

Most of the time, FWF forces responded impassively to our helicopters. The most notable exception occurred in early January as an Echo Troop AWT surveyed a faction brigade headquarters site. Parked outside the building were four M-36 tanks and a twin-barreled anti-aircraft gun. When the Bosnian gunners noticed our two helicopters hovering nearly a kilometer away, they raced to bring their gun into action against them. Through high-powered

A Kiowa Warrior from Echo Troop flying visual flight rules high above the heavy cloud cover early in the operation, February 1996 (photograph: Phil Nusbaum).

sights, our pilots observed this provocation. One aircraft quickly armed a Hellfire anti-tank missile to launch against the antiaircraft gun. Apparently, the gunners thought better of the move they had made and backed down from the gun.[61]

In February, Quarterhorse air cavalry troops expanded their aerial reconnaissance to cover the 10-kilometer Exclusion Zone on both sides of the IEBL. This zone extended the length of the 2 BCT sector, and covered a total area of 750 square kilometers. Once an initial reconnaissance was completed, the two troops flew periodic follow-up missions over selected areas of interest. We were seeking to confirm the absence or return of FWF forces, so our AWTs also paid particular attention to the miles of trench lines and bunkers along the ACFL. In March, our air cavalry troops expanded their focus once more and began flying reconnaissance missions over the entire 4,300-square kilometer 2 BCT sector.

Back when Quarterhorse was still in Schweinfurt preparing to deploy, our air cavalry troop commanders had reached an agreement on how they would divide responsibility for the huge brigade sector. They determined that each troop should develop in-depth knowledge of particular areas. Delta Troop assumed responsibility for Task Force 4-12 Infantry's sector in the middle of the 2 BCT sector. Echo Troop flew missions over Task Force 2-68 Armor's sector farther south. On several occasions, both troops flew missions over the Russian brigade sector as well.[62]

During a particular aerial reconnaissance mission early in the operation, an AWT reported locating a "bomb truck." Our TAC dispatched an attached counterintelligence team to the location. Some of the "CI guys" engaged the driver in friendly conversation while another snapped pictures of his two-and-a-half-ton truck. The "bomb" turned out to be a jerry-rigged rocket pod removed from a HIND-D attack helicopter.[63]

In mid–March, a visiting reporter asked a Quarterhorse pilot what he'd seen during the flight he had just completed. His answer reflected the great progress that we had made in identifying and removing FWF forces. "Today, we saw nothing in the Zone of Separation. Nada. No weapons. No troops. They have all gone home to rest, I guess."[64]

# 3

# DANGER AND BRAVERY

## Operational Conditions

January and February 1996 were the most difficult and dangerous months of Quarterhorse's tour in Bosnia. Stress was high because we anticipated hostile fire and mine strikes at any time. With so many armored vehicles and aircraft in motion over very rugged terrain in the depths of winter, snow, ice, mud, anxiety, and exhaustion were our constant companions.

Our cavalrymen were fortunate that all American soldiers serving in Operation Joint Endeavor had received a special issue of winter clothing — the multi-layered Extended Cold Weather Clothing System (ECWCS). This ensemble included polypropylene long johns, a synthetic fleece shirt for extreme cold, camouflaged Gore-Tex jacket and pants, two pairs of insulated boots, two pairs of insulated gloves and mittens, and thermal head and neck wear. Thus attired, the soldiers of Task Force Eagle were better equipped for cold weather operations than any American force in history.[1]

By the first week of February, most Quarterhorse cavalrymen had already moved into canvas tents equipped with space heaters and generator-powered light. Contracts were out to provide more permanent quarters.

By this point, we were also receiving two hot meals a day. Normally, these were "T-rats" for breakfast and dinner. Each tray-shaped can contained eighteen servings of food. We had few complaints about them so long as we received a sufficient variety. Eventually, Quarterhorse cooks were able to supplement our prepackaged meals with fresh bread, fruit, salad, and hot coffee.

For lunch, we ate Meals, Ready to Eat (MREs). Each MRE contained its own individual ration heater. This was great for morale, since nothing was worse than gnawing on frozen corned beef hash in the dead of winter. Sometimes we got ahold of the coveted humanitarian MREs in their distinctive yellow bags. These meals featured entrees not found in our standard-issue MREs.

A section of Bradleys from Bravo Troop's 1st Platoon prepares to depart on a combined patrol with Russian paratroopers, February 1996 (photograph: DoD Joint Combat Camera Center).

By the summer of 1996, cavalrymen in all three of our camps dined on "real food" for breakfast and dinner. For lunch, soup and sandwiches supplemented our MREs. Once civilian contractors took over feeding us, chow became one of the few pleasures we could enjoy.

Experts predicted that it would take years, if not decades, to rebuild Bosnia. The infrastructure was severely crippled from three and a half years of destruction. Everywhere we ventured, we saw entire villages reduced to rubble. Fields lay fallow and were scarred by trenches and craters.

Imagine walking down a street where everything that could be broken was broken. Street lamps were shot out. Road signs were bullet-riddled and bent-up. Curbs were crumbled. The roads were potholed like Swiss cheese. Buses and cars were gutted and blocked roads, or were tumbled down into ditches and streams. Telephone and electric wires hung limply from shattered poles. Large stores were bombed out and looted. The destruction that the Bosnians wreaked upon themselves was sobering.

A pall of brown dust hung in the winter air over Bosnia. The smog was from the low-grade coal used by Bosnians for heating and cooking. This dirty, crumbly, brown coal was mined from "the quarry" within the Quarterhorse sector. U.S. Army medical teams tested the air for toxicity and concluded that it posed minimal risk to our health.

Tests were also conducted on the soil and water. The water was full of natural and manmade pollutants and was unsafe to drink.[2] Contractors kept us supplied with pallets of bottled spring water from France and Italy. The availability of free bottled water was something we took for granted. It was a real shocker to have to pay for it once more after we returned to Germany. One day, Captain Mark Viney, the squadron maintenance officer, observed Chaplain David Brown washing his Humvee's windshield with bottled water. CPT Viney quipped, "We must be living the good life down here, Dave. Where else could we afford to use Italian spring water for cleaning windows?"

In late January, tensions mounted between IFOR and the factions. Sniper attacks on French peacekeepers in Sarajevo increased. An American lieutenant was also grazed by a sniper's bullet down there.

After six sniping incidents in one week, Admiral Smith, the overall NATO commander, vowed to retaliate against future attacks. "If we see somebody pointing a weapon at our forces, he will be attacked without warning, not warning shots, no 'drop your weapon.'" Soon afterwards, French forces killed one sniper and captured another.[3]

Quarterhorse probably never experienced any such sniper attacks, although one of our scout platoons reported that one of its Bradleys had been hit by a small arms round. There was a small gouge on the vehicle's turret, but the evidence was inconclusive as to whether it had been caused by a bullet.

For the first two months of the operation, Quarterhorse subsisted on improvised support. We knew beforehand that the conditions would be austere, but the actual extent to which we relied on improvisation to keep the squadron in operation was a surprise. We received no direct support-level maintenance or repair parts for almost forty-five days.[4] Thus, Quarterhorse mechanics relied on their ingenuity to keep our vehicles running. On one occasion, the Bravo Troop Maintenance Section modified a 5-ton truck starter to bring an inoperable Bradley back into service. To all of our mechanics' great credit, Quarterhorse sustained an operational readiness rate of 95 percent for all equipment during this challenging period. The significance of this achievement is apparent when it is considered that the U.S. Army standard for nondeployed units in garrison was only ninety percent.

Each of our ground cavalry troops carried their own fairly robust stock of prescribed load list (PLL) repair parts. Quarterhorse also had large fuel hauling capacity to support our helicopters.[5] Unfortunately, the Forward Logistics Element (FLE) provided to us by the 1st Armored Division brought with it only limited fuel, parts, and preventive medicine support.[6]

Not only was this all we had to sustain our squadron through the most difficult days of the operation, it was also all that was available to the entire 2 BCT. For reasons unclear to us, it took the 47th Forward Support Battalion almost sixty days to arrive and initiate its support functions. In its absence, Quarterhorse supported not only our own seven cavalry troops and attachments, but also the 4-29th Field Artillery Battalion, the 501st Military Intelligence Battalion, the 2 BCT headquarters element, and Task Force 2-68 Armor as well![7]

By itself, Alpha Troop provided all classes of supply and support to TF 2-68 AR for forty-five days because that battalion's headquarters company did not deploy until late in the movement flow. Likewise, Bravo Troop provided all logistical support to our attached Alpha Company, 40th Engineer Battalion for two months. Our support platoon hauled fuel and supplies all over the treacherous 2 BCT sector to sustain our sister units.

At the outset of the operation, all classes of supply were limited and hard to get. Our ground cavalry troops made frequent runs to Tuzla West to steal food and construction materials. Vehicles often drew fuel from any fuelers in the area. Generator fuel was so scarce that at one point each troop was limited to only eight gallons per day. The generators normally consumed ten gallons every two hours. We chopped wood to fuel our potbellied stoves. The logistics system gradually came to life and conditions improved for us once the 47th FSB finally got its act together.

It was very difficult to contact our families during the first two months of Operation Joint Endeavor. Initially, it took nearly a month for our outgoing mail to reach our loved ones in Germany. By the summer, though, mail traveling in either direction took only about a week to arrive.

In January, there were only five commercial telephones available at Tuzla Air Base for the more than 20,000 soldiers of Task Force Eagle. Nevertheless, Quarterhorse shuttled our cavalrymen over there to use these phones. By late spring, each camp had its own phone tent equipped with nearly fifteen pay phones. AT&T made a big publicity fuss to show how much it supported American soldiers by putting us in touch with our families. What AT&T didn't publicize were the hefty rates it charged us for its service.

As the stability operation settled into a sense of normalcy over the spring, the U.S. Army authorized limited, off-duty-hour usage of its phone lines for soldiers to make "morale calls" home. Some hardy cavalrymen endured the associated difficulties just to get five free minutes with their families. Using the military phone lines meant spending up to thirty minutes dialing over and over in hopes of making a connection with an operator in Germany. Once we got through and gave the operator our desired extension, we were lucky to get a full five-minute conversation. Use of these lines was considered a privilege. Official calls had priority and routinely cut off morale call traffic. Echoes and static were frequent, and military operators sometimes cut the line without warning once our time was up. A majority of us resigned ourselves to paying AT&T's outrageous fees to avoid these hassles.

E-mail saw only limited use within our squadron. For the most part, only a few officers and staff personnel took advantage of this means of keeping in touch with home. Computers were simply not available for this purpose.

Despite the real hardships and perceived inconveniences, we found our first three months in Bosnia tense, yet fulfilling. Many exciting things were going on, and operations continued at a very fast pace. Day-to-day activities grew more mundane, but they were frequently punctuated by memorable incidents.

In late January, President Clinton flew into Tuzla for a whirlwind eight-hour visit.[8] He didn't see any Quarterhorse cavalrymen because we were all hard at work around the sector.

The press reported on the mixed feelings that many in the U.S. military personally felt for President Clinton. He was our commander-in-chief, and there was no doubt that we would obey any order he issued. But it didn't sit well with many of us that President Clinton had avoided the Vietnam draft, had admitted in his youth that he "loathed the military," and had forced an unwelcome agenda of social experimentation upon our armed services.

During President Clinton's visit, the Task Force Eagle Public Affairs Office distributed pamphlets with stilted answers deemed appropriate for reporters' questions. If asked what we thought of the president, we were encouraged to answer, "U.S. forces are confident in our trained and competent leaders. We have pride in our leadership, from the President on down, and full trust in their decisions."[9] We found the pamphlets pretty amusing.

## Land Mines

One of IFOR's primary missions was to supervise the clearance of all mines, unexploded ordnance, booby traps, and fortifications that were emplaced during the war. We were not supposed to remove these obstacles ourselves, but to supervise, and if necessary train, the FWF forces that had emplaced them. This mission was vital since uncleared portions of the ZOS hindered the dismantling of FWF defenses. If minefields were not cleared, then trenches could not be collapsed and bunkers could not be destroyed. As long as Task Force Eagle operated in the ZOS, uncleared areas remained a threat.[10]

The former Yugoslavia had been a major producer of land mines. Most factories were located in Serbia. While some foreign-made mines were used in Bosnia, the vast majority were locally produced. Much of Yugoslavia's mine development focused on beating enemy mine detection equipment. Thus, many antipersonnel (AP) and antitank (AT) mines were completely nonmetallic. These mines had plastic casings and friction-sensitive chemical fuses encased in Bakelite. They were essentially undetectable by typical hand-held mine detectors, which required a metallic mass for detection. Many land mines were emplaced with anti-handling devices that greatly increased the danger of mine clearing.

Eight separate FWF elements had operated within the American sector. During the war, the factions emplaced millions of mines and other obstacles throughout the region.[11] One of IFOR's biggest challenges resulted from the very haphazard nature of fighting during the war. Minefield standards varied from unit to unit. Some militia emplaced mines without any set, recognizable pattern. Some minefields were simply not recorded. Yet, for the most part, the FWFs followed Soviet doctrine for the emplacement of mines and obstacles. Because battle lines shifted, minefields were frequently moved. Sizes, configurations, patterns, and AP-AT mixtures of minefields varied across the region. Factions used innovative emplacement techniques to increase the effectiveness of their minefields. Many were emplaced on or near roads and intersections, while bypasses were blocked with mines and other obstacles as well.

Most minefields were located along battle lines in or near the ZOS. Because of Bosnia's mountainous terrain, lines of communication and especially vehicle movement were constricted to a limited number of roads and trails. This was ideal for emplacing mines at critical points or strategic locations. Checkpoints and obvious rest areas alongside roads were also mined. Mines were emplaced in and around abandoned buildings and structures. They were sown around airfields, base camps, trench lines, and bridges as well.[12]

As IFOR units entered their sectors, engineers received some minefield information from UN forces already there. This information was disseminated to other units through sketches, copies of mine markers, and photographs. Extensive UN experience greatly facilitated our force protection efforts.[13]

Alpha Company, 40th Engineer Battalion was attached to Quarterhorse and was an important, integral player on our team. Captain Wayne Skill commanded "Alpha Fortieth." His job was to coordinate, oversee, and monitor mine-clearing operations by the FWF forces in our sector. Our initial mine-clearing operations focused on opening roads through the ZOS. This allowed freedom of movement for civilian traffic and helped IFOR to accomplish our peacekeeping missions.

Quarterhorse employed a standard IFOR battle drill for verifying mine clearance. This was a combined arms mission involving organic squadron elements and attached engineers. Once an FWF unit completed its clearing, we had to proof its work. Typically, a mine roller tank, an M113-mounted engineer squad, and an armored combat earthmover (ACE) were used. A section of tanks or Bradleys provided local security, while a medic team in an M113 ambulance track stood by in case of mishap.[14]

All across Bosnia, steady progress was made in the mine-clearing effort. But more minefields were discovered every week. This led some to estimate that mine clearing would probably continue for years to come. In May, Captain Skill confessed, "I don't know if they'll ever get this place totally cleared. We're still finding stuff in Germany from World War II and this place is just as bad. We're getting really good cooperation from both sides, though. In just this general area, we've cleared quite a few."[15]

By this point in the operation, minefield markers were a common sight around the Quarterhorse sector. Only four months earlier, it had been anyone's guess where the mines lay.

## First Casualties

Early in the operation, snow and mud made removal of the estimated 6 million mines a "slow and tedious affair."[16] Our squadron's first serious casualties resulted from two mine-related incidents in late January and early February.

While Bravo Troop's 3rd Platoon secured Mount Vis, its 1st Platoon conducted daily patrols along both sides of the ZOS. On January 12 and 13, it conducted a combined patrol with D Platoon of the Swedish 8th Mechanized Battalion. Our cavalrymen marked the ZOS boundaries with picket stakes. They also initiated a cordial relationship with Bosnian Serb Lieutenant Burnjakovic of the 3rd Battalion, 1st Brigade, VRS Drina Corps.[17]

Early on the morning of January 30, Sergeant First Class John Iacono led a detachment of four 1st Platoon Bradleys on a reconnaissance mission to clear a route through the ZOS. At one point near the village of Hadzici in the center of the ZOS, the only available route was an old trail marked by wagon tracks and footprints. SFC Iacono knew that the route had not been traveled by IFOR units before. He knew it was possible that his vehicles might run into mines. Nevertheless, SFC Iacono led his four tracks up the road.

Moving well forward of the other three CFVs, SFC Iacono's Bradley ran over a TMM-1 antitank mine. The explosion under its right track lifted the 30-ton Bradley up and to the left several feet. Fortunately, the explosion blew outwards and not up into the crew compartment. Four sections of track, a side armor skirt, and the first set of road wheels were damaged. The crew was shaken, but uninjured.

Within an hour, the Quarterhorse leadership descended on the scene. The squadron commander, the command sergeant major, Captain Ivy, First Lieutenant Michaelis, and some attached engineer officers all came out to "assess the situation" for themselves. Even our chaplain and the Task Force Eagle psychology team showed up. Back in the TOC, Major Sean MacFarland, our squadron executive officer, requested situation reports (sitreps) from the platoon nearly every five minutes.[18] 1LT Michaelis was amused by all the fuss, which he believed was an overreaction.[19] The incident suggested that President Clinton's paranoia over taking casualties extended all the way down our chain of command.

Captain Brown, our squadron chaplain, stood atop the disabled Bradley and said a prayer of thanks while an engineer squad probed up to the vehicle so mechanics could move in and tow it away. After the circus departed, Bravo Troop began the serious work of recovering the disabled vehicle. Mechanics short-tracked the vehicle and backed it out of the dangerous area in its own track marks. To their credit, the damaged Bradley was completely repaired and returned to service within twelve hours.

Soon afterwards, Lieutenant Colonel Harriman wrote about the incident in his command newsletter:

> We owe Him one. We owe Him the lives of the crew; we owe Him thanks for the ditch that allowed the blast to vent to the side instead of up and into the crew compartment of the Bradley.
>
> What God gave us was the opportunity to think through what we do again, using 20-20 hindsight. We know that we travel only on cleared routes. We know that on routes through the ZOS, we get the factions to clear the mines and to lead us through the first time. We know that deliberate route clearance with faction guides was exactly the procedure Bulldog Troop used to open the route to Mt. Vis. We know where the factions say the minefields are, and we know that faction records vary in accuracy.
>
> I will make certain that you plan and follow your routes with more deliberation. Using checkpoints, and asking that you report them each time, every time, I will make certain that the Troop TOCs and the Squadron TOCs know when you break new ground — and that we plan as troops and as a squadron to do it.
>
> I ask you to think this through with me, to review what you would have done and what you do, and will do. And then make our procedure in the future better. Today God gave us back a crew. Let's not squander that gift.[20]

A much more serious incident occurred just two days later. Apparently, LTC Harriman's guidance hadn't been disseminated to all Quarterhorse elements yet.

At about 2:00 P.M. on February 1, several Quarterhorse officers went back to the mine strike location to survey the area with a Bosnian Serb colonel and an American major from the 40th Engineer Battalion. The officers walked to the farthest reach of the path cleared two days before. They felt safe since the area had been probed. The group paused at the point where Bravo Troop's Bradley had hit the mine.

The VRS officer wanted to confirm the exact location of where the group was standing. First Lieutenant Bob Washburn, an engineer officer attached to Quarterhorse, moved to let the others see his map. In doing so, he stepped just outside of the Bradley tracks and onto an undiscovered PROM-1 antipersonnel mine. What the officers failed to realize was that, while the tracks themselves were clear, the area between them that had been underneath the disabled vehicle was not.

The explosion slightly wounded Second Lieutenant Parnell in the legs and SFC Iacono in the face. It took off half of 1LT Washburn's foot, blew him into the air, and dropped him square atop a modified TMM-1 antitank mine that had also gone unnoticed. The mine's fuse cap had been replaced with an antipersonnel fuse, making it a very potent antipersonnel mine.

First Lieutenant Jamie Wells took charge of the situation. He ordered one NCO to find and mark a landing zone for a medevac helicopter. Other cavalrymen moved to help the wounded.

Corporal Herbert Gadsden was a trained combat lifesaver.[21] He witnessed the explosion and immediately ran down the cleared path to help. He moved through the wounded and assessed their injuries. CPL Gadsden observed that the young engineer officer was the most seriously wounded.

In the same instant, engineer Corporal Francisco Alcantar grabbed his mine probe and ran to the edge of the minefield.[22] Seeing that there were wounded, he selected a route by which they could be evacuated. He donned a Kevlar blast protection suit, and then probed for mines on his hands and knees towards the wounded.

In spite of his own wounds, SFC Iacono got on top of 1LT Washburn to hold him still while CPL Gadsden applied field pressure dressings to the stump of his foot. CPL Gadsden stopped the heavy bleeding, and then prevented the officer from going into shock. As the NCOs worked, they noticed the edge of another mine underneath the lieutenant's body. Although it had not detonated with the weight of two soldiers on it, they feared what would happen when the pressure was removed. The slightest wrong move might kill them all.

SFC Iacono and CPL Gadsden called CPL Alcantar to come to their location. CPL Gadsden told the lieutenant what was going on and kept him calm. CPL Alcantar cleared around them. The two corporals stayed calm and collected as they worked.

By this time, another engineer had probed his way out to the group and widened the footpath for 1LT Washburn's evacuation. CPL Gadsden then moved out of the minefield to give the engineers more room to probe around him.

CPL Gadsden aided the other wounded, who had been collected by his Bradley. He then donned a Kevlar blast protection suit. He and CPL Alcantar went back to 1LT Washburn's location.

CPL Gadsden kept him still while CPL Alcantar inspected the mine underneath him. The fuse was pressure-activated, so as long as 1LT Washburn didn't move his leg in the wrong direction the mine should not detonate. With a deep breath, they gently moved his leg away from the fuse. Nothing happened. Then, they cautiously lifted him off of the mine. Again, nothing.

They carried him out of the minefield. 1LT Washburn and 2LT Parnell were loaded into a Bradley and moved to a landing zone about a kilometer away. CPL Gadsden rode along and kept 1LT Washburn calm. At the LZ, an aerial trauma team took over.[23]

2LT Parnell's wounds to both legs were only superficial. He was in good spirits as he was put aboard the medevac. Looking at his shredded uniform, 2LT Parnell quipped, "I guess I need a new pair of pants!" It was funny despite the circumstances.[24]

Eventually, CPL Gadsden, CPL Alcantar, and Sergeant Harris were all awarded the Soldiers Medal.[25] This is America's highest award for valor in times other than war. Each of them had risked his own life while working to save the lives of his comrades. None of them hesitated when help was needed. Each was a fine example of selfless service and gallantry for the rest of us in Quarterhorse to follow. Actually, these heroes were no different from most of our other cavalrymen. They simply had been in the wrong place at the right time and did what most of us would have done for our buddies.

Staff Sergeant Carver and Sergeant Foley both received the Army Commendation Medal for their assistance. They had been recommended for the award with a "V" device for valor, but they were declared ineligible for it since the incident was categorized as a "non-combat situation."

While these brave cavalrymen and engineers were risking their lives to save First Lieutenant Washburn, SFC Iacono noticed that the engineer major from 1LT Washburn's own battalion had mysteriously disappeared. Although the major was the ranking American officer in the survey party, he was notably absent while the wounded were being evacuated.[26]

1LT Washburn received a Purple Heart and was sent back to the United States where he also received a prosthetic foot. His engineers named the alley in front of their tents "Washburn Way" in his honor. 2LT Parnell and SFC Iacono both received Purple Hearts and returned to duty.

Toward the end of Quarterhorse's year in Bosnia, the Polish battalion commander said, "Mine-clearing operations may continue in Bosnia for the next 200 years." Twenty-three months after the operation began, only 2,147 of the 7,943 minefields emplaced in the American sector had been removed. By March 1998, Task Force Eagle had experienced 40 mine strikes in all.[27]

## Another Incident, More Heroes

Not more than a week later, Bravo Troop experienced its third serious incident. The troop sustained its scout platoon and mortar section on the summit of Mount Vis by means of daily logistics package (LOGPAC) convoys. LOGPACs carried food, fuel, ammo, barrier materials, and mail to our elements at remote sites like Mount Vis or Checkpoint Charlie. Typically, the troop first sergeants or supply sergeants led the LOGPAC runs. On February 8, Captain Ivy led the LOGPAC himself.

At about 1:00 P.M., Bravo Troop's LOGPAC departed the summit of Mount Vis after dropping off supplies and fueling up 1st Platoon's vehicles. The convoy departed sooner than it normally would have because of an approaching snowstorm. Heavy snow and sleet fell as the convoy wound its way down the steep, twisting road. About midway down the hill, the first sergeant's Humvee suddenly slid sideways on a patch of ice.

The driver, Specialist Jesse Miller, could do nothing as his Humvee slid toward the M978 fuel truck in front. SPC Miller and the Humvee's other occupant, Specialist Nathan Meyer, erroneously feared that a collision would result in a fire, which would not have occurred as the fueler carried diesel. They also did not want to slide into a minefield. They attempted to jump free.

SPC Miller jumped clear but dislocated his shoulder in the attempt. SPC Meyer caught his foot on the door on his way out. The Humvee rolled up an embankment on the driver's side and ended up pinning Meyer facedown underneath. The vehicle rested on a patch of ice. It was tilted precariously beyond forty-five degrees on its side. SPC Meyer could not breathe with the full weight of the vehicle on his chest.

Specialist Michael Grayson, a cavalryman from our support platoon's fuel section, saw the accident occur in his rear-view mirror. He responded immediately. Putting his own life in jeopardy, SPC Grayson dove underneath the Humvee to assist Meyer.

SPC Grayson was a trained combat lifesaver, and checked SPC Meyer's vital signs. He had a pulse but was not breathing. SPC Grayson saw that the Humvee's rollbar was across SPC Meyer's back. Using his own body as a lever, SPC Grayson attempted to lift the vehicle. SPC Meyer coughed once, but SPC Grayson's hands slipped on the ice. The vehicle leaned farther down onto them, and then it began to slide slowly.

In the meantime, other cavalrymen arrived to help. Private First Class Kyle Wren was CPT Ivy's driver.[28] Hearing about the accident over the radio, CPT Ivy ordered PFC Wren to turn around and drive back to the scene. PFC Wren pulled up, jumped out, and joined the others trying to lift the vehicle off SPC Meyer. The ice was too slick, and they could not get any good traction.

SPC Grayson kept lifting up on the vehicle. The slight movement was just enough for SPC Meyer to breathe each time. Finally, SPC Grayson could not lift anymore by himself. PFC Wren jumped underneath to help him. Together, they lifted the vehicle several more times. Each time the Humvee came down, SPC Meyer's breath was audibly forced from his lungs, and the truck leaned over more and more. Eventually, all three were trapped underneath. Other cavalrymen rigged some jacks to lift the vehicle. The jacks slipped on the ice but were reset. Finally, the Humvee was raised enough to pull the three out.[29]

CPT Ivy called in a medevac helicopter. An aerial trauma team loaded SPC Meyer aboard their UH-60 Blackhawk. He was unconscious during the short flight to the 212th Mobile Army Surgical Hospital (MASH). He later came to and was evacuated to a U.S. Air Force hospital in Landstuhl, Germany.

SPC Grayson and PFC Wren had saved SPC Meyer's life. Through their selflessness, quick reaction, and brute strength, SPC Meyer lived. But he had sustained serious internal injuries, broken ribs, and later contracted diabetes as a result of the accident. He was medically discharged from the Army not long after.

SPC Grayson and PFC Wren typified the 900 cavalrymen of Quarterhorse. They did the right thing to help their buddy out of a bad situation. Both of them later received the Soldiers Medal, the nation's highest peacetime award for gallantry.

This was the third serious incident for Quarterhorse and Bravo Troop in the first thirty days of the operation. It looked like we were in for an exciting, dangerous time. Miraculously, SPC Meyer was the last serious casualty that Quarterhorse sustained during our year-long operation.

Meanwhile, Alpha Troop returned to the Dawg Pound on February 12 after completing its mission at LA Linda. Task Force 2-68 Armor had finally replaced the troop in Olovo and had assumed control of the southernmost part of the 2 BCT sector.

LTC Harriman gave us an idea of what Alpha Troop had had to contend with besides conducting patrols, manning checkpoints, and setting up the camp. "Ask an Alpha Troop [cavalryman] what it feels like to be [with] four line companies and an HH[C] for a strange COL; they'll tell you. Alpha's Mess Team has been cooking for about 400 for a while now. Alpha's TOC was the whole task force TOC for a long time."[30]

# 4

# THE PEACEKEEPING LIFE

## *Joint Military Commissions*

For most American commanders in Bosnia, Operation Joint Endeavor was their first exposure to Joint Military Commissions. JMCs were formally established bodies in which guidelines for assistance to the FWFs were laid out. The nature of our stability operation required a great deal of direct personal contact and political interaction between IFOR commanders and factional military and civilian leadership. This interaction helped to resolve numerous conflicts before they became unmanageable. JMCs were useful forums for securing the cooperation or consent of local leaders.

Sometimes, IFOR forcibly brought factional leadership together to negotiate agreements or to mediate disputes. In such situations, our commanders could not have hoped to succeed by using purely military principles and logic. Success depended on their ability to balance a combination of political power and interests, cultural values, personalities, and perceptions.[1]

Lieutenant Colonel Harriman proved himself well-suited for command in stability operations. In fact, probably no other battalion-level commander within Task Force Eagle was as adept an arbitrator. Major Bryan Roberts, our squadron operations officer, demonstrated considerable talent as well. In one incident, LTC Harriman wanted to convince an FWF leader that his actions were undermining the peace. To illustrate his point, he held a raw egg up to the Bosnian's face. He told him the egg was peace, and asked him how bad he wanted it. Then, he dropped the egg at the man's feet to show him what would happen if he did not desist from his unconstructive activity.[2] LTC Harriman never failed to keep his translators amused.

Quarterhorse began participating in an increasing number of JMC meetings in February. LTC Harriman usually chaired the meetings, while our troop commanders were tasked to carry out the agreements that were brokered.

On February 22, LTC Harriman told us that he anticipated an improvement in our relations with the VRS military. The VRS Drina Corps had recently resumed dialog with 2 BCT after a long period of silence. He expected that Bosnian Serb families would soon evacuate Areas of Transfer ceded to the Federation under terms of the Dayton Agreement.[3] But recent evacuations of Bosnian Serb families from parts of Sarajevo ceded to the Federation suggested that RS leaders did not want Serb-Muslim coexistence to succeed.

Our Squadron Intelligence Section expected further Bosnian Serb evacuation of the 10-kilometer Exclusion Zone south and east of the ZOS. At the same time, however, the VRS military dragged its feet on the requirement to report its heavy weapons locations. The Serbs greatly resented having to request IFOR's permission to move them.

LTC Harriman thought the risk was low that either entity's forces would be foolish enough to engage Quarterhorse in a firefight. Such an encounter would cause them tremendous losses. Nevertheless, he cautioned, "Your attention to security, boresight, load plans, PMCS [preventive maintenance checks and services], and personal readiness directly affects the level of risk. You continue to stay ready; that is the reason the risk stays low."[4]

LTC Harriman advised us that Quarterhorse would soon begin to conduct or support inspections of FWF weapons and equipment storage sites.[5] In short time, these inspections became a daily routine for our patrols. By showing up with sufficient force, we compelled the factions to cede right of entry, although some of our later inspections sparked major incidents. During these inspections, our cavalrymen inventoried all the weapons and ammo present and checked for discrepancies. Whenever any were found, we required the offenders to fix the problem. Sometimes this took quite a while, but we were prepared to wait for as long as it took. On occasion, we found it necessary to bring in other patrols to press the issue. The Bosnians respected force.

One of the first inspections we conducted was in Zvornik, RS (Republika Srpska), on February 27. This was the occasion previously mentioned when Quarterhorse mechanics moved the ten disabled T-34 tanks.

That same day, compliance paid off for Republika Srpska. The UN Security Council voted to lift economic sanctions against the Bosnian Serbs.[6]

Meanwhile, our stability tasks continued on both sides of the ZOS. BiH police arranged with LTC Harriman for them to patrol Memici, the areas to the north, around Mount Vis, and the abandoned villages to the south. This gave the Federation control over areas in our sector that Republika Srpska would later transfer to them. It also delayed BiH entry into the contested Serb enclave of Kula until March 18. Thus, we helped give both entities time to negotiate any village swaps they wanted to make.[7]

Lieutenant Colonel Anthony Harriman (left) and an unidentified Quarterhorse cavalryman inspect a Bosnian Serb Army (VRS) heavy weapons storage site in *Republika Srpska* as VRS officers look on, February 1996 (photograph: DoD Joint Combat Camera Center).

The last week of February was an eventful time for Bravo Troop's 3rd Platoon, whose actions typified those of all six Quarterhorse scout platoons at that time. On February 23, the platoon located a previously undetected vehicle storage area used by the VRS Sekovici Brigade.

Six days later, 3rd Platoon conducted the first of several combined patrols with Russian paratroopers in the area north of Zvornik. Our seasoned cavalry NCOs who remembered the Russians as our former enemies found the experience particularly rewarding. It was during one of these combined patrols that the supposed evidence of a sniper attack was discovered on one of Bravo Troop's Bradleys.[8]

Not long after, 3rd Platoon confiscated a man-portable SA-7 antiaircraft missile on the outskirts of Osmaci.[9] This was an important find. Our Kiowa Warriors didn't need any unaccounted-for missiles roaming around in our sector.

On March 2, 3rd Platoon rotated back up to Mount Vis to replace Bravo Troop's other scout platoon there.[10]

While his two scout platoons conducted independent missions in separate

Scouts from Bravo Troop's 3rd Platoon and Russian paratroopers break during a combined patrol, February 29, 1996 (photograph: DoD Joint Combat Camera Center).

areas, Captain Ivy split his mortar section into two one-gun squads. One squad conducted combined patrols with the Swedes and helped to mark the ZOS boundaries. The other squad established a firing position on Mount Vis, where it also helped to construct perimeter defenses. Naturally, it also coordinated with the troop's fire support officer to establish priority targets on our patrol routes and checkpoints.[11]

By mid–March, factional police forces had become key players as FWF military forces were confined to their cantonment areas. LTC Harriman knew that Quarterhorse needed to understand these various police forces and how they operated. He told our ground cavalry troops to closely observe local police forces. Even aerial reconnaissance was refocused to gather intelligence on the police.[12]

Our Squadron Intelligence Section expected the FWFs to build new police forces on the old Yugoslav model, with municipal police, military police, and Ministry of Internal Affairs special police (MUPs). The municipal police traditionally handled routine police work, such as burglaries. Military police were soldiers first and were not permitted in the ZOS. We considered the MUPs as combat forces, too, since the factions trained, equipped, and employed them as such.

The BiH municipal police wore dark green or dark blue uniforms with large, Soviet Army–style visor caps. The BiH MUPs wore camouflage uniforms with shoulder patches or berets with "MUP" on them. BiH police, whose uniforms stated their station name and *Policija*, were recently demobilized soldiers. By this point, we still hadn't figured out what their purpose was.[13]

On the Bosnian Serb side, municipal police wore plain blue uniforms. We called the RS MUPs "purple people eaters" because they wore purple camouflage uniforms, black berets, and arm brassards. They had a distinguishing red, blue, and white shoulder patch with *Policija* written in Cyrillic on it. All Quarterhorse elements were instructed to report any RS MUPs wearing black, as this was the color of their combat uniforms.

LTC Harriman told us to identify what type of police manned each checkpoint by reporting uniform descriptions. As LTC Harriman pointed out, legitimate police elements wore proper police uniforms, had identification cards, were listed on local police rosters, and were only permitted to carry pistols.[14] Our patrols were told to ascertain the missions of all FWF police checkpoints and patrols. We kept watch for police elements restricting civilian movement, harassing people, or committing human rights abuses. We had orders to stop such violations.

## *Hillary and Chelsea*

In early March, First Lady Hillary Rodham Clinton and her daughter Chelsea toured selected American camps in Bosnia. The Dawg Pound was one of their stops. LTC Harriman met their helicopter and escorted their party around our camp. He explained to the First Lady how we performed stability operations. He told her that our cavalrymen understood their environment and the people in it. He explained how we interacted with the locals while on patrol, and how some cavalrymen invited Bosnian families to share coffee with them at our checkpoints. He told Mrs. Clinton how we gathered the intelligence we needed because we took notice of what went on around us; that we brought life back to dead villages; and that we also "protected our force."[15]

Mrs. Clinton gave us the impression that she enjoyed her visit. She was gracious when introduced to our cavalrymen. She spoke with them and posed for many photographs. Some commentators remarked that Bosnia was an odd location for Chelsea Clinton to spend her spring break, but the First Daughter seemed happy to visit with Quarterhorse.

Imagery by 55th Sig Co (Combat Camera)

First Lady Hillary Clinton and daughter Chelsea (not pictured) meet unidentified Quarterhorse mechanics during tour of the Dawg Pound, early March 1996 (photograph: 55th Signal Company, U.S. Army).

During the presidential election year of 2008, candidate Senator Hillary Clinton claimed to have been under sniper fire during her visit to Bosnia. She certainly was not exposed to any such threat while at the Dawg Pound. Amid much reporting that refuted her claim, she later recanted her story, much to her campaign's embarrassment.

Our cavalrymen had done a great job preparing for the First Lady's visit. According to her Secret Service detachment, the Dawg Pound was the most secure area they had taken a First Family delegation to in quite a while. They said that they normally ended up organizing site security plans even when those sites included military forces. Quarterhorse had planned our own security for the First Lady's visit. Her advance team had nothing to do but approve it. Secret Service agents asked for a copy of one our planning boards to help plan and brief other First Family visits.[16]

A few months later, we received several large manila envelopes from the White House. Inside were nearly one hundred 8 × 10 color glossy photos of the First Lady's visit — a very thoughtful gesture. We promptly distributed them to those appearing in the photos.

## The Storm

At about the same time as Mrs. Clinton's whirlwind tour of the Dawg Pound, another sort of whirlwind ripped through the Thunderdome and LA Molly. A fierce nighttime windstorm, described by some as a tornado, destroyed several tents and a Mobile Kitchen Trailer (MKT).[17] At the Thunderdome, Quarterhorse cooks retreated into a large MILVAN shipping container after their MKT flipped over. All but four of HHT's tents were blown down. Several were ripped. Cavalrymen in the Squadron Personnel Section placed their computers under tables, piled sandbags atop their collapsed tent, and rode out the storm. Mail, computer paper, and tents were blown all around. Not surprisingly, from then on, whenever anyone couldn't produce needed manuals or paperwork, it was conveniently blamed on the storm. A few claims for missing clothing and equipment were submitted also.

At 7:00 A.M. the following morning, HHT began to put its flattened tents back up. To the credit of Captain Wawro's cavalrymen, all the tents were erected within an hour. When some generals from IFOR headquarters flew over the camp three hours later to survey the damage, there was nothing unusual for them to see. The British Army cooks supporting Quarterhorse had the overturned MKT up and running in no time. By 10:00 A.M., they had hot soup and coffee ready. They served a hot T-ration breakfast at 2:00 P.M. and a hot T-ration dinner at the usual time.[18]

The storm caused havoc at LA Molly, too. Cavalrymen in the Squadron TOC had to tie-down their tent shelters to an M113 armored personnel carrier (APC) to prevent them from being blown away. Several military policemen were enlisted to help keep the squadron commander's sleeping tent on the ground. The storm lasted nearly an hour. Afterwards, only one tent on LA Molly remained standing.[19] All had been constructed with wooden floors, foundations, walls, and roof supports.

Patrols continued throughout March. Second Lieutenant Parnell — his leg wounds healed — led Bravo Troop's 1st Platoon on a series of daily patrols on the RS side of the IEBL. Two of the patrols were conducted with Russian paratroopers, many of whom considered Bosnia a vacation spot after their recent defeat in the former Soviet republic of Chechnya. One noteworthy patrol by Bravo Troop's scouts and mortarmen discovered skeletal human remains in a site we had suspected was an unauthorized weapons storage site.

For a seven-day period in late March, Bravo Troop's 3rd Platoon occupied the village of Glavica to prevent looting after an ethnic disturbance occurred there. Our cavalrymen also secured a meeting place for Serb and Muslim townsfolk to gather peacefully.[20]

At the end of March, LTC Harriman thought that we were very close to achieving our objective of moving all FWF forces into registered cantonment areas. He expected that we would continue to patrol the ZOS, the 10-kilometer Exclusion Zone, and areas beyond.

LTC Harriman instructed Quarterhorse to observe all police behavior, to report what faction civilians did and did not do, and to provide area security while international agencies began to investigate suspected war crimes sites.

We were also to remove illegal police checkpoints in accordance with the latest instructions passed down from the Commander of the Allied Rapid Reaction Corps (COMARRC). As LTC Harriman remarked, "The boys at the Carparde checkpoint don't know it yet, but their days are numbered."[21]

LTC Harriman also wanted us to keep an eye on the controversial village of Kula from OP Alpha. We would also henceforth keep Checkpoint Charlie open as a meeting place for both sides. Charlie Troop would take up permanent residence in the Dawg Pound.[22]

By the end of March, mission requirements had diminished sufficiently to allow our air cavalry troops to reduce their intense flying schedule. From then on, one troop typically flew from 8:00 A.M. to 8:00 P.M., while the other flew from 12:00 P.M. to 12:00 A.M. We would no longer fly in the early morning hours since previous missions had detected very little activity during these times. Quarterhorse always maintained an aerial Quick Reaction Force (QRF) on standby.[23]

LTC Harriman gave our ground cavalry troops the heads-up that we would soon be issued up-armored XM114 Humvees to use in our mounted patrols. As it turned out, we received only one in late March, and that became LTC Harriman's command vehicle. It was not until late July that our ground cavalry troops received their complement of six up-armored Humvees each.

We decided to stop using our SUSVs since they had been issued with no manuals or repair parts and were showing signs of hard use.[24] We wanted to maintain them, but simply could find no means of doing so.

## Redesignations

Back in the fall of 1995, the U.S. Army had begun a significant realignment of its combat units. This had been necessary following the Army's massive post–Cold War downsizing. Generally speaking, the U.S. Army retained on active duty only the oldest and/or most distinguished of its combat regiments. Most regiments were reassigned to the divisions in which the bulk of their combat service had occurred.

This realignment affected our squadron, too. On March 23, 1996, we held a ceremony to mark our redesignation from the 3rd Squadron, 4th U.S. Cavalry to the 1st Squadron, 4th U.S. Cavalry (Quarterhorse).[25] The most visible manifestation of this change was our switch from wearing 3rd Infantry Division shoulder patches to the Big Red One patch of the 1st Infantry Division. We also had to repaint many signs adorning our garrison headquarters in Schweinfurt and our Bosnian lodgment areas.

Two days after our redesignation ceremony, our cavalrymen at the Dawg Pound had another reason to celebrate. A small Post Exchange (PX) was now open for business.[26] Eventually, all of our camps had small PXs. They sold necessary toiletries, snack foods, drinks, reading and writing materials, audiocassettes, and CDs. They also did great business in IFOR–Operation Joint Endeavor souvenirs like coffee mugs, sweatshirts, T-shirts, hats, key chains, coats, flags, cigarette lighters, and bottle openers.

One item that our camp PXs did not sell was alcohol in any form. American soldiers of Task Force Eagle were prohibited from consuming alcohol anywhere in the theater except in a single tent in Taszar, Hungary. We watched with envy as our IFOR allies enjoyed their beers at local Bosnian cantinas and in their own unit pubs. Many within Quarterhorse detested this restriction, which was viewed as preemptive mass punishment. Since our senior leaders trusted us enough to operate multi-million-dollar vehicles in life-threatening situations, why wouldn't they allow us to drink responsibly in controlled situations?

Some of our junior officers contended that a far better approach would have been for commanders to make the standards of alcohol consumption plainly clear to their subordinates, entrust them to act within the boundaries, and then slam the hell out of any individual who failed to live up to expectations as an example to everyone else. These junior officers cited the fact that American soldiers respect their leaders who demonstrate genuine trust in them.

However, this philosophy assumed a degree of risk that senior military commanders in Bosnia were unwilling to assume. The logic went that zero alcohol would mean zero alcohol-related incidents, hence, zero bad press. Some young members of Quarterhorse argued that the ban on alcohol was only one dimension of the cover-your-ass, damage-control mentality that seemed to prevail among our senior leaders. Such timidity was incompatible with the confidence, audacity, and measured risk-taking that are the hallmarks of victorious combat leaders, they argued. How would we fight our next war, some wondered?

Some within Quarterhorse casually ignored the ban on alcohol, which allowed no exceptions. The policy was not culturally attuned to the Bosnians' custom of toasting with *slivovitz* plum brandy before getting down to business. In order to maintain cordial relationships with the locals in our sector, many of our junior leaders felt obligated to partake in these toasts.

Our camp PXs sold various brands of nonalcoholic beer for those willing to endure bloated stomachs and sour mouths. Few of us wasted our money on this "near beer."

During the year-long Operation Joint Endeavor, there was considerable concern among American politicians and senior military leaders over the potentially debilitating effects of stability operations on the fighting abilities of combat units like Quarterhorse. The concern was that we could not train for war if we were completely involved in an entirely different line of work. Acknowledging this dilemma, the Quarterhorse leadership also recognized that stability operations had proven beneficial to the squadron in some ways. LTC Harriman wrote in the training guidance he issued in April:

> Ongoing stability operations have improved command and control procedures, reconnaissance operations, and stability operations task performance. By contrast, skills associated with fire and maneuver, the ability to attack and defend against technologically advanced enemy have degraded. Personnel turbulence requires constant retraining of gunnery, stability operations, radio communications, and reconnaissance skills. Continued noncommissioned officer efforts to present innovative training during patrols, checkpoint operations, and base camp operations have done much to maintain the squadron's edge.[27]

LTC Harriman instructed Quarterhorse to "continue stability operations throughout the period. Continue maintenance with three goals: sustained FMC readiness rates above 90 percent for vehicle fleets and 75 percent for helicopters, a 100 percent self-redeployment capability, and a no-maintenance-recovery-required posture upon redeployment. Continue Soldier, crew, and platoon training to attain two goals: readiness to fight here and readiness to train upon redeployment." LTC Harriman wanted our squadron to "redeploy in a training posture that would allow us to take good advantage of gunnery, Warfighter, and CMTC once back in Central Region."[28]

In early April, our air cavalry troops changed the type of aerial missions they flew. During the first three months of the operation, Quarterhorse aerial weapons teams had predominantly conducted zone reconnaissance missions to locate unidentified FWF elements and route reconnaissance missions to assist the movement of our ground elements. Now they began to focus more on area reconnaissance of known areas of interest, such as weapons storage sites, disputed villages in the ZOS, and mass gravesites.[29] This mirrored the tactical situation on the ground, where our operations had shifted from locating and moving FWF forces to a situation where civil affairs and psychological operations activities held primacy.

On a particular aerial reconnaissance on April 1 near Han Kram, a village south of the VRS headquarters at Han Pijesak, one of our AWTs located a large cache of heavy weapons, including anti-aircraft artillery pieces, which had been secretly moved to this unauthorized location.[30] This was an important discovery. Quarterhorse turned over videotaped evidence of this violation to 2 BCT headquarters, who used this evidence to compel the VRS to move their weapons back to the approved storage site.

## More Visitors

On April 3, American Secretary of Commerce Ron Brown and a group of American corporate executives visited the Dawg Pound. Secretary Brown's party was in Bosnia on a fact-finding mission to explore economic opportunities. Economics, it was thought, was another incentive for stability. "Trade, not aid," as Secretary Brown put it.[31]

He told our cavalrymen how vital our mission was to stability in Bosnia-Herzegovina. As he did at other camps he visited, Secretary Brown treated us to freshly prepared McDonald's hamburgers.

Secretary Brown's party departed for Eagle Base, where the group boarded a flight to Croatia. Three hours after the delegation left the Dawg Pound, those of us watching CNN in the mess hall were stunned to learn that their plane had crashed on approach into Dubrovnik. All thirty-four passengers on board were killed. We were dumbstruck. We had been among the last to enjoy their company.[32] LTC Harriman wrote of their deaths:

> My sense is, thinking back, that their last day might not have been such a bad last day—given that they had to have a last day. They left here with what they came for: a sense of the Balkans. They left here having met many of you. They left with a glimmer of understanding for what you have done here and the kind of people you are. If what they said gives any indication at all, they left proud— proud because Quarterhorse is America's team—proud because they were Americans too. Last days, ever unexpected, rarely approach what a planned last day might be. If what they said gives any indication at all, they felt good about themselves, about you, and about Americans on their last day. And that is the best that you or anyone else could have done.[33]

In mid–April, the Bosnian winter suddenly yielded to spring. Almost overnight, the area around LA Molly and the Thunderdome sprang to life. That is, everything except the immediate area, which was nothing but barren, almost lifeless slag heaps. The surrounding hillsides grew lushly green. The gray skies parted, the fog lifted, and our cavalrymen saw mountain ranges many miles away that we had never seen before.

Major Zajac, the 2 BCT operations officer, cautioned all subordinate units

> to continue your fine record of deliberately planned, well rehearsed operations combining all appropriate battlefield functions required for success. Familiarity breeds contempt! It may not seem so, but danger lurks around every corner. Remain vigilant! Spring brings foliage and foliage equals concealment. Of course, concealment offers greater opportunity to probe or penetrate our lodgment areas.[34]

More succinctly, LTC Harriman warned us to look out for the sniper, the drunk, the thief, the bomber, and the complacent soldier.[35]

Around this time, LTC Harriman wrote an open letter to our families in Germany that eloquently captured the essence of spring in Bosnia:

> Spring planting has begun in Memici. Memici people move around the gutted, roofless houses, turning earth, pruning trees and shrubs, and planting vegetable gardens. Planting potatoes and corn mostly. Along the Memici street that formed the former Serb front-line, the bunkers have all but disappeared. The houses, still windowless, still doorless, have clean floors, swept floors, swept clean of furniture fragments, wadded clothing, vinjak bottles, ammunition boxes, shells, excrement — all those things your Soldiers saw when they first arrived. Yesterday, I saw toddlers in Memici yards, trying to divert their parents from the clean-up task at hand. And yesterday, lining each side of a walk-way leading up to a house, burned and bare, I saw the green leaves that precede coming flowers, not pushing up from some forgotten bulb, but planted there with a purposefulness that suggests the house may not have to wait long for a new roof. Your husbands, sons, daughters, mothers — your Soldiers, are part of spring this year. This year, in Memici, in towns around it, mother earth has an ally, garbed appropriately in green: Quarterhorse.[36]

By mid–April, a growing number of our cavalrymen asked why Quarterhorse had to remain in Bosnia since the faction armies had left the field and since our patrols were not seeing much of significance to report. Many wondered what was next. Why stay? What was our mission now? LTC Harriman addressed our concerns:

> The mission follows: we implement the peace agreement. As time goes on, we will increasingly implement the peace agreement simply by being — here. We will implement the peace agreement simply by being ever ready to defeat all comers — here. We will patrol a border area to understand our environment and understand the activities of the former warring factions. We will work on protecting the force ... to protect ourselves against the Mujahadeen and rogue elements. We will train to deploy and fight — the way we trained to fight the Soviet armies of the '80s and the armies of various cretans [*sic*] and miscreants today.

Finally, we will remain here. Hanging around (ready for a fight the whole time) works. We hung around Europe for forty years, training to keep ready, but just training. And we changed the political face of the world. We exist to fight our nation's wars. Remember that and you will understand most of what we do.[37]

Something always happened to break the monotony of our existence. Things livened up for awhile in mid–April after a shoot-out between Serbs and Muslims broke out in the cafe in the village of Osmaci.[38]

It was around the end of the month that normal garrison requirements caught up with us. Standard reports and meetings became mandatory, as did all the physical security and safety requirements associated with garrison life. Our seven cavalry troops initially had a hard time meeting these administrative requirements. During the pre-deployment period, they simply lacked enough time and sufficient container space to pack all of their records, manuals, and materials. Quarterhorse deployed to Bosnia expecting to have to fight, not to conduct some hybrid of stability operations overlaid with garrison activities. The reality turned out quite different.

LTC Harriman wrote about these "bullshit requirements" that caused our junior leaders and cavalrymen so much frustration:

> Some of you have noticed that we have begun to do Schweinfurt things in Bosnia. We train for one. We did it from the beginning because our noncommissioned officers led the way. Training in combat zones is the mark of a good Army. We inventory and account for our stuff, another mark of a good Army. We continue schools and skill certifications, safety council meetings, promotion boards, Audie Murphy boards. And we do the mission too.[39]

Like other American units in IFOR, Quarterhorse was not constrained by any "stop loss" program that could have prevented individuals from leaving Bosnia to attend professional military education schools or to rotate out to new assignments upon their DEROS dates. Our cavalrymen came and went. We simply worked around their absence, as we would have done with casualties in combat.

# 5

# UNSTABLE PEACE

## The IPTF

One of the many international organizations that Quarterhorse eventually came to work with on a daily basis was the International Police Task Force. We referred to this organization by its acronym IPTF. The IPTF was mandated under the Dayton Peace Accord. Its mission was to help create an impartial law enforcement system in Bosnia. Specifically, the IPTF was charged to monitor, assist, advise, and assess local Bosniac and Serb police forces.

The IPTF was authorized 1,721 officers to accomplish these tasks, but by early February only 215 officers had arrived in Bosnia. Out of thirty-six nations that pledged support, only twelve had so far provided any manpower. Some officers who joined the IPTF spoke little or no English, the organization's common language. Some were unqualified to drive over the treacherous mountain roads.[1]

Limitations specified in its mandate further handicapped the IPTF. Its officers could not carry weapons even for self-defense. They could not investigate crimes. And they could not patrol after sundown. The IPTF also lacked a sufficient number of vehicles and radios.[2]

In early February, American Admiral Leighton Smith, the commander of all NATO forces in Bosnia, said, "I'm a little bit disappointed that we don't have more of the international police task force in place."[3] But ADM Smith recognized the difficulties and delays encountered by UN efforts in a variety of humanitarian, refugee resettlement, and economic reconstruction projects.

The IPTF would require the complete cooperation and support of armed IFOR units to achieve its primary mission of observing faction police. But relationships at the highest levels of IFOR and the IPTF had gotten off to a rocky start.

NATO did not want to provide a strong arm for the IPTF out of fear of mission creep. Senior officers insisted that IFOR would not carry out police duties. American Secretary of Defense William Perry reiterated this stance in early January when he responded to criticism from the Bosnian government that the NATO operation was not fulfilling its obligation to protect Muslim civilians. Mr. Perry stated, "The task of the NATO Implementation Force is to ensure freedom of movement under the terms of the Dayton agreement. We are not set up as a police force."[4]

However, over time, Quarterhorse developed a close relationship with most IPTF officers operating in our sector. This was due in part to our having saved their asses on more than a few occasions. Almost daily, IPTF officers coordinated their operations with our staff officers in the Dawg Pound.

## Mahala Part One

From the beginning of the Bosnian Civil War in April 1992, the Muslim-led Bosnian government had successfully portrayed itself as the hapless victim of Serb aggression. It posed as the only entity within the former Yugoslavia that supported the ideals of a multiethnic, multicultural society so valued by the West.[5] But since the signing of the Dayton Peace Accord in November 1995, several actions and pronouncements contrary to the spirit of Dayton by senior BiH leaders dismayed some Western diplomats. What was Bosnia's true direction, and what success would Western engagement in the region enjoy? As early as late January, one diplomat previously known for his staunch pro–Bosnian views was quoted as saying, "As far as I am concerned the gloss is off the Bosnian government. I have tried to help these guys out, but now frankly I am tired of their talk."[6]

Colonel Batiste told us that he had to keep reminding himself that there were no good guys here in Bosnia. All were equally crafty and not above deception to further their own agendas.

IFOR intelligence officers predicted that as FWF military forces reorganized and consolidated into cantonment areas away from the ZOS, their influence on the populace would decrease. Authorized local police forces, monitored by the IPTF, were expected to fill the power vacuum.

On April 25, a significant incident occurred within the Quarterhorse sector that illustrated the deviousness of the BiH leadership. It also showed how ineffective the local police forces really were.

Nearly 200 Muslim civilians unexpectedly passed through Checkpoint Charlie to "visit their old homes" in the abandoned village of Mahala in Serb territory.[7] In reality, few of these civilians marching from Kalesija were bona fide former residents of Mahala. The movement was a political stunt organized by Dzevad Tosunbegovic, the Muslim mayor of Kalesija, who alternately played arsonist and fireman.

To Quarterhorse, the march appeared to be part of a deliberate effort to resettle Federation refugees in formerly Muslim towns on the RS side of the IEBL. This was particularly troublesome, as it purposefully exploited GFAP provisions in order to encroach on Republika Srpska territory.[8]

Captain Downey, our squadron intelligence officer, admitted that the march caught our squadron completely off-guard. Our intelligence-gathering assets were focused on the contested town of Dugi Dio. Other Quarterhorse elements were thinly dispersed across our sector. None of our assets anticipated the march, although it had been announced over Kalesija radio the day before. We were caught flat-footed. CPT Downey's section was surprised and confused when the first report of the marchers came in from our cavalrymen at Checkpoint Charlie.[9]

The Bosnian Serbs had been forewarned of the march since they also tuned in to the Kalesija radio. RS police and an angry mob of Serb "civilians" met the Muslim marchers. The Serbs, armed with sticks and rocks, chanted their intent of forcing the Muslims out of Republika Srpska. The Muslims met Serb harassment with violence. Some fisticuffs broke out.

An elderly Muslim man threw a couple of high-explosive grenades at the Serbs. One detonated directly underneath Captain Brunson's hovering Kiowa Warrior, but it caused no damage. The other grenade hit a tree and bounced back at the old man, wounding him. The Serbs responded by throwing two stun grenades into the Muslim crowd.[10]

Charlie Troop reacted immediately by sending a scout section to Mahala from nearby Rock (Alcatraz) OP. A tank from the troop's 2nd Platoon moved to block the east-west road at its intersection with the IEBL. In coordination with other Quarterhorse elements, including CPT Brunson's AWTs, Charlie Troop prevented the violence from escalating further. It provided safe passage for the IPTF to get to the scene so they could help Muslim and Serb police defuse the situation.[11]

LTC Harriman realized that it was critical for Quarterhorse to get our Kiowa Warriors overhead during incidents like Mahala One, as this incident was later known. We had made it well known to both entities that our helicopters had video cameras. Civilians on both sides were reluctant to commit acts of violence on film, lest the evidence be used against them later.[12] But our helicopters' presence did not deter all violence. In fact, many of our cavalrymen jokingly dubbed Mahala One the "Braveheart" incident. They were

**A Quarterhorse aerial weapons team on standby about to depart the Dawg Pound, June 1996 (photograph: Mark Viney).**

referring to a battle scene from the motion picture of that name. One of our cavalrymen recalled:

> We saw a bunch of young Serbs go into the police station and come out again armed with ax handles and the like. They rushed at each other just like in the movie. I saw one old man, I mean this guy must have been fifty-something, and he was kicking everybody's ass with an axe handle! I mean he went through five or six people before we could break it up. Unbelievable![13]

Following the incident at Mahala, Major Zajac, the 2 BCT operations officer, wrote:

> Our response to actions like this will be measured, deliberate and even-handed. Our mission is not changing to riot or crowd control. At higher levels (read Task Force Eagle/2 BCT), we will apply pressure to civilian leaders, encouraging them to refrain from initiating such activities. At task force and squadron level, civil affairs, PYSOP, and counter-intelligence teams will work with local leaders to discourage these events. Check points, patrols, and a solid information campaign will contribute to deterrence. Meanwhile the burden of responsibility for controlling or dispersing crowds will rest fully on the shoulders of local political leaders, FWF police, and the IPTF. We are not here to act as police. The media will scrutinize our activities in regard to civil disturbances with great interest — expect it.[14]

On the same day Quarterhorse kept the lid on Mahala, General John Shalikashvili, the Chairman of the Joint Chiefs of Staff, visited 2 BCT headquarters down in LA Lisa.[15] His message to soldiers there was also directed to our squadron:

I want to tell everyone who is involved in this great effort what an absolute superb job everyone is doing. It's hard to overstate how far we have come in the last four months because of the professionalism, the drive, the can-do attitude, the even-handedness, the diplomacy. But most of all, because of the professionalism of each and everyone involved in this effort.... None of us know where we're going to be in the next four months or in the next eight months, but if it's anything like what these men and women have accomplished in the last four months, we do have reason to be optimistic.... People here know what they are doing, and they are going about it with ... a smile on their face. I feel good about it.[16]

GEN Shalikashvili mentioned the situation still developing in Mahala. He addressed the concern that IFOR could easily become sucked into the middle of more incidents like this one:

I think we are all very much concerned about these kinds of demonstrations. But it is important to remember first and foremost the responsibility of the local authorities to keep them from happening. IFOR has not in the past, and IFOR will not stand idly by and see people get hurt. But it is wrong to assume that it's only IFOR's mission to deal with these matters. My worry is that we get the word to all the local factions to make sure that they do a lot more than they have done up to now to keep those from occurring.[17]

After our immediate response to the Mahala incident, Quarterhorse quickly implemented Operation Shortstop. Designed to prevent further riots from erupting in the ZOS, the initial four-day operation required our cavalrymen and attached engineers establish twelve additional checkpoints to limit access to Mahala. Our medical platoon sent an aid team to Checkpoint Charlie to provide more rapid treatment to any casualties that might occur. Female crew chiefs and armament technicians from our air cavalry troops were brought over from LA Molly to search civilian women crossing the ZOS for hidden weapons.[18]

Operation Shortstop evolved into a regular activity for our ground cavalry troops. They manned six additional checkpoints on both sides of the IEBL in addition to their usual tasks of patrolling, occupying remote sites, and assisting squadron intelligence-gathering activities. The operation was successful in preventing further violence around Mahala and Memici over the summer months.[19]

LTC Harriman later explained to Quarterhorse what had happened in Mahala and what issues were at stake:

Over the next few months the factions will sort through the freedom of movement issue. Since political power often comes from dissatisfied people, not every

A Bradley from one of Bravo Troop's scout platoons mans a temporary checkpoint near Mahala as part of Operation Shortstop, May 1996 (photograph: Mark Viney).

faction politician will act in ways to keep tensions low over freedom of movement. Some background follows.

BiH. Lots of Muslims want to go back home, some to live, some to dig up buried bucks, some just to visit. Some BiH politicians figure that if the Muslims go back home they will effectively reoccupy land in the RS. That's why 45 Muslims live in Dugi Dio, a broken village on the old confrontation line. They plan to move from broken village to broken village while the RS isn't looking. It's a squatter's movement — but some own the homes they squat in. The mass group that crossed the IEBL at Mahala wanted to force the RS to do one of two things: accept mass Muslim crossings, or beat up the people who crossed. BiH politicians figure beatings look dramatic on TV and might force IFOR to choose sides.

RS. Lots of RS people feel that the factions must live separately to get along. Like others have, they've noticed that Balkan peoples periodically kill large numbers of each other in factional fighting. They feel like they've given up lots of good land to the Muslims in exchange for separateness and in exchange for long-term peace. They figure the Muslims who cross the border just want more than their fair share of the land. And they fear the Muslims, since they just finished fighting them. RS people seem to want to live in RSville — a place of their own. Many have been willing to gather sticks and come to the border to beat up Muslims who cross. Some RS politicians support and encourage these homeboy hordes.

When the Muslim mass hits the homeboy horde, we got trouble — if we don't play heads up ball. First, police police civil disturbances. The BiH has police. The RS has police. Faction police have the civil disturbance ball. The International Police Task Force police work like referees; they watch faction police bounce the ball. What we do is set the terms of the game.

1. We use checkpoints to keep the size of the crowds down.
2. We let people cross the IEBL on foot.
3. We make sure faction police can get to the scene.
4. We encourage leaders of all factions to think and act smart.
5. We document what happens.
6. We help reporters catch the action.
7. We keep faction armies out of the fight.
8. We rescue IPTF in trouble.
9. We protect our own (remember, we respond to direct fire).
10. We don't let an atrocity happen.
11. We don't get between two crowds."[20]

Quarterhorse would later contend with two more incidents similar to "Mahala One." We nearly perfected LTC Harriman's list of eleven tasks — all but the last one. We never quite managed to avoid getting stuck in the middle. It was a "Catch-22" situation. If we got in between the clashing factions, we might take casualties. We wanted to avoid that. On the other hand, if we let them fight it out, the incident could easily spin out of our ability to contain and could jeopardize the tenuous peace. We obviously wanted to avoid that, too.

## The War-Torn Nation

By early spring, Quarterhorse was firmly established in our sector. Many of us took fresh stock of the desolation around us.

Bosnia-Herzegovina had always been a poor, backwards country long before its civil war. Nearly three and a half years of fighting and ethnic cleansing effectively destroyed much of its infrastructure. Nearly every Bosnian family subsisted on home-grown food. Instead of tending front lawns, Bosnians tended large gardens of tomatoes, beans, corn, squash, onions, potatoes, pumpkins, beets, and cabbage. Scrawny chickens scratched about while goats and sheep grazed under the care of young children. Every family seemed to own a milk cow. Bosnian Serb families, unlike Bosnian Muslims, also kept pigs. (This was one indicator that helped Quarterhorse determine who was who among the otherwise almost-same-looking factions.)

It was common during the summer months to see Bosnians taking their domestic animals for walks along the shoulders of roadways. It amused us to watch gray little old men in berets and jackets leading their cows on leashes just as Americans would walk their dogs through the neighborhood. Young children used thin, whip-like sticks to prod herds of filthy goats and sheep. Often, the sheep crowded into the lanes of traffic. At first, many of us chuckled at the Bosnians and their pets. Then we learned the practical reason for these walks. The animals grazed on common land in the summer in order to conserve harvested hay for the winter.

Very little commerce existed in Bosnia during our squadron's year there. What free enterprise there was consisted mostly of tiny Mom-and-Pop stands along the road. These stands were too tiny to be called stores. About the size of a small shed, they carried only a few convenience items, maybe an article of clothing or two, and their quantities of goods were severely limited.

Trash from American lodgment areas provided a lifeline for some of Bosnia's poorest people. Unemployed and displaced war refugees regularly waited at trash dumps for trucks to arrive with American refuse. People clamored and bickered over unopened MRE packets, uneaten fruit, cereal, and other items to supplement their meager meals. Others looked for wood, cardboard, or broken items that could be repaired.[21]

Everywhere we looked in Bosnia, just about everything that could be broken was. It was evident that the Communist government of Josip "Tito"

Muslim schoolboys in front of typical Bosnian "Mom-and-Pop" store, near Kalesija, summer 1996 (photograph: Mark Viney).

Broz had done much good work building up the national infrastructure. Bosnia once had good paved roads, railways, coal mines, and electric plants. But by late 1995, all suffered from many years of hard use, neglect, and war. The Bosnian people simply used items until they wouldn't work anymore, and then cannibalized them for other uses. There were very few junkyards in Bosnia. Broken-down cars were simply abandoned along the sides of roads and eventually pushed into streams and rivers after thorough stripping. What remained of these derelicts was usually nothing more than the bodies and chassis themselves. Everything useable had been removed.

Another example of Bosnia's ruin was the open strip mine near the Thunderdome and LA Molly. This mine was huge and had once been a massive operation using five or six large excavating cranes and a fleet of over thirty-five massive dump trucks, each capable of moving loads of nearly sixty tons. While Quarterhorse lived next door, the mine still functioned, but at a dramatically reduced capacity. Only one crane and three "monster trucks" were ever seen in working order. All the rest had been stripped for parts to keep the precious remaining few in operation.

# 6

# LATE SPRING

A hundred and twenty days after Operation Joint Endeavor commenced, Colonel Batiste informed us of what to expect in the coming summer months:

> What happens (next)? Initial compliance inspections are complete and the factions are busy fixing the discrepancies — the count is four BiH and thirteen VRS discrepancies. We will continue to monitor and compel compliance. Any violation demands action. Always treat people with dignity and respect.[1]
>
> I expect factions to be in full compliance by D+150. We will then transition to an operational tempo of 30 percent mission, 40 percent training, and 30 percent sustainment. Training will be METL related, planned, and resourced by the book — companies, batteries, and troops will conduct weekly training meetings. Training presence throughout sector will be a powerful deterrent until the day we redeploy. We set the preconditions for peace which permit the UNHCR (United Nations High Commission for Refugees) and OSCE (Organization for Security and Cooperation in Europe) to get about rebuilding the country and running the elections scheduled for mid–September. We give peace a chance.[2]

The "30 percent mission" that COL Batiste referred to included continual inspections of weapons storage sites, continued surveillance of the ZOS, and vigilance in the conduct of all force protection missions. He cautioned, "Take care of one another. I need Soldiers focused on the mission, supported by a great squad and platoon. Never has a fully integrated chain of command been more important. Leaders must know their Soldiers. Anticipate problems. Find solutions that work. Support your comrades. Team work is everything."[3]

As the spring temperatures rose and our purely military tasks tapered off, our focus on civil affairs missions and the scheduled national elections intensified. Lieutenant Colonel Harriman was the first senior commander in 2 BCT to anticipate this shift. Increasingly, we worked to assist the efforts of several non-governmental and humanitarian aid organizations by providing area security as they worked around our sector.[4]

The same was true of our support to the OSCE and the European Community Monitoring Mission (ECMM). These two organizations were responsible for determining the readiness of the region for democratic elections, as well as for monitoring the elections themselves. At this point in the year, IFOR's precise role in assisting them had yet to be clearly defined. Initial coordinations at echelons above Quarterhorse were already underway.[5]

The two civil affairs teams attached to Quarterhorse spearheaded our humanitarian assistance effort. Our "CA guys" helped to determine the needs and requirements of the people and infrastructure and reported this information to Task Force Eagle headquarters. Direct humanitarian relief was clearly beyond IFOR's official mandate, however.

With the shift in mission focus, many of our cavalrymen asked yet again why Quarterhorse had to remain in Bosnia. Our commanders replied that it was the presence of Task Force Eagle that gave Bosnians in both entities the confidence to continue the march towards peace and stability. LTC Harriman wrote, "Towards this end, the strong, combat ready squadron, ubiquitous in the Brigade sector, constantly and visibly training to sustain its fighting skills, [had] sent precisely the right message" in the first quarter of the operation.[6]

On May 4, Bravo Troop's 1st Platoon went out to look at Hill 425, an outpost manned by Alpha Troop. Our ground cavalry troops regularly rotated their cavalrymen through remote sites like Hill 425 to give them much-needed changes of scenery and activity. Unfortunately, our support cavalrymen had no such opportunity. Largely confined to the same small camps for the duration of our tour, they dubbed themselves "prisoners for peace."

Ever since IFOR units had first occupied Hill 425 several months past, an almost constant string of attempted incursions by locals had occurred. These forays into our perimeter were not hostile in nature. The impoverished Bosnians were simply trying to scrounge what they could from us. But their presence still posed a threat. In the first half of June, one of our platoons finally moved and reconfigured the perimeter atop Hill 425. It also established better fields of fire beyond. The incursions ceased very soon afterwards.[7]

## When Do We Leave?

Colonel Batiste was aware of the growing desire within the ranks for more information on our redeployment home to Germany. He wrote, "Do not listen to the rumors and remember that the press almost always gets it wrong. Plan for 365 days. The redeployment will probably span three or four months — you and your unit may get lucky."[8]

LTC Harriman also addressed our concerns in mid–May:

In about a year, we will go. Like you, I read the newspapers. I can see the politicians have begun dancing with ideas. We have to keep a presence through the elections, some say. We must extend the IFOR mandate, some say. We must postpone the elections, some say. IFOR can't leave until after the elections, some say. One year, some say. Till January. Till March. We don't know, some say.

Here is what I say. First, we leave last in the 2nd BDE as I see it. And plan to stay here a year. Nothing I have said thus far should strike anyone as news. I have said this much before. Second, politicians will choose how long IFOR stays here. Generals have a say in the length of stay decisions; politicians make them. Third, Generals know what living away from home for a year feels like. At least the ones I have talked to know what it feels like. The way I figure it, if the politicians decide to keep American Soldiers here for some longer period, we, Quarterhorse, will stay here for about a year because our Generals know what life away from home feels like.[9]

As Quarterhorse soldiered on, the politicians and diplomats wrangled over how long peacekeepers would be needed to provide a reasonable guarantee that the Bosnian peace would hold.

Since December 1995, President Clinton had continued to promise that American soldiers would be home in not more than a year. We in Quarterhorse knew that his claims were politically motivated for maximum palatability. We also knew firsthand how wildly unrealistic they were.

The length of the operation was already an issue when IFOR units first rolled into Bosnia. Lieutenant General Sir Michael J.D. Walker, the British commander of all NATO land forces in Bosnia, brought world attention to the issue. LTG Walker told his deputies that he favored a two-year time frame. A senior French officer agreed but wondered what the American response would be. "You must excuse me if I seem to value a real solution in Bosnia over the reelection of President Clinton," LTG Walker replied.[10]

By mid–May, some 10,000 NATO troops had been withdrawn from Bosnia with little fanfare. With most of the military provisions of the GFAP accomplished, IFOR strength dropped to about 50,000 soldiers. The number remaining included 16,000 Americans (down from a high of 20,000), and 7,000 each from Great Britain and France (down from 11,000 each).

A NATO spokesman said that IFOR had "hit a steady level now in numbers," and that our strength was unlikely to fluctuate in the foreseeable future.[11]

As it turned out, the American contingent of IFOR did return home in just short of a year. In its place, however, came a series of ever-smaller follow-on forces. It was not until 2005 that NATO officially concluded its stability operations in Bosnia.

## The Zvornik Seven

While the Bosnian Civil War raged back in July 1995, thousands of Muslim men and boys fled into the woods after the UN "safe haven" of Srebrenica fell to the Serbs. Most of them were chased down and summarily murdered before reaching Muslim territory. Their bodies littered the hillsides. Almost a year later, nearly 6,000 Muslims remained unaccounted for.[12]

On May 10, an unusual incident reminded Quarterhorse of this human tragedy. A group of seven armed men emerged from the woods four miles west of Zvornik claiming to be Muslim survivors of a fallen "safe haven."[13] American artillerymen from Alpha Battery, 4-29th Field Artillery were the first to spot this group, soon to become famous as the "Zvornik Seven." The artillerymen watched as the seven men, armed with Soviet-made pistols and grenades, disappeared into a nearby woodline.

By chance, a patrol of military police, civil affairs, and counterintelligence soldiers attached to Quarterhorse happened by. Just then, there were several bursts of gunfire and an explosion.[14] The mysterious men ran back out of the woods. They threw themselves at the artillerymen's feet and begged for protection from the Serbs, who had supposedly just attacked them. The seven claimed to be Muslim survivors from Zepa. They said they had been hiding in the woods for ten months and had followed the sun towards Tuzla.

Shortly after the seven men appeared, several Bosnian Serb policemen arrived. No IFOR unit had called for them.[15] Was it just coincidence, or were the Serbs on cue? We wondered.

Our military police took the men into custody. We called in the IPTF to decide whether the Muslims should be turned over to the Serb police. They were clearly in violation of the GFAP since they carried weapons and moved as an armed group. They were also in Serb police jurisdiction, so we turned them over. The *Star and Stripes* newspaper reported a discrepancy between IFOR and the IPTF over who had made this decision to hand over the seven men. Colonel Batiste said that we had deferred to the IPTF. The IPTF countered that their officers on the scene had only been observers and that IFOR had made the decision.[16]

Either way, the BiH government and international human rights advocates were furious. Critics argued that IFOR should have known better, given the Serbs' track record for beating, torturing, and killing prisoners.[17] On one hand, they were right. But Lieutenant General Walker, the COMARRC, defended our decision. The men had to be handed over even if they were survivors of the Srebrenica massacres: "The fighting is over. The tragedy that happened in Srebrenica has no legal bearing on crimes committed since."[18]

Realizing the danger in which we'd placed the seven men, LTC Harriman immediately flew to Zvornik. Major Roberts's patrol joined him at the Zvornik police station. LTC Harriman went inside to see what was going on. Our concern was not to try to get them back, since that would be seen as an IFOR move to undermine the Dayton Accord. Rather, we just wanted to guarantee humane treatment for the men.

The Serb police were very polite at first. Besides LTC Harriman, the International Red Cross and the IPTF both had representatives present for the group's initial interrogation.

MAJ Roberts stayed outside in his Humvee. Radio communications were causing problems, so he had to drive around in order to keep in contact with the TAC. Captain Downey and two MPs remained on foot outside the station. Soon, CPT Downey was instructed to take LTC Harriman's borrowed Black-hawk and fly to LA Molly to report the situation to General Nash, the Task Force Eagle Commander.

Rumors spread quickly through Zvornik that the seven were Muslim terrorists who had committed an incident a few days earlier. Just as CPT Downey's helicopter departed, a curious mob of civilians arrived at the station.[19] While discussions inside dragged on for several hours, the Serb crowd grew increasingly hostile towards MAJ Roberts's patrol.

Additional shifts of Serb police arrived. Some wore flak vests and carried AK-47s — sure signs of potential trouble. They set up a perimeter around the station. Was it to protect their new prisoners from the mob or to prevent any IFOR attempts to free them?

The mob surrounded MAJ Roberts's vehicles. He admitted, "We got a little nervous." He called the TAC and instructed them to be prepared to launch a rescue mission.[20]

MAJ Roberts was later quoted in the *Stars and Stripes* that his element then "went to a state of higher force protection."[21] When CPT Viney asked him what that meant, MAJ Roberts exclaimed, "We got the f___ outta there!"[22] But they could not simply move out because they were surrounded. MAJ Roberts complained to the Serb police, who promptly escorted his vehicles through the agitated crowd.

The seven Muslims remained in Serb police custody for many months. An internal UN report later stated that the men were beaten into signing confessions following "torture [that] was intentionally inflicted by, urged by or allowed by" Bosnian Serb officials.[23] Muslim media in Tuzla reported the confessions extracted from the "Zvornik Seven." The Serbs insisted that the men were guilty of the recent murder of four Serb lumberjacks down in the Task Force 2-68 AR sector.

The 2 BCT headquarters had not had a clear picture of our situation until CPT Downey gave his report at LA Molly. By then, it was already late in the day.

The next morning, Brigadier General Cherrie began discussions with ABiH and VRS military leaders, American military police, IPTF leaders, and other civilian authorities on how to investigate the incident in a neutral manner. Their meeting spawned broader discussions about human rights, the Dayton Accord, and the role of IFOR.[24]

No one was certain who the men were or where they had come from. Supposing their story was true, they had overshot Tuzla by nearly 15 kilometers. They had inexplicably recent haircuts and were either clean-shaven or had trimmed beards. Their shoes were relatively clean and bore no evidence of having trod over forested mountains for any length of time.

LTC Harriman told our officers that he felt it might have been a hoax to gain outside support for the Muslims. The names the men had given to authorities appeared to be Muslim names, but one man wrote his name in Cyrillic — the Russian alphabet used by the Serbs.[25] The Federation government denied that any of the names were on its army rolls. Two of the men wore military uniforms and all appeared to be in better health than one would imagine after having camped out in the woods for ten months.[26]

Colonel Batiste was skeptical of the whole affair: "Things in the Balkans are never as they seem. I am constantly reminded that there are no good guys here."[27]

Some NATO officers speculated that at least the two uniformed men might have been part of a covert military operation, possibly sanctioned by the Federation government. In recent months, IFOR had caught the Federation running clandestine paramilitary training camps in central Bosnia. But this theory had its holes, too. The men were not armed well enough for any serious mission. Between them, they carried five small knives, two grenades, and two pistols. Serb police later revealed a cache containing an AK-47, two shotguns, and extra ammo that they'd supposedly discovered.

The Zvornik Seven continued to draw international headlines several weeks after their capture. The *Los Angeles Times* reported, "Beaten and tortured into signing murder confessions, seven Muslim men who were turned over to Bosnian Serb police by U.S. troops are at the center of a heated controversy over law, human rights, and the actions of American peacekeepers."[28] During Quarterhorse's year in Bosnia, it was never resolved who the Zvornik Seven were or what they had been up to.

While the fallout from their capture occupied much of our attention, LTC Harriman gave our officers an assessment of the overall situation at this stage in the operation. He surmised that both sides probably felt threatened by a possible loss of power in the upcoming elections scheduled for September. Freedom of movement was the issue. Its loss would probably mean the breakdown of the country into separate ethnic areas.[29]

The Mahala incident that we had contained back on April 25 showed just what a difficult issue freedom of movement would be. Under the Dayton Accord, people were allowed to return to the areas they had fled or were expelled from during the war. LTC Harriman thought both governments were undermining the Accord. They had only allowed freedom of movement in certain areas and not in others where they felt threatened by the potential of being voted out of political control by returning refugees.[30]

Our biggest military threat, LTC Harriman warned, was an ambush against our many daily convoys of thin-skinned utility and logistics vehicles.[31] The threat of accidents and terrorist attacks was also very real. Accordingly, we issued FRAGOs and conducted inspections and backbrief rehearsals for every patrol and convoy departing our lodgment areas.

Those of us who traveled the roads all the time had to remain vigilant each and every trip. Those who maintained a healthy fear of the dangers prayed that we would make it through another day without incident. We checked to ensure that our weapons were ready and within arm's reach. As we drove the twisty, turny roads through the thickly forested mountains, we scoured the roadsides for potential ambush positions. We mentally wargamed what we would do if one suddenly occurred.

Regrettably, some of our cavalrymen did not maintain such vigilance. By late spring, many had lapsed into varying degrees of complacency. Quarterhorse had been in country too long, and many of us had been lulled into a false sense of security. We were accustomed to the routine. Our missions typically ran smoothly. Major incidents did not erupt all that often. So it was our great fortune that no one ever attempted to ambush us.

## Alcatraz/Rock OP

In order to maintain force presence and observation over contended areas of the ZOS, Quarterhorse occupied a series of remote sites throughout our sector. A few kilometers east of Checkpoint Charlie was a small observation post near the destroyed village of Carparde. We rotated our scout platoons and mortar sections through tours of duty at the OP. These elements scanned from the OP's observation tower and patrolled the surrounding area to detect any VRS military activity in and around the ZOS.

Quarterhorse scout observes from his Bradley at Alcatraz OP, summer 1996 (photograph: 1st Infantry Division Public Affairs Office).

The checkpoint was alternately known as Alcatraz OP or Rock OP, depending on whichever troop had responsibility for it. When Alpha Troop's scouts under First Lieutenant Dudley occupied it in mid–June, it was known as Alcatraz. It was not a very impressive post, just a bombed-out three-story building surrounded by a white brick wall topped with sandbags and concertina wire.[32]

Training was an important part of most days at Alcatraz. Some cavalrymen manned the radio retransmission site at the OP, while others conducted daily patrols. Our mortarmen practiced fire missions and crew drills. Staff Sergeant Anderson, Alpha Troop's mortar section sergeant, held competitions between his crews to break up the monotony. He rewarded the winners with relief from guard duty.[33]

Hot chow from the Dawg Pound was brought out to Alcatraz in morning and evening LOGPACs. Our cavalrymen slept in the ramshackle, three-story apartment or hotel building. A rumor circulated among them that the plywood laid down on the floors covered bloodstains from the war.[34]

The OP had modest recreational facilities. It had a small weight room, volleyball court, and sandlot basketball hoop. There was a television and videocassette player, although movie selections were understandably limited.[35]

To pass idle time, Staff Sergeant Johnson and Sergeant Cosme created a diversion called "Sniper Alley." From their sleeping quarters on the top floor, they plinked at plastic bottles on a nearby building with mail-order BB guns. They claimed that it helped them maintain their marksmanship skills.

A Quarterhorse civil affairs officer explained to a visiting reporter that "the cavalry is hard core combat arms."[36] He was right. The endless hours without action were hard on us. We were trained to conduct mounted reconnaissance and armored shock actions. The inactivity between missions didn't satisfy us at all.

SSG Johnson said, "When I came down [to Bosnia] I was expecting a punch up. But nothing's happening. I'd rather be back in Germany on exercise. If we ain't gonna get into to it, get me the hell outa here." But then he softened. "If it helps the kids, then I'll live."[37]

SSG Johnson's comments were typical among the Quarterhorse ranks at this point in the operation. The initial excitement had worn off. What remained were the mundane rituals of peacekeeping. It was hot, and we really missed our families. While many of our cavalrymen may have shared SSG Johnson's relish for a good fight, others privately questioned how mentally prepared we really were for one. One year in a stability operation seemed far too long. By this point, we hadn't even been in Bosnia for six months.

Alcatraz was very close to the contentious ZOS villages of Mahala and Memici. Many Muslims now living in Memici and Kalesija farther to the west had been ethnically cleansed out of Mahala. Although the Dayton Accord said they were allowed to return to their homes, Bosnian Serb authorities had made it difficult for them with illegal checkpoints and harassment. The resettlement issue was exacerbated by the substantial number of Serbs who were moved into the area after parts of Sarajevo were turned over to the Federation. Emotions ran high on both sides of the ZOS.

Nearly 300 vehicles passed through Checkpoint Charlie every day. Bosnian Serb police stopped many of them. But intimidation was not limited to the Serb side. Muslim police also beat Serb travelers on occasion.

Alcatraz became a way station for Bosnians crossing the IEBL. Many Muslims, fearful of the Serb police, stopped at the gate to request an IFOR escort. We had to turn them down because it was not our responsibility to provide such a service.[38]

In late May, RS police threw up one checkpoint that caused us particular ire. For the fourth time in three days, LTC Harriman had to drop his planned activities to evict the stubborn Serbs from this checkpoint just west of Zvornik.

LTC Harriman was impatient. "Move your checkpoint. You are in violation," he repeated over and over.[39]

A reporter was at the scene and recorded Major Roberts's explanation. "They're still playing their little game. We watch them stop cars and turn them back from our OPs, and then they deny it when we come down here."[40]

The Serb police continued to argue with LTC Harriman. They told some story about Muslim foot patrols, but he didn't buy it. A CBS News crew and a couple of other journalists began to record the tense exchange. Bosnians from all three factions hated to be filmed. Eventually, the Serbs decided to move out.[41]

Scout platoons from all three of our ground cavalry troops conducted frequent mounted patrols on both sides of the IEBL to prevent these illegal checkpoints from undermining the GFAP's promise of freedom of movement.

## Scouts on Patrol

A particular mounted patrol conducted by First Lieutenant Dudley's Alpha Troop scouts in mid–May was documented by a visiting reporter who had been granted full access to our activities. His account, paraphrased here, provides a good representation of how these daily missions were conducted throughout the Quarterhorse sector.[42]

Early that particular morning in Alcatraz OP, 1LT Dudley emerged from his platoon CP and briefed his scouts on their mission. On today's patrol, a scout section with attachments would venture deep into Serb territory to verify that a certain armored vehicle was still where it was supposed to be at a registered cantonment area. The section would then move through the hills above Sekovici to visit a local VRS headquarters. The patrol's basic mission was to maintain force presence within the Quarterhorse sector.

In short time, the patrol's three Bradleys and a U.S. Air Force Forward Air Controller (FAC) Humvee departed the compound. The wooded terrain closed in tightly along the road being traveled. Bosnian Serb men gave hostile looks as our scouts rumbled past. Serb children were always happy to beg from our cavalrymen, but Serb adults were contemptuous.

Locals glared as 1LT Dudley's scouts dismounted to inspect the Serb APC. The old 1950s-era BTR-50 command vehicle was right where it was supposed to be. It was completely inoperable.

A group of small children tagged along with our scouts, giggling and begging for bonbons. An old lady came by, gave a look of disgust for the vehicle, and gestured for us to drag the thing away. She had apparently seen enough of war and visiting IFOR patrols. Staff Sergeant Johnson climbed on top of the derelict vehicle. He was intent on salvaging whatever optics or instruments he could find for a souvenir, but they were already long gone. The young Serb men in the square just glared and did not acknowledge our scouts' greetings. 1LT Dudley's scouts mounted up and departed.[43]

They rumbled on through Sekovici, an important, yet typically dirty town brimming with activity. Election posters for the notorious warlord and paramilitary chief Arkan were everywhere. The weather was sunny, but the citizens' dispositions were not. Local men swilling their morning beers gave only angry looks and an occasional unfriendly hand gesture to our scouts. Serb MUPs in their "purple people eater" uniforms stood defiantly with hands on hips. The Serbs in this town merely tolerated our presence. They certainly did not welcome it.

SSG Johnson told the accompanying reporter a story about the town. "We used to go by this one place every day and these two little kids would always run out to wave to us. One day as we were going past, they came running out and their mother ran out yelling at them and chased them off with a switch. The next day we came by and the kids looked to see if their mother was looking before they started waving." Kids like these gave us hope that our hard work might not be in vain after all.[44]

Beyond Sekovici, the scout section rounded a steep turn that led farther up into the hills. The road grew narrower and the hills became steeper, almost closing in over the road. It was perfect terrain for an ambush or roadblock. The scouts continued past several ramshackle cabins, scanning for threats as they went.

1LT Dudley told the reporter, "We haven't had any real problems with people around here, but it only takes one with an axe to grind for it to get ugly in a hurry. We stay ready for anything."[45] As indicated earlier, this was a difficult task since nothing exciting happened very often. Only our scouts' professionalism kept them on their toes.

When the patrol reached the VRS headquarters, it found that the local commander was out. The place was active nonetheless. Soldiers shuttled about, turning the three-story building into a veritable "ski lodge," complete with bars and ballrooms.

"I wish the commander was here," 1LT Dudley said. "His office is quite a sight. He's an avid hunter and he's got all kinds of hunting stuff and fox pelts hanging up. We always like to swap hunting and fishing stories after we deal with the business side of things." Not surprisingly, none of the commander's subordinates admitted to having a key to allow 1LT Dudley to peek inside his office.[46]

As our scouts mounted up, a cold drizzle fell over the lush green hills. The vehicles were turned around, and the patrol headed down the narrow road it had come up. No Serbs paid them much attention this time, not even in Sekovici. Forty-five minutes later, the patrol rumbled back into Alcatraz.

On May 21, we were visited by a young Internet news reporter who had covered the Bosnian Civil War for almost three years. After dinner, he gave a class on Bosnian history to a group of Quarterhorse officers. His fascinating lecture traced the animosity between the ethnic groups back to the Battle of Kosovo in 1392. This battle began the ongoing cycle whereby one group always felt oppressed by the other.[47] The briefing really opened our eyes to the depth of hatred that the ethnic groups felt for one another.

Most of our cavalrymen were able to celebrate Memorial Day by taking the day off. LTC Harriman and Chaplain Brown led commemoration ceremonies at the Dawg Pound and LA Molly. LTC Harriman reminded us of our regiment's many hard-won victories:

> Today, as you pull on your boots, your American Army boots, remember the troopers who wore them before us. Some fought through the rubber trees on a Michelin rubber plantation in 1969. Quarterhorse troopers avoided roads and trails then. Different war. Some walked first onto Omaha Beach; the Big Red One wanted to wade ashore with its eyes open. Colonel Robert E. Lee left Quarterhorse in 1861 to fight against it. And Colonel John Sedgwick signed on to give Lee a run for his money. Leonard Wood, a contract surgeon at the time, took over B Troop in May of 1886, then chased Geronimo across Arizona and New Mexico. Leonard Wood gave up on surgery. He became Army Chief of Staff. PVT James Pratt wore your boots. He was a farrier. James earned the Medal of Honor in Red River, Texas, in 1872 — and it wasn't for shoeing horses. 1st Sergeant William McNamara earned the Medal of Honor — same river, same day. 29 September 1872. A rough day it was. And Sergeant John B. Charlton once wore Quarterhorse boots. He handled regimental distribution in 1874. Back then they were called distribution dispatches. John had to ride 580 miles from Fort Richardson, Texas, to Fort Sill, Oklahoma, to drop a buck slip. It took him six days. You didn't do distribution in 1874 unless you were like Sergeant Charlton: "zealous, energetic, reliable, always faithful, absolutely loyal ... perfectly trained and disciplined, all combined with intelligence and common sense."[48]
>
> Today we remember those who wore our boots before us: our Soldiers, some Quarterhorse, some not so lucky. Our distant relatives, those who lived long enough became our fathers and mothers. Some died too young to do anything but shape our souls. But all made us the Army we are, the country we are. Without them we wouldn't be here in Bosnia. Without them we just might not be good enough, without the moral horsepower needed to fill these American Army boots here. And that's why we pause to remember those who wore these boots before us, this Memorial Day.[49]

As a recording of "Taps" was played, many proud eyes rested on the Quarterhorse colors, the national flag, and a fallen cavalryman's monument of a helmet upon an inverted rifle between a spit-shined pair of boots. It was good for us to take the time to reflect on who we were as Quarterhorse.

## The Rear Detachment

Back in our home station in Schweinfurt, Germany, Captain Rich Spiegel commanded the Quarterhorse Rear Detachment (Rear-D). This was a provisional troop that kept our families informed and provided them with necessary assistance in the absence of deployed spouses. Specific Rear-D tasks included routine garrison activities, in-processing new arrivals and coordinating their pre-deployment training, out-processing departing cavalrymen, as well as providing logistical support to our deployed main body. This vital support allowed those of us downrange to concentrate on our stability tasks at hand.[50]

Because Quarterhorse did not require all of our tanks in Bosnia, each ground cavalry troop left behind one of its two tank platoons. These tankers and other non-deployable personnel provided manpower for the Rear Detachment.

A reporter who visited Schweinfurt in early 1996 wrote, "Soldiers who work the Rear Detachment during the Bosnia deployment would be welcome on most baseball teams because they can hit both right and left handed.... Family support specialists at 3rd Squadron, 4th Cavalry juggle and solve Soldier problems in Bosnia with one hand and at the same time help family members back in Schweinfurt with the other."[51]

Sergeant Grant Springer, a tank NCO from Charlie Troop, said, "I've never been back on a Rear Detachment or any kind of family support. I deployed to Desert Storm and always to the field for training. You think about what the guys back in the rear are doing but it's a lot more work than anybody would expect." SGT Springer figured that he worked ten to eighteen hours a day solving a variety of problems: "This is the hardest thing I ever did. It doesn't just happen during the day; it goes into the night. You get phone calls in the middle of the night all the time. Somebody goes into labor, you've got to go. The main thing is to make sure the families are happy and cared for."

SGT Springer was one of our Rear-D's point men for family problem solving. He also worked issues received from downrange in Bosnia. "When the Soldiers need something done, they send it back to me and I get it squared away and get it back out to them."[52]

Captain Spiegel said, "The family support representatives are completely self-motivated. It's just typical NCO initiative, like they would approach any other duty. They might not like the fact they didn't deploy with their unit, but they've got their job, and they're going to do their best just because they're NCOs."[53]

Our Rear-D established a family room in the squadron headquarters building where family members could stop by for the latest news from "downrange." Donated toys kept children occupied while mothers received assistance and information.

LTC Harriman kept Quarterhorse families up-to-date on our activities through periodic open letters. In late February, he wrote:

> You can be proud. Greetings from Quarterhorse, from Lodgment Area Saber (Molly) and Lodgment Area Quarterhorse (the Dawg Pound). I'd like you to know this — you who are cavalry family, you who have a husband, a wife, a father, mother, son, daughter, lover, or even a distant relative in Quarterhorse. They who make up the Quarterhorse are good at it. They have stability operations right. They care for each other. They will and have saved lives and risked their own to do it. They stand ready to defend themselves. They know their environment. Quarterhorse Soldiers affected the Rome summit directly by executing a synchronized air-ground mission at Han Pijesak. Quarterhorse Soldiers brought together a brother and sister — long separated by the conflict at Memici. Quarterhorse Soldiers talk to the people surrounding them and treat those they meet with respect. Quarterhorse troopers — the Soldiers, Airmen, the Navy guys too — they have it right.
>
> Read the Sunday, 25 February *Stars and Stripes* article on Checkpoint Charlie. Checkpoint Charlie Soldiers serve ready to fight, but they have human ties here. The Checkpoint Charlie article talks about the Bosnia half of our cavalry family — the Soldiers you know and love. Then read the *Soldier of Fortune* article in the February edition. *Soldier of Fortune* soldiers here talk tough talk and walk around with pornographic stickers on their Squad Automatic Weapon magazines. Quarterhorse Soldiers don't; they do stability operations right. You have every reason to be proud.[54]

The guest speaker at one Quarterhorse Family Support Group (FSG) meeting in mid–March was Lieutenant Colonel Gene Kamena, the commander of 3-12 Infantry in Schweinfurt. He had just returned from a trip to Bosnia and told our families how we were doing. He narrated a recent videotape showing construction underway at LA Molly.[55]

First Sergeant Jeffrey McGinnis, the Rear-D first sergeant, also spoke to our families. He told them, "They've just about got their showers all built. It's a lot different than Hungary where they complained they didn't get a hot shower this week. Some of the guys in Bosnia didn't get a shower in a month.... The tents and hard stands are being built. They're upgrading the area. Daily it's becoming better. They all should be in tents by now."[56]

Later, on June 1, our Rear-D hosted a Family Fun Day for all Quarter-horse families to enjoy food, games, and companionship. Cavalrymen helped our children climb all over the vehicles on static display. Wives enjoyed competing in numerous contests and events.[57]

Quarterhorse was separated from our families for almost a year. It was too long to be gone, and some disreputable things happened while we were away. Conflicting demands, insufficient personnel, and lapses of leadership were all blamed for the loss of accountability of nearly $60,000 worth of barracks furniture. Eventually, most of the furnishings were accounted for after our squadron's return to Schweinfurt.

Our barracks themselves were scenes of debauchery. Drug use was rampant. Almost twenty Rear-D cavalrymen were arrested for drug use and distribution following our return. One turned out to be the second-biggest drug dealer in the Schweinfurt military community. Some lonely wives found their way into the barracks, one of whom became pregnant. These incidents are worth mentioning because they are the same sort of issues that all deployed units must be prepared to address.

# 7

# SUMMER

## Support for the ICTY Investigations

The International Criminal Tribunal for War Crimes in the Former Yugoslavia (ICTY) was the first international war crimes tribunal convened since the Nurnberg and Tokyo trials following World War II. Based in The Hague, the ICTY was responsible for bringing to justice those responsible for the worst atrocities committed in Europe since 1945. Richard Goldstone, a South African, headed the ICTY team, whose mission it was to collect evidence and pursue the fifty-six men Goldstone had indicted for war crimes. Among them were Bosnian Serb political leader Radovan Karadzic and the VRS military commander General Ratko Mladic.[1] Goldstone emphasized the imperative behind his mission. An enduring peace in Bosnia would not be possible unless some form of justice was delivered.

During IFOR's first month in Bosnia, the ICTY struggled to establish its legitimacy. It needed considerable help. Goldstone pressed IFOR leadership to provide his team with office space, transportation, and security at suspected gravesites. Goldstone also expected IFOR troops to dig up a particular gravesite in northwestern Bosnia.[2] Admiral Smith, the overall NATO commander in Bosnia, refused. "NATO is not — I repeat, NATO is not — going to provide specific security or, in other words, guarantee security, for teams investigating these grave sites.

"Our job," ADM Smith continued, "is to provide an environment in which they can accomplish their missions. That does not mean that we will guard individual gravesites. That does not mean that we will provide security for individuals as they go about [their investigations]."[3]

However, on the same day ADM Smith made these comments, American Assistant Secretary of State for Human Rights John H.F. Shattuck made a contradictory statement while touring suspected war crimes sites. Mr. Shattuck said that one of IFOR's missions was "to provide security for investigations of the kind that will be conducted by the International War Crimes Tribunal.

"Clearly, security will be needed," he said. "That task will be taken up [by NATO] as soon as the primary task is completed.... It is the responsibility of the international force to do so.... The underlying fact here is that ultimately justice and long-term peace must go together."[4] ADM Smith lost the argument. Once IFOR had guaranteed freedom of movement, and many of the GFAP military provisions had been met, IFOR units, including Quarterhorse, did provide significant assistance to the ICTY investigations.

During several periods from late May through October, the ICTY searched for evidence of war crimes atrocities within the 2 BCT sector. Quarterhorse assisted the ICTY by providing site security and ground and aerial quick reaction forces (QRFs). The site security mission normally involved two platoons and the Squadron TAC for 24-hour periods.[5]

The investigations were not without incident. On three occasions — at Luke, at the Vlasenica police headquarters, and at the Panorama Hotel on the Drina River — Bosnian Serb authorities attempted to block ICTY access to investigation sites. Military police and Bravo Troop elements compelled the Serbs to move aside.

The ICTY mission received a lot of attention from the IFOR chain of command, the press, and American political leaders. Major Zajac, the 2 BCT operations officer, surmised that "perhaps by fairly determining guilt and responsibility for war crimes, the ICTY will mitigate revenge motives that could fuel another conflict."[6]

The fourth round of ICTY investigations was conducted in July. The foul task of exhuming putrefied corpses was particularly awful in the strong summer heat. Bravo Troop's Second Lieutenant Parnell was one of several Quarterhorse cavalrymen who took an up-close look at the exhumation. The stench of decomposed bodies was so intense that it permeated his clothing. Immediately upon his return to the Dawg Pound, members of 2LT Parnell's platoon insisted that he remove his uniform and burn it. He had no issue with complying.[7]

Investigations in August centered on the town of Lazete in Republika Srpska. The main investigation site was a mass grave filled in after the fall of Srebrenica.

Another round of investigations began on October 10. The ICTY resumed their exhumation of mass graves and documented mass execution sites. Once again, Bravo Troop provided area security. Our cavalrymen were careful to avoid having their pictures taken near the gravesites. Our civil affairs and counter-intel guys thought such pictures could trigger an undesirable political response from the Serbs.[8]

During war crimes investigations in our sector, Quarterhorse provided living spaces at the Dawg Pound for ICTY personnel. Lieutenant Colonel Harriman suggested that "sleeping near the evidence might give the Docs the creeps."[9] ICTY forensic experts examined the bodies they recovered just down the road in the bombed-out ice cream factory outside Kalesija. None of us liked to sit near them in our mess hall.

## War Crimes

While our three ground cavalry troops continued their myriad missions, our two air cavalry troops flew daily reconnaissance missions over the 2 BCT sector. The most dramatic of these aerial recons was the one in May when Chief Warrant Officer Three John Roberts's aerial weapons team (AWT) discovered the ridgeline near Vlasenica that was littered with the remains of several hundred slain civilians.[10]

Hilltop trail intersection near Vlasenica littered with bones and clothing, evidence of ethnic cleansing discovered by CW3 Roberts's aerial weapons team from Echo Troop, May 1996 (photograph: Phil Nusbaum).

While Bravo Troop provided security for the ICTY investigations, it discovered other previously unknown sites of partially buried corpses. Some of these sites dated back to the Serb campaign to seize the UN "safe haven" of Srebrenica. UNPROFOR failed to halt the Serb advance, and the city fell on July 11, 1995. An estimated 40,000 Muslims were then expelled from this pocket, to which many had fled from Serb attacks elsewhere. UNPROFOR's failure to stop the Serb assault reflected the overall failure of the UN mission in Bosnia and led to stronger American diplomatic and military efforts to stop the war.[11]

Nearly 25,000 Muslim women, children, and elderly were forcibly transported to Tuzla. About 12,000 Muslim men attempted to break out of the Serb noose around Srebrenica. Moving on foot, they attempted to reach Muslim-held territory some sixty miles away. Thousands survived, but between 3,500 and 5,500 remained unaccounted for, according to a report by UN Secretary General Boutros Boutros-Ghali published in November

Echo Troop's First Lieutenant Devin Weil (left) and Chief Warrant Officer Three John Roberts await their pre-mission briefing, LA Molly, summer 1996 (photograph: Mark Viney).

1995. CW3 Roberts's AWT uncovered the fate of several hundred of these men. The UN report stated that an unknown number of men might have been executed and buried in six mass graves near Srebrenica. These mass executions were the worst atrocities committed in Europe in over fifty years.[12]

After throwing out the Muslim inhabitants, Bosnian Serbs moved their own war refugees into Srebrenica. A drunken VRS fighter boasted to a reporter, "Look at those hills—they used to be covered with woods, but the Muslims cut them down, and that ruined this town. It used to be so pretty, so we killed them. We killed them all.... Let's have a coffee."[13]

The Federation government hoped that the ICTY investigations would help to resolve the fate of nearly 24,000 Bosnians still missing from the war.[14] Nearly 2.5 million people had fled their homes. During Quarterhorse's tour in Bosnia, nearly 300,000 civilians remained displaced. Nearly one-third of all family dwellings in Bosnia had been destroyed during the three-and-a-half-year civil war. As with other civil wars, the Bosnian Civil War was proof that the conflicts a nation's people wage with each other are the bloodiest and most brutal of all.

An interesting American newspaper opinion column blasted Western policymakers for their weak-hearted stance on pursuing indicted war criminals:

> It would be tempting to blame ... the eventual failure of the new Bosnia-Herzegovina on historic enmities. But it can also be blamed on the lack of enough international will, beginning with that of the United States, to help create the conditions for the rebirth of the multicultural, multiethnic Bosnia that existed during much of its history.[15]
>
> The key failure was the refusal to arrest war criminals indicted by the international war crimes tribunal in The Hague. After setting up the tribunal and sending 60,000 troops into Bosnia to help police the Dayton peace agreements, the Western democracies shied away from allowing them to arrest either ... Karadzic or war chief Ratko Mladic for fear of getting someone hurt in the attempt.
>
> The tribunal's chief prosecutor, Judge Richard Goldstone, was properly scornful ... in remarks addressed pointedly to Washington, where the decisions are made. What is the use of having police, he demanded, if they are afraid to arrest the worst criminals? And why create a war crimes tribunal at all only to refuse to carry out its warrants?
>
> The official line is that they are here to keep the peace, not go after war criminals. If war criminals are seen, of course, if enough troops happen to be around, of course, they will arrest them.[16]

Lieutenant General Walker, the NATO Commander in Bosnia, announced to a news conference of nearly 200 journalists that if IFOR saw any war criminals and if "the circumstances were right"—meaning that their bodyguards were not around—then they would arrest them. The journalists hounded him with sustained, derisive laughter.[17]

The newspaper commentator concluded, "Without their arrest, the message will be clear: Crimes will go unpunished; anything goes in the name of nationalism; the United States and other Western democracies are paralyzed by fear."[18]

Many of us in Quarterhorse shared these same questions about IFOR policy. This newspaper commentator was not simply bashing the U.S. government, but making an astute observation about the Achilles' heel of our operation. Recent history weighed heavily on senior American leadership, who recalled the loss of public support as casualties mounted during the Vietnam War. Then there was the terrorist attack that killed over 200 U.S. Marines in Lebanon. Most vivid, of course, was the mission creep that spun out of control in Somalia in 1993.

Our National Command Authority's extreme anxiety over American casualties was demonstrated immediately after the first death of an American soldier in Bosnia on February 3. Phones rang urgently day and night at the Task Force Eagle headquarters in Tuzla. Calls came in from senior officers in Sarajevo, from the ISB in Hungary, and from USAREUR headquarters in Germany. A number even came directly from the Pentagon. President Clinton himself was said to be "closely following developments" while campaigning in New Hampshire. A day later, he personally phoned the soldier's family to express his condolences. A senior officer in Tuzla said, "We were all astounded by the reaction to [Sergeant First Class] Dugan's death."[19]

Army veterans from the Vietnam era found our chain of command's alarmed reaction to the accidental death of a single soldier unusual, to say the least. But after all, Secretary of Defense William J. Perry had clearly identified our number-one priority in Bosnia as the protection of our force.[20] His concern was that any combat-related loss could jeopardize our operation because the American people had little commitment to our cause. Major General Nash said:

It's obvious that there's a political agenda to have low casualties, although nobody's overtly pressuring me to have low casualties. My feeling is that there's two ways to do this, the dumb way and the smart way, and I want to do it the smart way every chance I get.... If my Achilles heel is the low tolerance of the American people for casualties, then I have to recognize that my success or failure in this mission is directly affected by that.[21]

Lieutenant General Abrams, the Commanding General of Fifth Corps in Germany, said, "In peace enforcement operations, there is a high expectation for a low number of casualties.... It's clear that we have to deal with this expectation — that's part of the environment. It's not a bad thing, not a good thing. It's the nature of the mission."[22]

A senior staff officer at Task Force Eagle headquarters said:

In an operation like this ... something you do at a tactical level may have strategic implications. The terrorist threat is an example. If you get a half-dozen Soldiers killed because they didn't have at least a four-vehicle convoy for protection [as was the requirement for all American forces in Bosnia], that could cause the whole mission to collapse.[23]

Therefore, force protection remained one of IFOR's top priorities throughout Operation Joint Endeavor. Colonel Gregory Fontenot, the commander of 1 BCT, said, "You've made us policymakers. And it's not just me, not just Colonels. It's every Private with a rifle. That Private is now a policymaker."[24]

LTG Abrams acknowledged that "there are going to be junior people who do things that have strategic consequences. If I'm uncomfortable with that, I'd have to engineer the operation so that junior people never do anything. And that's impossible."[25]

While the ghosts of ethnic cleansing haunted Bosnia, the ghosts of American soldiers killed in Somalia haunted American political and military leaders. The mission there was seen in hindsight as a classic case history of good intentions gone awry. The UN force, particularly the American component, was allowed to forfeit its neutral, moral high ground by hunting wanted faction leader Mohamed Farah Aideed and his subordinates. "I have still have ringing in my ears ... what horrible things we did by allowing ourselves to be drawn into mission creep," said General Shalikashvili, Chairman of the Joint Chiefs of Staff. "It's a useful lesson that we learned that I'm not about to unlearn."[26]

American commanders adamantly refused to chase indicted war criminals in Bosnia. In private, however, they acknowledged that allowing leaders like Mladic and Karadzic to roam free could destabilize the country whenever NATO troops departed.[27] U.S. military leaders portrayed the issue as a civilian responsibility, although that raised the question of how civilian authorities could bring indicted war criminals to justice without military firepower at hand.

Lieutenant Colonel Harriman explained the IFOR position on war criminals as best he could. "Yes, [Radovan Karadzic] is a criminal, and should go before a judge. But we are doing more important things like building the peace, rather than chase him around."[28]

In May, Karadzic told Western journalists that he was "ready to be tried under any charge if they can bring forward enough evidence." At the same time, however, he told the Greek Macedonian News Agency that he did not accept the ICTY's authority.[29] By July 19, intense international political pressure forced Karadzic to step down from official power.[30] Remarkably, Karadzic would not be apprehended until twelve years after his indictment for war crimes. Mladic was finally captured on May 26, 2011.

Meanwhile, some Quarterhorse cavalrymen were diverted from the harsh realities of the Bosnian civil war for a short while. During the first week of June, the U.S. Army's Morale, Welfare, and Recreation (MWR) service sponsored a visit by the popular TV game show *Jeopardy*. The host, Alex Trebek, took the show on a tour of lodgment areas looking for eligible contestants to participate in the actual show in Hollywood.[31] Several Quarterhorse officers and cavalrymen took the prerequisite test, but none of us possessed the minimum intelligence to compete! Regardless, our cavalrymen enjoyed meeting Mr. Trebek and participating in a mock *Jeopardy* contest.

## An Injured Boy and Dancing Girls

On June 5, an eleven-year-old Muslim boy riding a tractor past the Dawg Pound fell off and was injured. It was not clear whether he had had a seizure and then fell off, or vice versa. A *Stars and Stripes* photographer saw him fall and called for our medics. The photographer and a reporter tended to the boy until help arrived.[32]

Quarterhorse medics cut the boy's shirt off, checked his eyes, and listened to his heart. An ambulance came out of the gate and moved the shaking, bleeding, and unconscious boy back inside to the Squadron Aid Station. The boy regained consciousness and vomited while one of our medics examined him. Captain Bradford Williams, our squadron surgeon, instructed Second Lieutenant Scott Zimmermann, our medical platoon leader, to call the 212th MASH for a medevac helicopter. CPT Williams feared that the boy could have torn an artery, causing blood to flow into his brain.[33]

Since the patient was a local civilian, CPT Williams had to wait anxiously while permission was sought and finally granted from the first general officer in the chain of command. In his exasperation, CPT Williams made an offhand remark to the reporter that, as the attending doctor, he should be making the decision on whether to medevac the boy, instead of having to defer to some general leaning on a water cooler up in headquarters.

The helicopter finally arrived and flew the boy to Camp Bedrock nearly twenty-four miles away. Doctors examined him, and he was later released once his condition had stabilized.

The reporter observed our entire effort to get the boy to the MASH. 2LT Zimmermann told him, "We don't differentiate between Bosnians and Americans — we help anyone. And if we're in a combat situation, we would treat enemy soldiers. That's just what we do. That's the medical profession."[34]

The reporter also cited CPT Williams's juicy remarks in his story. The proverbial shit soon hit the fan. Immediately after the story ran, the aggrieved general officer gave LTC Harriman a call. He was not the type to lean around on the water cooler. Rather, Brigadier General Stanley F. Cherrie was a Vietnam veteran whose shattered hand and foot bore testament to his combat service. LTC Harriman, in turn, expressed his outrage to CPT Williams. The doctor sheepishly admitted his carelessness in front of the reporter, but stood by his conviction that doctors on the scene should be entrusted to authorize medevacs. When summoned before General Cherrie, he told him the same thing.

This incident confirmed our squadron's mistrust of this particular reporter. His previous articles had also smacked of sensationalism. We denied him further access to our units.

Ironically, this incident occurred only two months after LTC Harriman instructed us, "Reporters will tell our story if we let them. Tell them what you know. Don't speculate. Speed them through checkpoints. Welcome them to your camp, your lodgment area, your vehicle. INFORMATION HELPS HERE."[35] LTC Harriman soon amended his open-arms approach. Quarterhorse had rediscovered the painful truth that our predecessors had known so well in Vietnam — that reporters care about their stories, not about the asses of the participants in them.

Most of our cavalrymen in the Dawg Pound had no idea of the drama surrounding the injured boy. Instead, their minds were fixed on a visiting dance troupe, and to a far lesser extent, some magician named Dr. Bob. Several hundred cavalrymen crammed into the Quarterhorse mess hall to get as close as possible to the first "real women" most of us had seen in a very long time.

The same *Stars and Stripes* reporter who wrote the sensationalized medevac story also wrote, "Hundreds of dusty, dog-faced American Soldiers, most of whom have seen very few women in the last five months, gazed upon a Las Vegas–style revue of dancing showgirls ... like starving men gaze upon food."[36] It was far from Las Vegas quality, but enjoyable, especially for those cavalrymen who were cajoled into dancing.

One cavalryman said, "It gave us a chance to see something different — females. We don't get to see too much of them here. It's nice to know someone cares."[37]

Another added, "The outfits were great. We've been here six months and we enjoyed this show a lot. It was a big morale boost."[38]

# 8

# SABERS READY

## *Training*

In April, Lieutenant Colonel Harriman issued his guidance for the training that Quarterhorse would conduct from May through September. Besides the need to sustain our ability to maneuver in a high intensity conflict, this training had a second, more immediate purpose: "Faction leaders will notice that we continue normal training throughout the year. That we continue training will prove of substantial assistance in force presence operations. Our training that maintains the fact of a ready force will also maintain faction perceptions that we are a ready force."[1] Accordingly, our three ground cavalry troops rotated between a focused training period and tours at Checkpoint Charlie and Mount Vis.

Over the summer, our cavalrymen and engineers constructed a twenty-five-meter small arms range at the Dawg Pound. Targets were posted next to the railroad embankment along the camp's south side. It was known as Dead Dawg Range for the several stray intruders that were shot in the area out of concern that they carried Hantavirus. Quarterhorse used the range to qualify our cavalrymen on personal weapons such as 9mm pistols, M16A2 rifles, M60 machine guns, and M203 grenade launchers. Other IFOR units utilized our range, too. We also employed the Weaponeer and MACs simulators for remedial and night marksmanship training.

LTC Harriman observed, "The range allows us to practice live — to shoot tracer at night. Soldiers ... know peripheral vision allows you to kill at night — know how to move their eyes at night to see. We are getting good with illumination flares, with night sights, with low light apertures on M16s. Guys are coaching each other. Guys shoot at the range to get good."[2]

To keep American tank and Bradley crews proficient, Task Force Eagle established a gunnery training area in Taborfalva, Hungary. Company-size units rotated through this leased former Soviet garrison for a week at a time. Located on the open Hungarian plains, Taborfalva Training Area (TTA) would have been perfect for large-scale maneuvers but for the many unexploded artillery shells lying everywhere. Tank and Bradley crews fired Table 8 gunnery at TTA. This was a live-fire qualification table in which crews engaged simulated moving and stationary targets.

Quarterhorse first learned of the plan to rotate units up to TTA in mid–March. We scheduled Bravo Troop to go first in April. Charlie Troop followed in June. Alpha Troop went last in August.

It would have been unfeasible to road-march our tanks and Bradleys through Bosnia, Croatia, and Hungary just to fire them at TTA. Instead, the 7th Army Training Command pre-positioned other tanks and Bradleys at TTA for us to use.

Even though our own vehicles would not be used for this live-fire training, they were still in dire need of thorough maintenance. Quarterhorse mechanics and the supporting LARS representatives at the Dawg Pound conducted "Ghostbusters" pre-gunnery services on all tank and Bradley weapons systems. This intensive turret maintenance gave us some assurance that our vehicles could shoot accurately, should we ever need them in a crisis.[3] We had not fired any live rounds from them since our pre-deployment gunnery back in October.

The vehicle hulls were another story. We had put significant mileage on our tracks over the past five months. They were due for semi-annual services, but this proved to be a task that we could not perform with quality until after our return to Germany seven months later.

Quarterhorse armored vehicle crews wondered whether we would be expected to achieve the same qualification score that was the standard back in Germany. The concern was that we did not have U/COFT simulators — our primary gunnery training tool — with us in Bosnia. TTA had some of these simulators, and our crews were afforded a few short hours in them.

In Bosnia, Quarterhorse tankers conducted the Tank Crew Proficiency Course (TCPC), which incorporated the Army's new Tank Weapons Gunnery Simulation System (TWGSS) on a miniaturized range. Our Bradley crews conducted the Bradley Crew Proficiency Course (BCPC) using the similar Precision Gunnery System (PGS). We also certified all of our tracked vehicle crews on their respective Bradley Gunnery Skills Test (BGST) and Tank Crew Gunnery Skills Test (TCGST).

LTC Harriman addressed our crews' concern over gunnery standards:

This gunnery isn't about scores — or marksmanship. Prepare for combat. Do the Age Old thing. Work your crew drills in the tank or Bradley the way Patton's crews did — without advanced simulations. Work crew drills on the tank in the motor pool — in chairs, in the tents. Use the snake board. Master TCGST/BGST. Do the New Age thing. Do what the WWII crews didn't know how to do. Visualize every engagement, every switch, every command, every move, through round on target. Then practice combat in Hungary. You will do fine. You'll return better able to kill here, if need be.[4]

In mid–April, Bravo Troop's crews boarded a C-130 transport at Tuzla airfield for the flight to Hungary. Landing at the Intermediate Staging Base (ISB) in Taszar, the troop then boarded buses for a three-hour drive to TTA. Bravo Troop's eight-day rotation was the first for any element within 2 BCT.[5]

Staff Sergeant Robert Anderson, one of Charlie Troop's Master Gunners, evaluated the Bravo Troop crews on Table 8 engagements. He said, "This training will be standardized throughout the 1st Armored Division, and basically everyone will run the same tasks."[6]

Normally, Quarterhorse fired our tanks and Bradleys on separate, purpose-built ranges in Germany. But TTA had only one range for us to use, so our crews had to alternate firing days.

SSG Anderson explained, "The biggest problem we had was that we aren't used to shooting the CFV and the Abrams at the same time, so it's an integration of two different types of firing tables.... When you work with both tanks and Bradleys, they shoot different targets. Basically, you have twice as many targets on this range than you would have on another range."[7]

Despite any initial misgivings, Bravo Troop qualified all thirteen of its Bradley crews and all five of its tank crews. We were proud of the troop for performing to standard on unfamiliar terrain against an unfamiliar "enemy." The range at TTA was significantly more difficult than those we normally used at Grafenwoehr. For one thing, it was much wider and really forced our crews to scan for targets.

LTC Harriman informed the rest of Quarterhorse:

What Bulldog Troop did was train to fight. What Bulldog Troop did was fight the range and train hard, not dick around worrying about scores. What Bulldog Troop did was hit targets in time, with proper crew coordination, and proper fire commands. And that's just what I want everybody else to do too.... I see all of you doing the training that keeps crews lethal. Crews do crew drill. Crews do the minitank range; crews use the snake boards. Everybody seems well on their way to Taborfalva and a qualification, toward maintaining crew and platoon lethality. Keep it up.[8]

Charlie Troop trained at TTA during the week of June 8 to 15. Temperatures in the 90s made it uncomfortable for crews inside their vehicles, where temperatures climbed to nearly 120 degrees. The heat also tended to wash out the resolution on our vehicles' thermal sight pictures. Regardless, Charlie

Troop's crews shot very well. LTC Harriman's command tank killed ten of ten targets.

"Alpha Fortieth" sent some of its engineers to TTA along with Charlie Troop. They went along to fire their M249 squad automatic weapons (SAW). The SAW was an excellent light machine gun that would have been better suited for our ground cavalry troops' three-man dismounted scout teams than the heavier, more cumbersome M60 machine guns that they were armed with instead. LTC Harriman observed :

> Soldiers liked the wide range and the challenge of new ground. They kept the edge on lethality.... Everybody learned lots about the business of fighting. We can control fires. We can maintain fire superiority — the thing that allows combat maneuver.... Sergeants impressed me again and again as they taught Soldiers to move and fire in the dismounted assault.[9]

Alpha Troop conducted its TTA gunnery in mid–August. Besides firing tank and Bradley Table 8 exercises, some of the troop's cavalrymen also qualified with their assigned personal weapons. Three Quarterhorse staff officers established a dismounted squad assault course to give our cavalrymen and engineers practice in moving under enemy fire.

The U.S. Army Europe (USAREUR) command sergeant major paid a visit to Alpha Troop's ranges. The U.S. Army's senior NCO in Europe was reportedly pleased with what he saw, although we didn't hear it from him directly. Our cavalrymen were eager to meet this VIP who had risen from the ranks to the top. They were disappointed that he didn't bother saying hello to any of our junior enlisted men. They assumed correctly that sergeant majors go around asking people how they are doing to gauge morale and to ascertain any pressing soldier issues. It didn't matter. Alpha Troop's crews achieved the highest cumulative scores to date within Task Force Eagle.

Once range training at TTA was complete, our ground cavalry troops boarded buses for the beautiful Hungarian capital city of Budapest. There, our cavalrymen enjoyed two days of R&R with our families, who had taken chartered buses down from Schweinfurt.

The air crews and pilots of Delta and Echo Troops spent all of June preparing for their own gunnery coming up in July. LTC Harriman instructed:

> The squadron was given permission to waiver just about all [flight training] requirements. However, we must strive to waive nothing as an aircrew training goal. All aviators in Delta and Echo Troops will maintain RL1 and night vision goggle (NVG) qualifications. The squadron will complete aircrew coordination training, and as many gunnery tasks as ranges will allow.[10]

Our aerial gunnery was conducted in the British sector of Bosnia near Glamoc on July 10–31. Quarterhorse pilots needed to hone their gunnery skills as much as our tracked vehicle crews did. They looked forward to this rare opportunity to fire all of their aircraft weapons systems.

Resolute Barbara Range (RBR) was the site of this aerial gunnery training. It had been constructed by the British Army along a series of ridge lines in an isolated portion of their sector. Our pilots fired their air-to-ground ordnance in simulated tactical scenarios, not too unlike those simulated by our armored vehicle crews. Captain Brian McFadden's Echo Troop completed its ranges first. His pilots flew both day and night gunnery tables and a rare engagement with live Hellfire antitank missiles. Delta Troop then rotated up to Glamoc, as Echo assumed responsibility for our ongoing aerial reconnaissance missions. Captain Kerry Brunson's aviators and crewmen had nothing but good things to say for the gunnery and the range itself.[11]

Our air cavalry troops qualified all sixteen crews. Thirteen of them earned the highest "Distinguished" rating. Their success would not have possible without the tremendous efforts of maintenance teams from Delta, Echo, and Fox Troops. These support cavalrymen worked hard to keep our helicopters operational through the intense flying hours that we maintained all year. They received great assistance from a small group of civilian maintenance experts and contractor teams, who lived with Quarterhorse and who used satellite communications with the States to procure scarce parts for us in amazing time.

The 2 BCT headquarters credited Quarterhorse for our continued emphasis on live-fire training, which had significantly enhanced force protection and our ability to deal with any situations that might arise.[12]

On July 26, Delta Troop participated in Quick Thunder II, a joint live-fire training exercise conducted at Resolute Barbara Range.[13] The 2 BCT conducted this exercise in response to difficulties the VRS had given our forces during our most recent weapons site inspections. Quick Thunder II was a complex mission incorporating the suppressive effects of artillery from 4-29 FA, heavy mortars from Task Force 2-68 Armor, Kiowa Warriors from Quarterhorse, and U.S. Air Force ground attack aircraft. These assets were synchronized to suppress simulated enemy air defenses to support a follow-on air attack. In military parlance, it was called a joint air attack team (JAAT) mission. Quick Thunder II was an expanded repeat of our brigade's first JAAT mission — Quick Thunder — conducted back on May 30 in Glamoc.[14]

Both Quick Thunder exercises were controlled by 2 BCT headquarters with a Fire Support Element (FSE) and a U.S. Air Force Tactical Air Control Party (TACP). Both exercises gave us practice in mustering and controlling adequate combat power for any situations requiring greater force protection.

Several dignitaries watched the joint exercise in July. Among them were the Task Force Eagle commander, the Russian airborne brigade commander, and several FWF civilian and military leaders.[15] The scenario was a situation in which an IFOR inspection team was denied access to a weapons storage site. As the situation escalated, the factional unit opened fire on the IFOR team and a factional motorized rifle battalion moved out of its cantonment area. This MRB then seized a key village south of the IEBL. Colonel Batiste massed combat power to destroy the battalion. As it approached the IFOR engagement area, attack and scout helicopters fired an initial aerial salvo, complemented by heavy mortar and artillery fires. Sorties of U.S. Air Force A-10s and allied Jaguar fighters provided close air support.[16] The result was an intense display of synchronized firepower that, while staged, well illustrated the concept of American combined-arms doctrine. The foreigners in attendance were certainly awed with what they witnessed. Many American officers doubted that the FWF militaries possessed the expertise to cohesively employ armored formations as large as battalions.

COL Batiste said, "We are out here honing our skills to synchronize combat power.... The idea is that the brigade will always be prepared to defend itself and protect the force.... If called upon — and when ordered — we will compel compliance with the Dayton Peace Accord."[17]

Captain Gary Stephens's support crews from Fox Troop conducted split support operations to make the Quick Thunder II exercise a magnificent success while sustaining normal Quarterhorse flight operations within our sector. His "Three-Five" Platoon operated a forward air refueling point (FARP) that provided fuel and ammo to all Task Force Eagle helicopters participating in the exercise.[18]

The training requirements of our ground cavalry troops' heavy mortar sections were not neglected. Our mortarmen needed an opportunity to "drop some rounds" in a live fire situation. Quarterhorse combined our three mortar sections for a consolidated live-fire exercise in Glamoc from July 27 to August 4. Captain Lisowski, our squadron fire support officer, led this training.[19]

Back in the Quarterhorse sector, HHT cavalrymen continued to provide the same great maintenance, food, and fuel support as they always had. HHT did not let the extended distances between our camps hold them back.

Physical fitness training was essential. Our cavalrymen had to be in good shape to wear their heavy battle gear all day, every day. LTC Harriman encouraged small unit leaders to find innovative ways to do PT at their respective locations.[20] For a time, our cavalrymen in the Dawg Pound were actually allowed to run out the east gate and down the road towards Checkpoint Charlie. Each morning during PT hours, individuals and small groups of unarmed cavalrymen in PT uniforms made tempting sniper or ambush targets of themselves as they jogged, often individually. Another threat was the likelihood of being run over by speeding traffic. Eventually, our leadership acknowledged the risk. Our cavalrymen then had to content themselves with running laps within our tiny camp perimeters.

## Operation Gryphon

Colonel Batiste reported in early June that both entities in the 2 BCT sector still had some GFAP violations to correct. He had met with FWF commanders of the 28th Federation Division in Zivinice, the 16th Federation Division in Vares, and the III VRS Corps. Both sides were moving in the right direction, but COL Batiste was impatient with the pace of progress.[21]

A series of incidents at Han Pijesak had compelled 2 BCT to stage the Quick Thunder II exercise in July. The first occurred back on February 14, when COL Batiste and a small patrol were prevented from inspecting a weapons storage site by heavily armed VRS soldiers. COL Batiste backed off despite the Serbs' clear violation of the GFAP. Subsequent radio intercepts indicated that the Serbs were ready to shoot it out had he pressed the issue.

Another patrol was denied access the following day. This time, COL Batiste returned in force. He bluntly told the Serbs that he would inspect the site "with or without your permission." Apache attack helicopters, artillery, and NATO fighter planes were all standing by. The Serbs relented, and the site was inspected without incident.[22]

Had COL Batiste forced the issue on the first day, a firefight probably would have ensued. An officer from our brigade said, "If somebody had taken a shot down there, it would have all gone to hell and Clinton wouldn't get reelected."[23] He was only partly joking.

The next incident occurred on June 6, when VRS soldiers prevented an officer from TF 2-68 AR from inspecting General Mladic's VRS General Staff headquarters at Han Pijesak. As before, 2 BCT responded with an aerial show of force of NATO fixed-wing aircraft and AWTs from Quarterhorse.[24]

Again, COL Batiste personally went to inspect the site the following day. He was also denied access. For dramatic effect, one of our Kiowas hovered just behind him as he argued with the Serb guards. CPT Brunson flew swooping gun runs back and forth in his Kiowa. COL Batiste's party finally had to point their locked and loaded weapons at the Serbs to force an entry.

To Major Zajac, the 2 BCT operations officer, the operation illustrated the value of deliberate, planned, and rehearsed missions that synchronized all available battlefield functions. It also indicated that there were "hard cases out there who don't understand their place in life." MAJ Zajac asserted that "our discipline and professionalism will eventually convince them that non-compliance will trigger an appropriate response from us — they cannot out-escalate the 2 BCT."[25]

Under the military provisions of the GFAP, the FWFs were forbidden from using helicopters. Yet, General Mladic had supposedly reacted to IFOR's beefed-up patrols and checkpoints by getting around via helicopter. IFOR units had orders to seize him if he happened to fall into our hands.

On June 16, IFOR instructed 2 BCT to conduct aerial reconnaissance missions of helicopter landing zones around the VRS General Staff headquarters.[26] Naturally, the mission was passed on to our Delta and Echo Troops, who were ordered to observe, record, and report any unauthorized flights. It seemed that we were finally going to get tough on the war criminals. This mission was just one component of the much larger 2 BCT operation called Operation Gryphon.

In support of Quarterhorse AWTs, 2 BCT massed more combat power than it had ever assembled in any previous operation. The main effort on the ground included tanks and infantry from TF 2-68 AR. This force surveyed the area between Han Pogled in the north to Han Kram in the south. TF 4-12 IN conducted night patrols along Route South Dakota to observe the eastern approaches into the Mount Zep area. Artillerymen from 4-29 FA provided indirect fire support, while Alpha Company, 501st Military Intelligence Battalion provided Ground Surveillance Radars (GSRs) and a host of other intelligence gathering assets.[27] Within the Quarterhorse sector, Bravo Troop increased inspections of FWF cantonment areas.

Over Han Pijesak and Mount Zep, Quarterhorse pilots surveyed aerial avenues of approach into the area. We pre-positioned one AWT at nearby LA Lisa as a quick reaction force ready to pounce on any unauthorized flights. Our Kiowas were armed with Stinger anti-aircraft missiles for this operation. NATO air forces provided AC-130 Spector gunships and close air support sorties.

After the operation was concluded, 2 BCT described it as "a great mission employing a slice of each battlefield function in a well-synchronized effort."[28] While no unauthorized flights were detected, the operation did set favorable conditions for another armed confrontation that unfolded just one week later.

## Foot Patrols

In addition to our routine stability tasks, Quarterhorse had to maintain continuous security at all of our lodgment areas and remote sites. Securing our camps meant manning sandbagged observation towers, bunkers, and gates along the perimeter, as well as conducting foot and mounted patrols in the surrounding local areas.

In the spring, Quarterhorse foot patrols noticed how previously deserted areas sprang back to life as residents returned to their homes and began rebuilding. Charlie Troop's Private James Sabourin said, "We get to talk to a lot of people on patrols. We see kids now going to school, out walking around, and it's great."[29]

In mid–July, a *Stars and Stripes* reporter accompanied Sergeant Dwaine Myers on a typical foot patrol. SGT Meyers's six-man element was ordered to recon the area around Motovo in RS territory. Like most patrols, it was a real workout, and it went without incident. Nonetheless, foot patrols helped Quarterhorse to maintain force presence throughout our sector.

Our squadron headquarters was collocated at LA Molly with our air cavalry troops, several support detachments, and a State Department aviation unit. These elements constituted a tempting target for would-be attackers, thus requiring ground combat elements to secure them. For this purpose, our three ground cavalry troops rotated tank platoons down to Molly.

On occasion, the resident tank platoon rolled its four M1s out the gate on local mounted patrols, but this occurred infrequently, as we wanted to minimize wear and tear on the already-poor roads. About once every five to six days, the dismounted tank platoon conducted foot patrols around the quarry and the surrounding hillsides.

On one such patrol, tankers from Bravo Troop's 2nd Platoon met a Muslim militia officer who was eager to show his support for the IFOR mission. He offered the platoon leader a couple of hand grenades. The lieutenant did not know what to do with them, so he told the officer just to hang onto them for the time being. He should have confiscated them.

By mid–June, the Bravo Troop tankers had already conducted several foot patrols around LA Molly. MAJ Roberts, the squadron operations officer, felt that they still required more formal instruction on patrolling. He tapped CPT Mark Viney to provide some basic infantry training to the platoon. CPT Viney was the new squadron maintenance officer and had recently branch transferred from Infantry to Armor.

On the designated morning, the wary tankers reported to CPT Viney in an open gravel area in the center of LA Molly. He taught them how to

Swedish infantrymen inspect Charlie Troop tanks securing Quarterhorse head-quarters and airfield at LA Molly, summer 1996 (photograph: Mark Viney).

move tactically as a squad and how to react to contact from various threats they might encounter. By the end of the day, the tankers moved like proper infantrymen. They needed a graduation exercise to complete their training, so CPT Viney planned a dismounted zone reconnaissance mission in the rolling foothills of the Konjuh Range south of LA Molly.

For several weeks, the Tank Platoon Leader had badgered a grizzled State Department pilot to give our tankers a lift in his modified UH-1 Huey. The pilot was an old cavalryman who had flown combat missions in Vietnam. He was happy to be "back with the Cav" and readily obliged in giving the patrol a lift. But he was adamant about not having his picture taken with us.

On June 23, the ten-man patrol reported to the airfield. Accompanying them was a female Bosnian Serb interpreter named Tiana. The retrofitted Vietnam-era Huey would have to ferry the patrol on two sorties because of all the extra surveillance gear taking up so much of the cargo area.

After a short flight, the Huey flew past the landing zone to check for obstacles. Then it came back around and dropped the patrol in a high, grassy saddle overlooking a destroyed Serb village. Five cavalrymen jumped out, formed a perimeter in the high grass, and readied their weapons as the Huey flew off to get the others. Three curious young shepherd boys saw the heli-

A Quarterhorse aerial weapons team lands behind parked Kiowa Warriors at LA Molly. At left rear is a State Department UH-1H Huey based at our airfield whose pilot was an air cavalry veteran of the Vietnam War, summer 1996 (photograph: Mark Viney).

copter land and ran over to investigate. Tiana told the Muslim boys not to be alarmed by us.

Once the patrol was consolidated, it moved out. As they were traversing the open, rolling highlands, CPT Viney chastised the Bravo Troop tankers over some finer points of dismounted movement. At one point, Sergeant First Class Michael Tucker, the platoon sergeant, reminded him that they were tankers. They had been moving so well that CPT Viney had actually forgotten that they were not infantrymen.

The patrol descended through dense old-wood forest into grassy pastures overlooking the quarry. Heat and rain made the movement more difficult. The tankers were not accustomed to such strenuous hikes, and they did not enjoy themselves. For the most part, though, they kept their misery to themselves. All of the tankers were unanimous that helicopters were definitely not for them.

The patrol located a line of old fighting positions and identified several usable LZs and OP locations, but there were no signs of recent military activity. It did observe evidence of ethnic cleansing in the area. On a gravel road leading out from a destroyed village, five pairs of men's shoes were lined up in neat order. It was apparent that the shoes belonged to some detainees who had been ordered to remove them before being marched off to an unknown fate. Without shoes, the men could not have run away so easily.

A serious incident occurred towards the end of the patrol. The platoon leader was having a hard time navigating. The junior NCO at the head of the formation wanted to ignore the lieutenant's instructions and kept leading the patrol off in his own direction. The lieutenant suddenly lost his cool,

*Top:* Captain Mark Viney on reconnaissance in mountains south of "The Quarry," June 1996. *Bottom:* Bosnian wagon passes dismounted patrol from Bravo Troop's 2nd Platoon, June 23, 1996 (both photographs: Mark Viney).

threw down his radio, and pitched a childlike temper tantrum in front of his men. CPT Viney quickly pulled him around a corner and straightened him out.

The underlying problem was that the lieutenant had already forfeited his authority. Quarterhorse had assigned living spaces within our lodgment areas for the sake of convenience afforded by maintaining platoon and section integrity. This meant that company grade officers lived in the same open bay tents with their NCOs and men. This led to unacceptable familiarity between the ranks and bred contempt in cases such as with this particular tank platoon, whose platoon leader was weak from the start.

A few days before the patrol, CPT Viney entered the 2nd Platoon hooch and found the lieutenant playing cards with several of his subordinates. The platoon seemed to have a nickname for everyone, including the platoon leader. CPT Viney was shocked to hear one junior NCO address the lieutenant as "dumb ass." He observed further evidence of insubordination later that day during a leaders' recon with the lieutenant and two of his young sergeants.

Now that the platoon leader had humiliated himself out on patrol, CPT Viney reminded him of the previous incidents of insubordination that he had observed. After the patrol, he informed the lieutenant's troop commander and the squadron operations officer about all he had seen. This incident should have been a wake-up call for Quarterhorse, but it wasn't. The tank platoon's mixed-ranks billeting was partially to blame for its breakdown in discipline.

Living arrangements in the Thunderdome were also inappropriate. CPT Viney shared an open bay tent with several of his junior enlisted men. Later that summer, when HHT had to give up some of its tents to make room for an incoming U.S. Marine Corps unit, he suggested to the HHT commander that all Quarterhorse officers in the Thunderdome move into one tent together. CPT Wawro quickly dismissed the idea and offered no rationale.

Our squadron's billeting arrangements flew in the face of time-tested tradition that appreciated the need to maintain some measure of physical separation between the ranks in order to maintain good order and discipline. Peers should have been billeted with their peers.

When CPT Viney assumed command of Bravo Troop after Quarterhorse's return to Germany, he reestablished rank-segregated billets during training deployments. Initially, several young leaders complained about the inconvenience. Eventually, though, everyone came to appreciate the freedom to let their hair down since their supervisors were not in the bunks next to them.

## Intelligence and Information Operations

The United States operated a vast intelligence network to support IFOR's mission in Bosnia. The exact number of American intelligence personnel involved and the cost of the effort were not made public at the time, but their scope was large enough to provoke some Clinton administration officials and lawmakers to complain that excessive resources were being diverted from other important missions.[30]

The nerve center of the intelligence effort was a brigade-sized unit from V Corps. This unit included more than a thousand intelligence and signal personnel, analysts, and counterintelligence specialists. Contributing to their effort were dozens of small teams from the Central Intelligence Agency, the National Security Agency, and the Defense Intelligence Agency. These teams were deployed throughout the region.[31] The State Department kept a special-purpose aviation element at LA Molly with our Squadron Headquarters.

As our purely military tasks tapered off over the spring, Quarterhorse focused more and more on civil affairs (CA) missions and support to non-governmental organizations (NGOs) and humanitarian aid organizations.[32] Captain Jim Dirisio was one of our CA officers from the U.S. Army Reserve. He observed in September that our primary reconnaissance effort was focused on civilian governments and infrastructure "since no one [was] killing anyone."[33] Intel gathering on the FWFs remained a priority, though, since good intel enabled Quarterhorse to respond quickly and effectively whenever incidents arose or whenever GFAP violations were discovered.

By design, Quarterhorse was a combat intelligence-gathering organization. For our stability operation in Bosnia, the squadron gained additional capability through our attached civil affairs, counterintelligence, and psychological operations (psyops) teams. Besides helping to gather the intel we needed, these teams established and maintained healthy relationships with local Bosnians within our sector.

Officially, psyops, CA, and counterintel teams each have their own unique but complementary responsibilities. During Operation Joint Endeavor, however, the lines distinguishing them blurred considerably. There was significant overlap and duplication of effort. Even our three ground cavalry troops performed some typical civil affairs missions.[34]

Quarterhorse could not have hoped to be successful by limiting ourselves to merely receiving information passively. Instead, we actively shaped the mindset of locals within in our sector. Our information operations were intended to "win the hearts and minds" of the Bosnian people. More specifically, we wanted them to embrace the peace process and to view IFOR not as an enemy but as the facilitator of peace. This mission fell primarily on our attached psyops team, although everyone played a part.[35]

Several psyops teams rotated through short tours with Quarterhorse. The first was a Regular Army team from Fort Bragg, North Carolina. When this team rotated out, its replacement was an equally capable U.S. Army Reserve (USAR) psyops team, which had been activated for a six-month tour. Eventually, a second USAR psyops team rotated in to support our squadron. Each of these teams was led by a company-grade officer and included four psyops soldiers and a mechanic to maintain its vehicles.

Like the psyops teams attached to other task forces, ours informed local civilians about IFOR plans and their impact on daily life. Psyops used a multimedia approach. Teams distributed pencils, pens, and other school supplies to children — a typical civil affairs activity. They also printed handbills and newspapers and distributed them in towns throughout our sector.[36]

Bosnians from all three ethnic groups were gullibly susceptible to the inflammatory, ethnically motivated propaganda generated by their leaders. It was vital, therefore, that our psyops teams spread the truth so that people could make proper, intelligent decisions for themselves. One method was with a newspaper called *The Herald of Peace*. Task Force Eagle psyops personnel printed this paper, which our teams distributed and contributed information to. The paper was printed in both Roman and Cyrillic letters so that both entities could read the same news. Typical articles covered freedom of movement, road construction projects, the Dayton Peace Accord, and mine awareness.[37]

By late September, all the psyops teams within 2 BCT had distributed more than 200,000 printed products. Nearly 24,000 were distributed in just the week prior to the September elections.[38] In practically every weekly squadron command and staff meeting, our psyops team leader passed around samples of the printed products his team was distributing that week. On one occasion, he showed a poster that he had already taken into Kalesija to test out on some locals. The poster showed the sweet, innocent faces of three young children. The message read, "For their sake, peace." He reported that one old Muslim woman took a quick look at the poster and immediately concluded that the kids were Serbs. She said, "I'd like to take them home ... and cut their eyes out."[39] Likewise, the Bosnian Serbs who had been shown the poster thought the kids were Muslim. Our psyops officer said he would run it by some Croatians to see who they thought the kids were. The responses to this seemingly innocuous poster opened our eyes to the magnitude of ethnic hatred in Bosnia.

Quarterhorse psyops teams were not limited to merely disseminating

Quarterhorse civil affairs convoy in front of bombed-out store in Kalesija, May 1996 (photograph: Mark Viney).

materials. They assumed greater responsibility for collecting information than they typically would have. Psyops teams provided current local opinion assessments to our squadron, just as our CA and counterintel teams did. Typically, our teams on intel-gathering missions formed a convoy of Humvees, grabbed an interpreter, drove into a town, and simply talked with the residents. Shopkeepers were important to talk to since they could help disseminate information to their customers.[40]

Local Bosnian radio was another way of spreading IFOR's message. On several occasions, both Lieutenant Colonel Harriman and Major Roberts accepted invitations to discuss current events and the GFAP on the air. Broadcasts typically featured a translation of the officer's prepared text, then a call-in question-and-answer session. By the end of September, the 2 BCT psyops teams had logged almost eighty hours of radio information broadcasts.[41]

Two USAR Civil Affairs Direct Support Teams (CADST) were attached to Quarterhorse on respective six-month tours. The first, CADST 1-4, was led by First Lieutenant Hradil and hailed from the 401st Civil Affairs Battalion (USAR) in Rochester, New York. It joined Quarterhorse on June 25. The second team was CADST 2-3, which was from the 422nd Civil Affairs Battalion (Airborne) from Greensboro, North Carolina. First Lieutenant Slade McCalip was its team leader. Like our attached psyops teams, our CA teams also had one officer, four soldiers, and one Humvee. They also came with an extra officer who served as our squadron civil affairs officer (S-5). This officer was responsible for advising the squadron commander on our moral and legal obligations towards the local populations.[42]

Our "CA guys" were responsible for coordinating with NGOs, private

Muslim villagers watch as an M88 recovery vehicle from Workhorse Troop pulls a disabled Bosnian truck back onto roadway near the Quarry, fall 1996 (photograph: Mark Viney).

volunteer organizations (PVOs), and other IFOR units to enhance the legitimacy of our peacekeeping effort.[43] They eased relations between IFOR and the local populations by reaching out to communities, by completing civilian damage claim forms, and by monitoring local economies and opinions towards IFOR. Our CA teams frequently met with local mayors, police chiefs, and other officials to discuss problems and programs. They spent considerable time with refugees and on civil action projects like agricultural and food programs.[44]

In one such action in late June, Quarterhorse cavalrymen and CA guys helped to rebuild a partially destroyed house in a nearby village. The residents greatly appreciated our goodwill gesture. LTC Harriman joked that we should finish the project by painting the whole house cavalry red and white.[45] By September, our two attached CA teams had completed over forty civil assistance projects and had allocated over $350,000 in aid to improve local infrastructure.[46]

Quarterhorse did not want to compromise our CA teams' standing with the locals by tasking them to actively collect intelligence for our operations.

They did have a passive collection mission, however. They kept their eyes and ears open for anything of use. For the most part, however, our CA guys focused on what they needed for civil assistance projects. Some information came down from the Task Force Eagle G-5, but most was collected on patrols throughout our sector.

One type of fact-finding mission was an "economic indicators assessment." Every two weeks, our CA teams visited local markets to determine price changes in key staple goods. The Task Force Eagle G-5 compiled and analyzed this information, and made broad assessments of economic effects on local attitudes.[47] In September, our CA guys noticed that more luxury goods were being offered for sale. Basic necessities had previously dominated the shelves. We interpreted this as a sign that the economy was improving, since people could apparently afford to spend more on nonessentials.

Our CA teams provided Quarterhorse with great insight into local perceptions about the peace process. Bosnian Serbs wanted to keep the ethnic groups separated. They also believed that the Muslims were getting more than their share of humanitarian aid. Despite their animosity towards each other, people in both entities seemed friendly and appreciative of IFOR's work to maintain the peace.[48]

In late September, our CA team conducted an area ethnicity assessment of the entire Quarterhorse sector. In order to help our squadron prepare for the municipal elections, tentatively scheduled for November, they had to determine the ethnic composition of every city and village before and after the Bosnian Civil War. Captain Scott Downey, our squadron intelligence officer, reviewed this assessment and considered information provided by our counterintel and psyops teams. He then made his own assessment of possible areas of violence during the elections. The Quarterhorse staff used CPT Downey's assessment to develop appropriate operations plans.[49]

A human intelligence (humint) success story was Staff Sergeant Thomas Daniels, the NCOIC of our Squadron Intelligence Section. SSG Daniels "ran a source" who gave us the inside story on attempts by the Federation 281st Brigade to slip its soldiers into groups of refugees. His source also told us which contended ZOS villages would be targeted for resettlement next.[50]

Our air cavalry troops also made significant contributions to our intel-gathering effort. In several major incidents, our pilots had a pressbox view and provided videotaped evidence for analysis by higher IFOR headquarters. Our ground cavalry troops made contributions whose importance also cannot be overstated. Their patrols, many led by young, junior NCOs, were often the first to report and respond to significant activity.

Our troop commanders, the squadron commander, and many Quarterhorse staff officers all made valuable points of contact with local officials and influential leaders in their innumerable patrols around the sector. In September, an election monitor from the Organization for Security and Cooperation in Europe (OSCE) remarked, "I've been here three years and I can't believe the number of people you know!"[51]

# 9

# MID-POINT SITREP

By late June 1996, the NATO peacekeeping mission in Bosnia was six months old. The *Chicago Tribune* pessimistically described the Muslim-Croat Federation as a "dysfunctional union concocted by Washington to counterbalance Bosnia's Serb Republic and keep the country in one piece."[1]

The article pointed out that while the Dayton Accord guaranteed freedom of movement for all displaced persons to return home, by this point in time it was still a dream for many. As the months wore on, Quarterhorse and other IFOR units increasingly focused our efforts on this issue. The problem we faced, though, was that resentments still ran too high in some areas for people to willingly allow their former enemies to return. Ostracism and open scorn were common. Civilians crossing from one entity to the other were often harassed or beaten. Quarterhorse witnessed many such acts in our portion of the ZOS.

And yet, halfway through the planned yearlong mission, IFOR had succeeded in keeping the Former Warring Factions from killing each other. While there was little we could do to erase their deep-seated hatred for one another, our hope was that universal love for peace would eventually overcome ethnic hatred.

Carl Bildt, the NATO High Representative, wrote:

[I] admit quite openly that there is still a very long way to go, further than I would have hoped six months into the peace process.... Indicted war criminals are still walking around in many parts of Bosnia.... There is a climate of fear, which inhibits freedom of movement between the two parts of Bosnia, and has been deepened by a number of ugly incidents, mostly but not exclusively on the Serb side of the inter-entity boundary line. The media on both sides still take refuge in the rhetoric of war, with Pale television and radio often churning out propaganda of the most objectionable, Stalinist variety.[2]

The 50,000-man Implementation Force was the most visible manifestation of the Dayton Accord. As such, IFOR military leaders came under increasing pressure to somehow resolve these political problems. The expectation was unfair.

American Brigadier General John B. Sylvestor was the Deputy Chief of Staff for the Allied Rapid Reaction Corps, from which the IFOR ground forces were drawn. He insisted, "This problem has got to be dealt with by the people who signed the peace agreement.... Put the pressure where the pressure belongs — on the factional leadership."[3]

BG Sylvestor realized that the wounds of war would take a long time to heal — longer than our operation's planned twelve months. He said, "It is gonna take a long time to ease some of these fissures. Some, I predict, will never be eased. There will never be an embracing of someone who has killed your family or burned your home or destroyed all your livestock. Some of those people will move away and will never want to come back."[4]

British Major General Sir Michael Jackson echoed this sentiment:

> Look at the Dayton agreement — a most ambitious agreement, indeed. I'm reminded of the time it took the Western Allies and Germany and Japan to become reconciled after the end of the Second World War — arguably six, seven, eight years. If we're really expecting the same thing to be done in six, seven, eight months, it seems to me that's unrealistic.... Reconciliation takes time.... If the people wish to act in an ethnic manner, as opposed to a multiethnic manner, at the end of the day, that's what they're going to do. I'm not going to change it with the big stick of possible military action.[5]

However, by the summer of 1996, several hopeful achievements had been made. Fighting had stopped. IFOR troops covered the entire country. The FWFs were separated, out of the ZOS, and limited to their cantonment areas. IFOR units had good accountability of FWF weapons and ammo caches. IFOR had also overseen the mandated transfer of numerous tracts of land.

All of this had come at a surprisingly low cost in lives. Although American soldiers accounted for one-third of the 50,000-man IFOR, only three Americans were among the twenty-eight IFOR soldiers killed thus far. IFOR had sustained 130 additional casualties from fires, traffic accidents, suicides, and mine strikes.[6]

Seven months into Quarterhorse's tour, we still wondered when we would return home. LTC Harriman wrote, "Look to leave theater at about the one year mark. Politicians will decide if forces replace us or we just leave. Meanwhile, the Generals busily prepare us to do either one."[7]

## Force Protection

While the term "force protection" referred to a combat-ready, protected stance during all activities, it also meant taking active risk reduction measures to prevent accidents. When not out on patrol, Quarterhorse cavalrymen alternated between performing maintenance on our vehicles and equipment and pulling guard duty. Standing for hours on end in a bunker or guard tower was boring as hell, but it was vital for the security of our camps.

Over the spring and summer, Quarterhorse was concerned about frequent attempts by local civilians to penetrate our perimeters at night. The would-be intruders were not intent on launching any sort of attack, but merely on scrounging badly needed food and building supplies.

Infiltrations were particularly frequent at the Dawg Pound. Bravo Troop finally blocked off the section of railroad track running along the south side of the camp. This area had been a regular point of penetration. We encircled the entire camp with trip flares for early warning. For a time, the camp's QRF was kept busy responding to flares going off on the perimeter. Oddly enough, in June, local infiltrators shifted their efforts toward stealing the trip flares themselves.

One QRF member said, "We caught an old man out front of the main gate the other day with some of our trip flares. We saw him kind of eyeing our wire so we called him over. He had two of them in a bag on his bike. God knows what they want 'em for, but we always have a couple go off at night, either from dogs or the LNs (local nationals)."[8] The perpetrators may have wanted the flares as early warning devices for their homes. Our squadron leadership was not overly concerned. Our guards checked the wire regularly and made sure any missing flares were replaced.

Stray dogs searching for food also set off trip flares. Some of our officers were concerned about rabies and the Hantavirus that the dogs might have carried. Captain Bob Ivy gave his troop authorization to shoot stray dogs on sight. Several of his cavalrymen felt this was a draconian measure.

A significant shortcoming in security at the Dawg Pound was the camp's immediate proximity to the heavily trafficked road running from Kalesija to Zvornik. Rows of canvas tents stood just 75 meters from the road and were dangerously exposed to the threat of small arms or grenades from passing vehicles. In late June, engineers from "Alpha Fortieth" erected a barricade of sand-filled, wire-mesh Hesco bastions to shield our living areas from the road. LTC Harriman praised their work and said that the wall helped him sleep much better. Our other Dawg Pound residents agreed.[9]

In the last week of June, our sense of security was jolted when we learned that a massive truck bomb had been detonated outside a crowded American military compound in Saudi Arabia. On July 1, Task Force Eagle received a tip that a similar bombing would occur at an American lodgment area in Bosnia. As a precaution, our Squadron Headquarters deployed a full perimeter defense at LA Molly that afternoon. Besides the fully manned bunkers and fortified guard towers, the camp's QRF, which was then 2nd Platoon, Bravo Troop, manned their M1A1 tanks for three hours before stand-down was called.[10]

For seven months now, Quarterhorse had worried about terrorist attacks against us. On May 8, Delta Troop AWTs flew an important mission in search of a suspected Mujahadeen training camp in the area west of Banovici. No camp was found, but one AWT did locate some topless women sunbathing by a small pond. The women covered up when they realized that they were being observed from afar. During the mission debriefing, one pilot reported that the aircraft "pulled back and worked their way up to alternate OP locations." Grinning, he added, "It was good training!"[11]

In late June, someone set off a small bomb outside a local office of the Organization for Security and Cooperation in Europe. The OSCE was a protected organization under terms of the Dayton Accord. It was "off-limits" and IFOR was responsible for its security.[12] Major General Nash immediately ordered Quarterhorse to investigate. A cavalry staff sergeant surveyed the scene and gave a detailed, accurate report. Nerves at Task Force Eagle Headquarters were quickly assuaged. It turned out that the tiny bomb had not been meant for the OSCE. Someone had left it on the first-floor doorstep of the local Socialist Party office. The OSCE occupied the second floor. The bomb had not been meant to kill anyone. It only blew out some windows and gouged a hole in the doorstep. It had been placed after all the OSCE and ECCM monitors departed for dinner. LTC Harriman suggested that the Socialists might have worried the SDS party in Zvornik. We were concerned that whoever laid the bomb had inside knowledge of OSCE and ECCM activities.[13]

In mid–August, our attached counterintelligence team reported that three local civilian fuel trucks and one dump truck had recently been stolen. A government license plate had also been stolen. This development gave credence to the threat of possible vehicle-borne improvised explosive attacks against IFOR.

Quarterhorse implemented a bomb threat reaction plan called Operation Vigilance.[14] Countermeasures included replacing metal and wire barriers at camp gates with either tanks or Bradleys. After guards confirmed the identities of all passengers by checking IFOR identification cards, and inbound vehicles were searched with mirrors on rollers, the armored roadblock was pulled back to allow the vehicles to enter. Perimeter guards maintained high alert as well.

Another example of force protection measures undertaken was the special issue of modification packages for our thin-skinned utility and transport vehicles. Humvees were issued "Kevlar blankets" designed to minimize the deadly effect of mine strikes. The term "blankets" was a misnomer. They consisted of four rigid Kevlar panels connected inside a canvas cover. They covered the floor and front seats of the crew compartment. They were only slightly padded, so sitting on them while traveling over rugged, potholed roads was terribly uncomfortable. Besides, they were too long and took up too much foot room. The Kevlar blankets also forced taller passengers to bend well forward to look out the window at anything above the horizon.

The blankets were well intended, but we detested them. By the time we got them in the summer, few of us were concerned about the mine threat anymore. However, a mine-related incident occurred in August (related later) that made us realize how dangerously overconfident we had become. Until that time, we were more concerned about the loss of visibility that the blankets created. This made us a lot more vulnerable because we couldn't see as much around our vehicles.

Several Quarterhorse 5-ton cargo trucks and HEMMT heavy cargo trucks were fitted with fully armored cabs as protection against mines and small arms fire. These were more satisfactory, although the modification did not come with stronger door hinges. Many hinges broke under the weight of the heavily armored doors.

Throughout our tour, safety remained a prime consideration in all Quarterhorse activities. By the end of June, 2 BCT reported having set a record for safe operations, "despite terrible roads, a harsh winter, and unsafe Bosnian vehicles and driving habits."[15]

From late December to mid–February, accidents averaged about two to three per week in just the American sector alone. By March, the number dropped to about one per week. From April through the summer, military vehicle accidents occurred only about once per month.

In April, LTC Harriman reminded us:

Americans expect their Army to operate safely and in full compliance with the law. I know I do. By operating to published standards we will operate safely. By maintaining our high leader and Soldier self-discipline we will operate safely. By assessing risk and adopting measures to reduce it during the planning and preparation phases of training and operations, we leaders and Soldiers will operate safely. So do it right. Plan thoroughly. Brief Soldiers thoroughly. Rehearse. Concentrate when you execute; pay attention. Account for sleep deprivation, weather, task difficulty, and training with the risk assessment process. The

squadron will conduct a safety day each quarter, gather lessons learned information, [and] discuss safety issues in AARs.[16]

LTC Harriman's message touched upon the requirement to minimize casualties, an enduring consideration in modern American military operations. He
also cautioned:

> Every Soldier has a personal weapon, for which he or she remains personally
> accountable.... Load it right. Clear it right. Train to kill with it under all condi-
> tions, day, night, bad weather, all. Never forget where its muzzle points. Know
> where and when you might use it next. And never think about anything but
> your weapon when you work it. In other words, continue to do what you do
> well: bear arms with discipline.[17]

Outside our camps, members of Quarterhorse carried loaded weapons
every day, all year. Occasional accidents were bound to occur. They did, but
fortunately no one was ever hurt. Most rounds went into specially constructed
clearing barrels at the front gate of every camp. One cavalryman accidentally
fired a pistol round through the floor of his tent. Accidental discharges such
as this one cost the offender a field grade Article 15.

American soldiers in Bosnia were healthier than was expected in estimates
made prior to our deployment. Based on recent experience in Haiti, Somalia,
and the Gulf War, military doctors predicted that ten out of every one hundred
soldiers would be injured or sick enough to have to report to sick call per
week. The average actually worked out to between seven and eight.[18]

With warmer weather, the number of sports-related injuries went up.
One of the prime sources of injuries within Quarterhorse was our homemade
bull-riding device in the Dawg Pound. This contraption was fashioned from
a 55-gallon drum attached by heavy ropes to four posts. Cavalrymen pulled
guide ropes on the front, rear, and sides to give the "bull" its realistic motion.
Few mastered the bull, but many suffered minor injuries in spectacular, hilarious wipeouts while trying. It was definitely a spectator sport.

IFOR soldiers suffered fewer cases of disease than expected. A primary
concern was Hanta viruses, which can be found in areas with large rodent
populations. As a precaution, Task Force Eagle highly encouraged, but did
not compel, soldiers to take an experimental Hanta virus immunization not
yet approved by the FDA. Many of us opted for it after reading a precautionary
memo and signing a waiver. As it turned out, only one confirmed case and
one suspected case ever occurred within IFOR during our one-year tour.[19] A
few small outbreaks of salmonella occurred, but none was very serious. The
rate within Bosnia was comparable to that of units back in Germany. Major
Sharon Ludwig, the Army doctor in charge of preventive medicine and epi-
demiology for Task Force Eagle, said the lower injury and disease rates

occurred because "there are several things that we do here that are better for our health."[20]

Many American soldiers resented the restrictions placed upon us by General Order Number One and the many other policies aimed at "protecting the force." But by late in the operation, Task Force Eagle had some pretty convincing statistics to demonstrate the positive impact of these policies. American IFOR soldiers had committed only a few disciplinary problems. Senior officers felt the total ban on alcohol had helped a great deal.

There were other active countermeasures that helped to sustain low injury and disease rates. Confining us to base camps limited our exposure to contagious diseases. Eating only in Army or contracted facilities reduced our exposure to food-borne diseases, which we could have contracted in local restaurants lacking strict quality control. Drinking only bottled or treated water reduced our exposure to germs. Bad roads forced drivers to drive more slowly, thus reducing accidents. Housing soldiers in wooden-floored tents or metal shipping containers improved cleanliness and protected us against rodents. Another factor was the similarity of the Bosnian climate to that of Germany and some parts of the United States. This supposedly put less strain on our soldiers' immune systems.[21]

From our senior commanders' perspective, all the precautions paid off. As of October 14, only five American soldiers had been killed since IFOR's arrival in December 1995 — one by a mine, one in a vehicle accident, one from a burner that exploded, and two from heart attacks.[22]

By the end of our 351-day tour, Quarterhorse sustained no loss of life and no serious injury-causing accidents since those in February. Considering that our dangerous stability operation lasted ten months, this was a considerable blessing.

We reported on June 29 that Quarterhorse "continues to focus its efforts on peace enforcement, maintenance, and training Soldiers. Site inspections [of factions' cantonment and storage areas] and [previously undiscovered] SA-7s provided the highlights of the month ... the squadron continues to make sure that the former warring factions have the right things in the right places."[23]

LTC Harriman praised Alpha and Bravo Troops for their reconnaissance efforts. He said, "Keep up the good work. Capture detail. Report it quickly and accurately. You do reconnaissance very well."[24]

In numerous weapons storage site inspections, our ground cavalry troops recorded important details like numbered storage boxes, weapons types, accompanying ammo boxes, and faction soldier remarks. This information led our Squadron Intelligence Section to conclude that VRS forces had packaged arms and ammo for rapid mobilization — an important piece of intel.

During the warm summer months, Quarterhorse took advantage of our close proximity to allied IFOR units. We conducted a series of professional development exchanges with the Swedes, Norwegians, and Russians. HHT maintained a close relationship with the Swedish 8th Mechanized Battalion, exchanging soldiers for fatigue details and conducting several social and professional development events.

## Training and Arming the Federation

The Dayton Accord permitted foreign shipments of small arms and equipment to the Muslim-led Federation beginning in mid–March, 1996. This provision was meant to enable the Federation army (ABiH) to thwart any renewed Serb aggression after IFOR eventually departed.[25] When the U.S. Congress approved the deployment of American ground forces to Bosnia, lawmakers demanded American support for an international effort to help the Federation gain military parity with the Serbs.

In late February, the Clinton administration was under pressure from Capitol Hill and considered sending large quantities of excess American uniforms and outdated equipment to Bosnia. Because IFOR had to maintain its neutrality, American officials did not want IFOR soldiers to directly train or equip Federation forces. One exception was the Turkish IFOR contingent that provided considerable instruction to the predominantly Muslim ABiH. A private American contractor selected by the U.S. Department of Defense conducted the lion's share of the actual training. This contractor, Military Professional Resources, Inc. (MPRI), was a corporation of retired American officers, some of whom had recently trained Croatian forces.[26]

At the end of July, LTC Harriman announced that Quarterhorse would make a small contribution to the training effort.[27] Shortly thereafter, we gave several introductory tours of our camps to local Muslim unit commanders. Our air cavalry troops briefed them on the awesome capabilities of our Kiowa Warriors. Our ground cavalry troops explained our methods of Bradley and tank pre-gunnery training. LTC Harriman taught a class on U.S. Army training and warfighting doctrine. By their own admission, the Muslim leaders were suitably impressed with our discipline, professionalism, and military hardware.[28]

When MPRI began its work in mid–August, President Clinton said, "The [train and arm] program will help ensure that upon IFOR's departure, a military balance exists among the former warring parties so that none of them are encouraged to resume hostilities."[29] Initially, the program delivered nearly $100 million of refurbished American surplus equipment, including rifles, machine guns, radios, tanks, armored personnel carriers, light anti-tank weapons, and utility helicopters.

The program's start hinged on BiH compliance with GFAP provisions to release all Serb prisoners, withdraw all foreign forces, and end its intelligence cooperation with Iran. The Federation also had to pass a law integrating its military forces and creating western-oriented defense institutions. President Clinton certified that the BiH had met its commitments before any military hardware was shipped.[30]

But the BiH hadn't really, as far as the withdrawal of foreign forces went. Although by late January most of the estimated 1,000 Mujahadeen had departed, over a hundred remained. Some included highly indoctrinated Iranian Revolutionary Guards. Others were volunteers from all over the Islamic world — from Algeria to Afghanistan.[31] From the beginning, NATO considered these militants a threat to IFOR.[32] On December 18, a group of Mujahadeen in Zenica blew themselves up while assembling a vehicle-borne improvised explosive device.[33]

It was doubtful that all unauthorized foreigners had left Bosnia as mandated. As late as the national election day on September 14, the U.S. government still called for the expulsion of fifteen non–Bosnian-looking people in Bocinja Donja, a village fifty miles north of Sarajevo.[34]

Land mines were another ongoing threat to IFOR. Quarterhorse rejoiced in early July, though, when "Alpha Fortieth" reported having completed the marking and clearing of all minefields in our sector.

Early that month, recent adjustments to the IEBL went into effect. LTC Harriman hosted a ceremony with local leaders to mark the occasion. It was a success and fostered a measure of goodwill.[35] That goodwill was nonexistent when it was first announced that the IEBL would shift in some areas of the Quarterhorse sector. Back then, we cooled local reactions and protests with an information campaign. Our effort incorporated the assistance of local governments and police to educate the people and address their concerns. LTC Harriman said, "It was the right way to go. A potentially explosive situation was diffused [*sic*] with just a little common sense and quick analysis of what was wrong."[36]

# 10

# LATE SUMMER HEAT

## Han Pijesak Again

On the Fourth of July, Quarterhorse and our attached units enjoyed a much-needed day off from our continuous stability tasks. Cooks from HHT served up a traditional American barbecue at each of our three lodgment areas. Our cavalrymen at the Dawg Pound and the Thunderdome also enjoyed visits from a team of San Francisco 49er cheerleaders, who performed dance routines and signed autographs for hordes of appreciative cavalrymen. It was a restful day. Most of us had no indication of the brewing confrontation that would soon bring IFOR the closest it would ever come to a fight with the Bosnian Serb Army.

In early July, tensions flared between Western governments and the Bosnian Serb leadership. For months, the international community had demanded that Radovan Karadzic step down from power as mandated by the Dayton Accord. Indicted for war crimes, Karadzic simply ignored the demands. Threats of economic sanctions followed, but the Serbs managed to hem and haw their way out of them without actually reducing Karadzic's political influence.[1]

On the one hand, Western leaders wanted to arrest Karadzic and General Ratko Mladic and to bring them both to trial. Bosnian national elections were just two months away. As the leader of hard-line nationalist Serbs who rejected the goals of the Dayton Accord, Karadzic simply had to leave power. On the other hand, Western leaders were afraid of provoking reprisals. Therefore, they were reluctant to use NATO forces to capture the Bosnian Serb strongmen. The United States still reeled from the humiliation of the failed Somalia mission and did not push the issue.[2]

When warrants for the arrest of Karadzic and Mladic were distributed, some low-level VRS officials vowed to retaliate against UN and IFOR personnel. Many Serbs thought the warrants marked the beginning of an IFOR manhunt for the two leaders. But the warrants had no major impact on IFOR's mission. Units like Quarterhorse did not actively search for indicted war criminals, but we did increase our patrols to make it more difficult for the fugitives to move freely around the country. Senior IFOR leadership said that we would detain war criminals and deliver them to the appropriate authorities — only if they were encountered in the course of our normal duties, and if the on-scene commander determined that the tactical situation favored the move's success.[3]

During the period of July 5–7, a battle seemed imminent between IFOR and the VRS. Once again, it was in the forested mountains around Han Pijesak and Mount Zep. Tensions ran high all around. In recent weeks, witnesses at the UN tribunal in The Hague had placed Mladic at the scene of several atrocities.[4] Meanwhile, Bosnian Serb civilians, in groups as large as fifty, occasionally blocked traffic to hinder IFOR troop movements through the area.[5]

Our air cavalry troops' routine aerial reconnaissance flights detected eight combat vehicles deployed northwest of Mount Zep at the VRS General Staff headquarters.[6] This complex was only twelve miles from the 2 BCT headquarters at LA Lisa outside Vlasenica.

On July 3, Colonel Batiste and the commander of TF 2-68 AR went to the VRS weapons storage site south of Mount Zep on a no-notice inspection. They wanted to confirm that the eight tracked vehicles normally kept there had indeed been moved without IFOR approval. At the same time, another group of IFOR officers went to the location where we knew the vehicles were. Both groups were denied access.[7]

On July 5, AWTs from our Delta and Echo Troops began aerial patrols over the area. AH-64 Apaches from the 4th Aviation Brigade assisted. Our Kiowa Warriors returned with conclusive videotaped evidence of the VRS combat vehicles outside their approved storage site.

Captain Downey, our squadron intelligence officer, reviewed the tapes, which showed tanks and armored personnel carriers that he identified as from the VRS 1st Protective Regiment. They were in covered and concealed defensive positions about 300 meters outside Mladic's base. CPT Downey counted four dug-in, well-camouflaged tanks and two APCs. The vehicles were very hard to detect under the tall evergreen trees. The Serbs were aware of our Kiowas' thermal sights, and so had applied thick foliage to the vehicles to reduce their heat signatures.[8]

IFOR aircraft flew frequent overflights to remind the VRS of our resolve to uphold our mandated military function of enforcing compliance with the GFAP. The constant buzz of aircraft rattled some junior VRS officers, who made some threatening remarks about having weapons at their disposal to shoot down IFOR helicopters.[9]

The VRS had clearly violated the GFAP in three ways. First, it had moved the eight combat vehicles without requesting prior IFOR approval. Second, it had threatened to engage American helicopters during their aerial reconnaissance. And third, the VRS had refused to let IFOR units inspect the sites where the vehicles belonged and where they were actually positioned.[10] The GFAP specifically required that all places used for military purposes had to be declared and open for IFOR inspection. No exceptions were authorized. IFOR had authority to set the conditions for the inspections. They could be conducted anytime, anywhere.

Under orders from Major General Nash and Lieutenant General Walker (the COMARRC), 2 BCT devised a plan on the night of July 5 to force an inspection of the site. Dubbed Operation Gryphon II, this operation was executed barely a month after the original Operation Gryphon had similarly forced an inspection of the VRS headquarters.[11]

Simultaneous with our military planning, Western diplomats made several late-night phone calls to Serbian President Slobodan Milosevic, the Bosnian Serbs' mentor, urging him to convince them to back down.[12]

The plan called for COL Batiste and his immediate command group to demand to inspect the site on July 6. They would be supported by two company teams from TF 2-68 AR and two from TF 4-12 IN. This force counted nearly 18 tanks, an equal number of Bradleys, and over a hundred infantrymen. Quarterhorse would provide multiple AWTs for aerial reconnaissance and reporting. The 4th Aviation Brigade would provide Apaches to loiter overhead for immediate, devastating firepower. Three tube artillery platoons and an MLRS platoon from the 4-29 FA would stand by for immediate fire support. The 40th Engineer Battalion would send mobility teams to clear obstacles on order, and NATO fighter-bombers would circle overhead just in case.[13]

With nearly twenty fixed- and rotary-wing aircraft and a ground force of almost forty tanks and Bradleys, we were prepared to use overwhelming force if the Serbs demanded it. By noon on July 6, all elements were set.

COL Batiste arrived at the VRS base and demanded entry. As expected, the Serbs refused. He insisted. He also told them that with so much artillery trained upon their headquarters, and with NATO fighters and helicopters zipping past overhead, any attempt by the VRS to shoot down an IFOR aircraft would be the worst mistake of their lives.

The Serbs argued, complained, and held their ground. By 3:00 P.M., though, they backed down somewhat. The VRS agreed to let COL Batiste see the eight armored vehicles but not the fortified positions they were in.[14]

At that point, LTG Walker and one of his British deputies, Brigadier Charolton Weedy, became involved. After long and intense negotiations, the Serbs finally agreed to allow Brigadier Weedy to inspect the site.

As the brigadier set off on his inspection, a mob of nearly 800 Bosnian Serb civilians converged on Han Pijesak.[15] The VRS had whipped them up by falsely reporting that IFOR had killed two VRS soldiers and had captured General Mladic. In the intense summer heat, the angry mob pounded on the encircled IFOR vehicles and shouted anti–American slogans. They also physically assaulted some IFOR officers and their escort from the 501st Military Police Company.[16] To the MPs' great credit, they maintained their discipline and professionalism despite being spat upon and stoned. Their steadfastness prevented the dangerous situation from becoming deadly.[17]

Eventually, Brigadier Weedy did tour the VRS vehicle defensive positions. Later that afternoon, a second crowd of nearly 200 Bosnian Serb civilians congregated outside Mladic's compound. IFOR soldiers at the scene were later cited in the press for handling "the situation very calmly. They were very professional." The confrontation was defused without injuries.[18]

That evening, VRS leaders apologized for their belligerent actions. They allowed COL Batiste and an armed IFOR entourage to inspect their headquarters. The VRS was "very apologetic" about the threats and insults hurled by the civilian mobs. Senior VRS officers explained that they had been misinformed about Mladic's impending arrest.[19]

July 6 was the day on which IFOR came closest to using deadly force against a faction's forces, although none of us knew this at the time, of course. Throughout the day, Kiowa Warriors from Quarterhorse enforced the GFAP no-fly restrictions and contributed to the constant, overwhelming pressure on the Serbs.

After the standoff was resolved successfully, CPT Downey reflected on what might have played out had it come to use of force. Our Kiowa- and Apache-mounted, laser-guided Hellfire missiles probably would have been ineffective against the VRS armored vehicles hidden in the dense forest. Instead, he felt that we would have used our considerable artillery to neutralize the area before sweeping it with tanks, Bradleys, and dismounted infantry.[20]

COL Batiste later wrote to his soldiers:

> The teamwork of the entire Brigade Combat Team during recent operations around Han Pijesak serves as an inspiration to us all. Combat power was synchronized as well as I have ever seen it done.... In the end, the application of force was not necessary; the VRS complied and moved armored vehicles back to approved storage sites. I am very proud of every Soldier, from the point of the spear to the brigade support area. Well done.... Be patient. The tactical situation

could change in a heartbeat.... We must remain absolutely impartial. Treat people within the Federation and Srpska with dignity and respect. Never point a weapon at anyone unless you intend to use it. Discipline remains our foundation. Take care of one another.[21]

For some time after Gryphon II, Quarterhorse maintained higher force protection levels in our lodgment areas and checkpoints, and on our patrols within Serb territory.

As it turned out, this incident was not IFOR's last run-in with the Serbs. Just two months later, the VRS again prevented 2 BCT from inspecting the same headquarters site. However, that incident did not rival the tension of the one on July 6, because 2 BCT anticipated Serb resistance and planned accordingly.

Strong pre-positioned forces reinforced the small inspection team. TF 4-12 IN positioned mechanized infantry to the north and west. Quarterhorse provided AWTs for reconnaissance and precision fires. The 720th MP BN (CBT) positioned Quick Reaction Forces and reconnaissance patrols to the south. 4-29 FA trained sufficient artillery on the site and had quick, accurate fire support standing by. Each element, including the inspection team, had a "wingman" to watch its back.

The inspection began smoothly enough. Then the MPs confiscated four undeclared wheeled armored vehicles — another clear violation of the GFAP. What could have turned into a confrontation was quickly resolved. The inspectors convinced the VRS that it had no viable option other than to cooperate. The Serbs acknowledged the overwhelming combat power that 2 BCT was ready to bring to bear.[22]

The mundane task of maintaining our equipment proved a challenge to the success of Quarterhorse's stability tasks. By late July, our Squadron Maintenance Section realized the impending dilemma that we faced. Winter would set in within three months, and we would eventually road-march back to Hungary on our way home. Once we got back to Germany, maintenance funds would almost certainly be slashed.

With all this in mind, Captain Wawro initiated an aggressive plan to conduct semiannual services on all HHT vehicles prior to the fall. His effort was hampered because the HHT motor pool was largely submerged in the Thunderdome's deep, gooey mud. CPT Wawro's mechanics needed hard surfaces on which to jack up the vehicles. Their solution was to "borrow" several more pallets from Tuzla Air Base. Some relatively dry ground was set aside as a special service area. The work proceeded very well despite the austere conditions.[23]

A report submitted by Quarterhorse in July evidenced how busy we were.

Stability tasks "continued at a fast pace ... to enforce the GFAP and in training to maintain proficiency in individual and collective skills. Aerial and ground zone reconnaissance, traffic OPs to monitor the flow of civilian vehicles, site inspections, security operations, and lodgment area protection all continued."[24]

All seven cavalry troops and our attachments were humming. The success of our stability operation had made it possible for repairs to begin on the major Tuzla-to-Zvornik road and for adjacent communities to begin rebuilding. Our ground cavalry troops' round-the-clock compliance checkpoints had forced the FWFs to conduct military activities in accordance with GFAP restrictions. Our air cavalry troops flew daily missions over the entire 2 BCT sector. Besides participating in the recent Operation Gryphon II, our AWTs also located some potentially illegal police weapons storage sites. As always, our success in the air and on the ground would have been impossible without the dedicated support of our cavalrymen in HHT and Fox Troop. LTC Harriman reported that morale was high throughout Quarterhorse.[25]

Secretary of Defense William Perry visited the units of 2 BCT in mid–July. He said, "Everybody had forecasted that you wouldn't be able to do this. That when you came into Bosnia, you'd meet armed resistance. Well, we came in heavy. We came well-trained, well disciplined.... We came in with robust rules of engagement — and there wasn't anybody wanting to mess with the 1st Armored Division."[26]

Major Dixon wrote from 2 BCT headquarters, "1-4 CAV ... has significantly enhanced the stability in this contentious area by conducting very deliberate, frequent missions to control their area of operations."[27]

In a letter to Quarterhorse families, LTC Harriman captured a cross-section of our squadron's diverse activities on a typical day in late July[28]:

Today, in the town just across from the Dawg Pound, folk no longer walk around the burnt bus that has blocked the road there since 1992, rusting. HHT, SGT Stevenson's M88 crew, cut up the bus and hauled it away. Today, Echo Troop photographed the railway from Zvinice to Zvornik so Hungarian and Italian rail engineers can predict problems they will have when they rebuild the line this August. Bravo Troop went door-to-door today toward Zvornik, delivering IFOR papers, asking folk about the elections, and clearing possible ambush sites along the way. Today, Alpha Troop began the gunnery training that will lead them to a successful Hungarian gunnery. Delta Troop flew aerial gunnery missions in Glamoc, near Croatia, ground crews and the Chaplain reloading helicopter rockets between missions. Fox [Troop] kept them flying. Today, the S-4 assigned tent living spaces to physicians collecting forensic evidence for the Hague Tribunal.... And today, we all helped to do the chores, the maintenance, the putting things away, the guards, the details. Today we worked hard.[29]

Quarterhorse also helped 2 BCT maintain good relations with the neighboring Russian airborne brigade up north. We conducted occasional combined patrols with the Russians and attended ceremonies with them. One evening, we hosted several Russian officers at a partnership dinner in the Dawg Pound.

Bear in mind that all these activities occurred within a hostile fire zone. Bosnia remained a dangerous place to work and live throughout our squadron's year there. Occasional reminders of this fact helped ward off the complacency that always threatened to creep into our minds.

The standoff at Han Pijesak in July heightened our concerns for force protection.[30] This prompted our Squadron Intelligence Section to analyze possible locations from which our patrols might be ambushed. Second Lieutenant Jordan Friedman generated a list of likely spots along major roads. Our ground cavalry troops were then tasked to check them out.

While handing out IFOR newspapers door-to-door, Bravo Troop discovered four previously unknown bunkers that could have supported an ambush along the major Tuzla-Zvornik road. 2LT Friedman was justifiably proud of his analysis. A few days later, Quarterhorse sent a team of engineers from Alpha Fortieth to blow up the bunkers.[31]

On August 8, we received another important reminder of the danger surrounding us. A Muslim man flagged down a Bravo Troop patrol as it passed by the man's newly reoccupied house in the ZOS. He had been burning the overgrowth along the shoulder of the roadway in front of his house. The man pointed out to our cavalrymen what he thought was a land mine. We sent a squad of our attached engineers over to probe around the area. They made a surprising discovery — two TMM-1 antitank mines and an unattached pressure plate from another mine. A little research revealed that the mines were from a minefield that we believed lay farther north. The map graphics that we had been using to depict this minefield for eight months were 200 meters off![32] Our vehicles had driven past this spot countless times, oblivious to the hidden hazards just inches away. Had any vehicle happened to swerve off the road at that particular spot in order to avoid some hazard in the roadway, the results could have been disastrous. Our leadership used this unpleasant discovery to remind Quarterhorse of the dangers that still lurked within our sector.

Around this same time, LTC Harriman announced that Quarterhorse would soon be reinforced with several military police platoons from the 64th and 536th MP Companies. We needed them to help secure our large sector during the upcoming September elections.[33] We shifted our cavalrymen around to make tent and motor pool space available to them in the Dawg Pound.

## *Brief Escape*

Boredom was the biggest threat to our morale in Bosnia. The endless hours our cavalrymen spent manning checkpoints and OPs and performing mundane work in our camps led many to proclaim themselves "prisoners for peace." The year-long operation proceeded at a snail's pace, despite the fact that all of our camps eventually featured small post exchanges, weight rooms, and phone tents.

One Quarterhorse NCO remarked, "I came down here expecting to get into it and kick somebody's ass, but there's nothing happening. If we're not going to get into it, get me outta here."[34] This sentiment was widespread by the summertime. Many IFOR soldiers were pessimistic and believed that Bosnia would lapse into civil war after we departed.

But some within Quarterhorse had had personal experiences that kept them motivated for the tasks at hand. Staff Sergeant Johnson of Alpha Troop remembered:

> When we came into Olovo, we were the first Americans in. They had been surrounded on three sides, and I've never seen a place so blown to hell. The Serbs on the hill had been shelling them with artillery for four years and the place was a wreck. We were always patrolling and maneuvering down there, so we got to see a lot of people.... One thing I will never forget was one day we were moving through a town and this little girl maybe eight years old was out there with her family. They were all dressed up in their Sunday clothes and she was holding up a sign with a big heart on it with IFOR in big letters across it. It was really moving. We said to ourselves, "That's why we're here." And we always try to remember it.[35]

Quarterhorse scouts and tankers were fortunate in that they frequently left the close confines of our camps. But our cooks, mechanics, and headquarters and support personnel were largely confined to the same tiny camps for the duration of our tour. To them, Operation Joint Endeavor was little better than a prison sentence.

Task Force Eagle had already begun work on a plan for Rest and Relaxation (R&R) Leave by the end of January, which was when our cavalrymen began inquiring about one. Initially, it looked like we would only get seven days of leave. Fortunately, the number was increased to fifteen once the plan went into effect in April. All Task Force Eagle soldiers deployed to Bosnia for more than six months were eligible for fifteen days of R&R leave either in the U.S. or Germany.[36] Each unit received a monthly quota of slots to both destinations. "Freedom birds" departed Tuzla four times a week. Quarterhorse cavalrymen began taking leave in late April. Small groups continued to depart on R&R through October.

Units also received a limited number of four-day Fighter Management passes to Hungary. Soldiers lucky enough to score one of these passes had to endure a long bus ride through Croatia before reaching either Budapest or a resort on Lake Balaton. Soldiers did not have a choice and did not learn where they were going until the bus was underway. At Lake Balaton, the largest lake in Europe, American soldiers relaxed and enjoyed water sports and other activities at the simple but clean Hotel Zeus.[37] Fighter Management passes were primarily intended for soldiers serving less than 180 days in Bosnia.[38] But extra slots came down occasionally, and Quarterhorse had plenty of volunteers to snatch them up.

An article in one issue of the 2 BCT command information newspaper raved, "So you have been waiting with bated breath to indulge in civilization again — a bed, bath tub, and TV.... If you are slated to participate in the Morale, Welfare, and Recreation Pass Program to Budapest, prepare to get four-star service."[39] The MWR pass program actually began as a highly unauthorized boondoggle by our Bravo Troop. When the troop rotated to TTA for gunnery, it quietly worked into the schedule two days with families in Budapest. Surprisingly, senior IFOR leaders were not upset with the detour. It was a great idea, so all other units rotating through TTA were officially granted a brief stay in Hungary's lovely capital city.

When Task Force Eagle Soldiers arrived in Budapest from either Taborfalva or "downrange," an NCO with the most coveted job in IFOR gave them a safety briefing about the city and passed out handbooks before cutting the eager soldiers loose. The briefing was interminably long for both soldiers and family members who'd been ushered together into one room without even a second for greetings first.

American soldiers enjoyed special discount rates at the Hilton, Ramada Grand, and Thermal Hotels. The latter two were located on Margit Island in the Danube River. The island was like a larger version of New York City's Central Park. It had paths for strolling, a water park, petting zoo, and romantic thermal baths.

At the Ramada, MWR personnel and the hotel staff converted a basement room into the "Peacekeepers' Pub" for those Americans strangely inclined to experience as little Hungarian culture as possible. The pub served alcohol, had billiards and cable TV, and was limited to U.S. soldiers and their guests.[40] Not one of our single soldiers patronized the pub. They wondered who in their right mind would want to seclude themselves in a basement with the same soldiers they'd been cooped up with for so many months down in Bosnia, especially when some of the most beautiful women in all of Europe were right outside.

The five-star Hilton occupied a choice spot in the middle of Budapest's castle district. Overlooking the Danube, it was built into the ruins of a 13th century cloister and was adjacent to the famous Mattias Church and the scenic Fisherman's Bastion.[41] For the most part, only officers were privileged to be billeted there.

MWR provided a shuttle bus service for us to get around the city. Many opted to take optional sightseeing tours or Danube River cruises. Nightclubs and restaurants were popular hangouts.[42]

Our Quarterhorse leadership shared Task Force Eagle's desire that soldiers should enjoy their R&R while avoiding potential pitfalls in their relationships that reunion might bring about. Accordingly, Captain Dave Brown, the squadron chaplain, briefed our departing cavalrymen on the "do's and don'ts for R&R at home." This information also appeared on troop bulletin boards and in unit newspapers.

Down in Bosnia, our cavalrymen engaged in a variety of activities to pass the time. LTC Harriman informed our families, "Most of us have become volleyball fanatics, basketball fiends, movie mavens, or literature lunatics."[43]

Back in December 1995, the expected high operational tempo our impending mission compelled LTC Harriman to issue a policy memo denying our cavalrymen the opportunity to take leave to witness the births of their children. However, within thirty days of our departure he relented. The situation appeared such that individuals could be excused for a few days for this momentous family occasion. The revised policy allowed expectant fathers to return home a few days before the birth date, and to remain with the mother and child for about a week after the birth.[44] It was a tremendous boost to morale.

During the summer, LTC Harriman reaffirmed his commitment to send Quarterhorse NCOs back to Germany or the States to attend professional military education schools. He cautioned our Troop Commanders to ensure that "only qualified, prepared Soldiers attend school. Other Soldiers must work extra so school-bound Soldiers can attend school. Prevent shortfalls; then the unit's short-term sacrifice becomes well worth the effort."[45]

## August

As Operation Joint Endeavor entered its eighth month, peace had taken a tenuous hold. Quarterhorse sensed that it would take the Bosnians considerably more time to erase six hundred years of animosity and to get past their recent civil war. Practically every Bosnian man still wore a uniform, usually of American camouflage pattern. Their uniforms reminded us that war was just a stone's throw away for these people.

COL Batiste wrote, "I remain extremely proud of the brigade combat team, which includes Rear Detachments and Family Support Groups. We have had a dramatic effect on the peace process in Bosnia. Look no further than the faces of the children. This is a defining moment in all of our lives; we will look back on it with enormous pride."[46] The destruction and poverty were in sad contrast to the innocent faces of young Bosnian children. The kids struck a chord with many of us. They abounded in roadways, always in danger of being run over. They waved and shouted at us for candy, "Hey you! Gimme bonbon!"

In early August, Brigadier General George W. Casey, Jr., became the new Assistant Division Commander for Maneuver for the 1st Armored Division. Soon after his arrival in country, BG Casey visited the Dawg Pound with COL Batiste.

Incidentally, nine years later, *Major General* Batiste commanded the 1st Infantry Division during its first year-long tour of combat duty in Iraq, while *General* Casey held the top position there as the Commanding General of the Multi-National Forces — Iraq. After relinquishing command, MG Batiste retired and vocally protested American strategic handling of the war in Iraq. General Casey ultimately served as Chief of Staff of the Army from 2007 to 2011.

LTC Harriman assembled all of the squadron's field grade officers and most of our captains next to the helipad. After a round of handshakes, our weary officers gaggled behind as LTC Harriman gave BG Casey a walking tour of the camp. He took him atop the guard tower by the main gate for a better view.

After eight months, Quarterhorse observed that our presence was having a real impact. Political commentators credited IFOR for having increased the Bosnians' general level of confidence and security. A sign of their confidence was the incredible period of reconstruction over the late summer and early fall.

In August, rebuilding of the devastated city of Kalesija and its neighboring villages really took off. Bullet holes were patched over. Rubble was pushed into large piles for removal. Broken windowpanes were replaced. The terribly potholed roads were repaved. Shot-up road signs were replaced. Lines were painted on the roads for the first time ever in some places. Civilian workers and furloughed Muslim soldiers hacked away four years of undergrowth and pollution from the clogged shoulders of roadways.

As summer turned to fall, the pace of IFOR activity increased. Everyone in Quarterhorse was busy with peacekeeping operations, training, ICTY support, election preparations, the occasional serious incident, and then "force reshaping"—a new term entering our lexicon. Maintenance also became more of a priority than ever before. Many vehicles were overdue for annual services, and we expected to redeploy within the next few months.

LTC Harriman wrote:

> I expect squadron troopers to maintain equipment. Preventative maintenance checks and services remain the foundation of the squadron maintenance program. Troops will continue to integrate the service schedule with the operational schedule, and conduct services as an 8-step exercise. Troops will continue to train operators and maintainers on equipment. Once we redeploy, we will not get nearly the money we get now to maintain our equipment. Keep it fixed. Defer nothing. Get all required parts on order now. Install all parts before we redeploy. Fix even the very small things. These must be our goals while we have the bucks, the parts priority, and the time to do them.[47]

About this time, when LTC Harriman notified Quarterhorse that we would soon receive several up-armored XM114 Humvees for patrolling, he warned, "Remember the rule old cavalry troopers followed. Treat 'em rough! [refers to the enemy]. Treat 'em right [refers to the horse, the HMMWV, the SUSV, etc.]. Assign a single driver to these vehicles; I won't tolerate pass-around wheels."[48]

In mid–August, IFOR intelligence identified a serious terrorist threat from Muslim Mujahadeen fighters. This news came only weeks after the terrorist attack on Khobar Towers in Saudi Arabia.[49]

Once again, we ratcheted up force protection in our camps. All reasonable and prudent precautions were taken. Armored vehicles remained in use as rolling gates for the duration of our operation. LTC Harriman was particularly concerned that gate guards should keep their weapons at the ready for immediate use.[50]

Collocated in the Thunderdome with HHT were the 47th Forward Support Battalion and the Field Trains elements from the other 2 BCT task forces. HHT was responsible for securing a portion of the camp perimeter. Its sector included the 100-foot slag heap overlooking the camp. Atop the hill, cavalrymen from Workhorse Troop manned the fortified observation tower located next to the helipad. In the event of an attack, we would have reinforced the position with two armored vehicles. The camp conducted several perimeter readiness drills in August and September. These drills paid off when an incident actually occurred in November (related later).

Our stability and sundry tasks churned at a frantic pace. In the strategic parlance of our NATO leadership, our focus remained on "enforcing GFAP provisions to ensure a safe environment for Bosnia's future." We kept up our

*Top:* Lieutenant Colonel Anthony Harriman provides tour of the Dawg Pound for newly arrived Brigadier General George Casey, August 1996. *Bottom:* Staff Sergeant Huber (left) and his mechanics from Team Cav at work in the Thunderdome, November 1996 (both photographs: Mark Viney).

Newly issued XM114 up-armored Humvee leads Bravo Troop convoy through ZOS checkpoint on Route Hawk, the "highway" connecting Zvornik with Kalesija, Summer 1996 (photograph: 1st Infantry Division Public Affairs Office).

site inspections. We monitored FWF weapons movements and training. We conducted reconnaissance missions throughout our sector, and we also manned our checkpoints and observation posts. Still, we also found time to conduct individual and crew skills training.

An issue of the 2 BCT command information newspaper praised the brigade's soldiers for having earned and maintained a reputation with the factions as a tough, disciplined, and credible force. Reportedly, military leaders from both entities consistently expressed their respect for our brigade because of the way in which we completed our day-to-day tasks.[51]

In late August, 2 BCT shifted focus towards supporting preparations by the Organization for Security and Cooperation in Europe (OSCE) for the Bosnian general elections in September. Our brigade was tasked to provide area security for the 291 polling sites that had been designated within its sector. We were also tasked to provide logistical support and on-call emergency evacuation to the OSCE. Election support operations were closely coordinated between the OSCE, the International Police Task Force (IPTF), local mayors, and civilian police forces. Quarterhorse was designated as the brigade main effort. We would secure the most territory, including a few areas projected for violence.[52]

Quarterhorse also assumed another new mission around this same time. We were to provide intelligence for the Italian *Regimento Genio Ferrovieri*— the Railroad Engineer Regiment. This unit was tasked to repair a fractured, forty-five-kilometer segment of rail line running the length of the Tuzla valley. The track had to be brought up to minimum military standards in order to create a connected rail network across the country.[53] During the forty-three-month civil war, the rail line received no maintenance and was rendered useless by bombs, explosives, and fighting positions dug into the railroad bed, as well as by landslides and vegetation growth.

Prior to the Italians' arrival, both Quarterhorse air cavalry troops dispatched AWTs to conduct an aerial route reconnaissance of the line. This was a standard mission for our Kiowa Warrior crews. They provided videotapes to the Italians that showed the extent and exact locations of damage. Our support was greatly appreciated.[54]

Meanwhile, our ground cavalry troops provided security escorts for a German non-governmental organization named "Brandenburg Helps Bosnia." This group was one of several NGOs providing much-needed aid to the Bosnian people.[55]

Throughout the summer, Quarterhorse civil affairs and psyops teams continued their informational radio shows. They generated and distributed more printed materials, conducted polling site surveys, and continually explained IFOR's purpose for being in Bosnia.[56]

In midsummer, Task Force Eagle gained another aerial intelligence gathering asset meant to complement our squadron's Kiowa Warriors. This was a squadron of unmanned aerial vehicles (UAVs) from the U.S. Marine Corps' Unmanned Aerial Vehicle Squadron 1.

This squadron flew two types of UAVs. The majority were smaller, older Pioneer models, which were multi-million-dollar, oversized, remote-controlled planes. They featured zoom-lens cameras capable of rotating 360 degrees, and they could provide real-time video imagery — a capability that our Kiowas did not yet possess.[57] But these UAVs were constantly plagued by mechanical and design problems. A significant flaw was that they were controlled by line-of-sight radio. The aircraft would crash if it lost the radio signal directing it. This was a significant shortcoming in the heavily wooded, mountainous terrain of the 2 BCT sector.[58]

The Marines also operated a couple of the larger, more advanced Predator UAVs, which were controlled via satellite and were generally more dependable.

IFOR had additional Predators at its disposal in Taszar, Hungary. Those aircraft were controlled by European Command (EUCOM) in Germany.

Engineers from 40 EN BN constructed a short runway within a fortified perimeter next to the Thunderdome. When the Marines arrived in early July, they moved in alongside HHT. Our cavalrymen did not appreciate having to pack it in tighter in order to open up tent space for the newcomers.

The UAVs had a dubious impact on the operation. The Marines finally packed up and left on October 10 after having crashed six of their aircraft. Over half of the Marines' three-month deployment was spent in a grounded status between accidents.

Another materiel shortcoming of the Marine UAV squadron was that it lacked sufficient transportation assets to recover downed aircraft. Quite often, it had to beg for help from other units. During their last operational week, the Marines lost one of their Predator UAVs somewhere up in the Russian sector. In rainy darkness, First Lieutenant Matt Mock, the HHT executive officer, scrambled a convoy to recover the downed aircraft. It was very late when his convoy finally returned.[59]

The Marines themselves were an impressive lot. They looked sharp, acted serious, and marched in formation wherever they went. It was sad to see these proud Marines in such a lamentable situation with such pathetic equipment.

In order for President Clinton to keep his disingenuous promise of getting American soldiers out of Bosnia in a year, IFOR began a rotation of units — called "force reshaping" — in late August. As the original IFOR units rotated out of Bosnia, fresh units were introduced into the region. Within 2 BCT, redeployment dates were set fairly early on for TFs 4-12 IN and 2-68 AR. The fate of Quarterhorse was less clear. We faced the likelihood of being the last combat element of the original IFOR to depart. We expected to redeploy sometime in early December.

When TF 2-68 AR began redeploying its company teams, it needed another unit to come in and maintain security in its volatile sector. Since our Alpha Troop had opened up their sector for them, it was the logical candidate to receive it back. On August 18, the troop was attached to TF 2-68 AR and road-marched down to LA Linda. Alpha Troop's mission was to cover the task force sector during the upcoming elections. Eventually, it would assume control of the entire sector once TF 2-68 AR completed its withdrawal. Alpha Troop remained in Olovo until the third week of October. In turn, it was relieved by an incoming task force from the 1st Infantry Division.

The military police companies that had recently joined 2 BCT also helped to fill vacancies created by departing elements of TF 2-68 AR and TF 4-12 IN. Quarterhorse heard that these Humvee-equipped MPs were intended to make IFOR "a lighter, more mobile force with increased ability to ensure GFAP compliance and to support civil implementation efforts."[60] Higher-level commanders believed that these MPs would be adequately armed to conduct security and patrolling missions.

One of the new arrivals was the 64th Military Police Company, which was attached to Quarterhorse. The "64th MPs," as we referred to them, were part of the 720th Military Police Battalion from Fort Hood, Texas. The MP company quickly established itself as an integral player in our operations.

Throughout September, Quarterhorse ground elements continued to support the efforts of the International Criminal Tribunal for War Crimes in the Former Yugoslavia (ICTY), the Office of the High Representative (OHR), and the OSCE. In the air, Delta and Echo Troops flew daily aerial reconnaissance missions over the entire 2 BCT sector and maintained an Aerial Quick Reaction Force. The value of this QRF was demonstrated once again by another major incident in the ZOS.

## The Mahaladay Madness

Just two weeks prior to the September elections, Quarterhorse was reminded yet again of our sector's potential for violence. On August 29, a major armed disturbance between Muslims and Serbs erupted in the ZOS village of Mahala for the second time. This occasion proved the closest that Quarterhorse ground elements came to armed conflict during our year in Bosnia.

A group of Muslim refugees had recently returned to Mahala for the stated purpose of rebuilding the ruined homes they had vacated during the war. During a routine patrol of the area, our cavalrymen recognized several of the settlers as soldiers from the local 281st Brigade of the ABiH 28th Division. This brigade was a regular force unit that counted many Muslim refugees among its ranks. The brigade had close ties with the Muslim SDA party in Tuzla. The Social Democrats were orchestrating and funding Muslim resettlement efforts in Republika Srpska territory.[61] Since neither faction was authorized to move military forces into the ZOS, the presence of these armed Muslim soldiers was a clear violation of the GFAP.

At about 7:00 A.M. on August 29, a busload of Bosnian Serb military police arrived in Mahala. The MUPs fired their weapons into the air to intimidate the Muslims. In Captain Downey's words, "They came in, piled off the buses, and started cracking heads."[62] The Muslims responded with sporadic fire and by throwing rocks and bottles at the Serbs.

Captain Torch, the 2 BCT Intelligence Officer, had just tipped off CPT Downey that the MUPs were coming moments before their bus passed by Rock OP. Quarterhorse acted quickly to contain the violence before it spun out of control. CPT Downey called Major Gregory Tubbs, a new arrival to Quarterhorse, who was in the area with a patrol. CPT Downey told him to get out of the way and to find the IPTF and senior MUP commanders on the ground in Mahala.[63]

Captain Ivy and his patrol of Bravo Troop cavalrymen were the first to report on the violence. The MUPs fired right past CPT Ivy's men at the Muslims, who retreated with the MUPs in hot pursuit. Ten Muslims were wounded.

MAJ Tubbs and his element were also caught in the middle. MAJ Tubbs was the incoming squadron operations officer and had only been in country a short time. He was apparently unaware of LTC Harriman's instructions from the previous Mahala confrontation to try to keep the entities apart, but once they clash, to get out of the way. With map in hand and radio operator at his side, MAJ Tubbs waved at the Serbs to stop firing and chasing the Muslims. He reported several times that he was trying to get our cavalrymen back in between the two groups in order to separate them. Our officers later gave MAJ Tubbs a lot of good-natured ribbing for having exposed himself so dangerously.

The rest of Quarterhorse quickly went into action. Cavalrymen from Bravo and Charlie Troops, who had been manning checkpoints nearby, flooded the village. Joining them were our military policemen, engineers, and civil affairs soldiers. Together, the elements rounded up about sixty-five Bosnian Serb MUPs in two separate groups.

A crowd of Muslims then gathered and threatened to assault the MUPs. We held them back, and allowed the Serbs to withdraw. At one point, the MUPs opened fire, again endangering our cavalrymen. The Muslims responded by pelting them with rocks. Our AWTs hovered overhead and filmed all this action, including footage of a MUP firing several rounds past two of our Bradleys.

These vehicles were from Bravo Troop's 1st Platoon. Sergeant First Class John Iacono had positioned them as an obstacle to the advancing Muslim crowd. One angry Muslim climbed on top of SFC Iacono's track. He ignored SFC Iacono's screams to get down until a cocked pistol was shoved in the man's face. Another man tried to open the rear door and was dissuaded by similar means.[64]

Eventually, Quarterhorse was able to separate the two groups. Our quick response stopped the battle just one hour after it had begun.[65] We then brought in Bosnian Serb and Muslim authorities to take control of their respective sides. Quarterhorse officers and our attached civil affairs team negotiated for the withdrawal of the Muslims back to the IEBL.

At the first reports of violence, LTC Harriman raced to Mahala from Zvornik. His speeding, swerving Humvee clipped an unfortunate bicyclist — "a martyr for the process of democracy."[66] (The man was not seriously injured.)

But the day's excitement was far from over. With negotiations underway, another angry crowd was en route to Mahala. This was a group of Bosnian Serbs from Zvornik. Some of the MUPs had apparently returned to the town and agitated a large crowd of soccer spectators with livid tales of IFOR's assistance to the Muslims. They claimed that we had arrested the Serb MUPs, who were only exercising their legitimate authority. A mob formed to challenge this unfair and partial treatment.[67]

Many of the Serbs were drunk. Their first stop was just across the street at the local IPTF headquarters. Some of them overturned IPTF vehicles, while others effectively barricaded the unarmed policemen inside their building for several hours. The only thing the IPTF officers could do was to bar the doors. But no serious harm came to them, and the mob headed west towards Mahala.[68] Their approach threatened to disrupt ongoing negotiations between the RS Minister of the Interior, other factional leaders, and IFOR's LTG Walker.[69] BG Casey and COL Batiste were also on the scene by this point as well.

Our cavalrymen and attachments threw up several roadblocks, which the Serbs simply bypassed. Our hasty barricades slowed them down somewhat and progressively thinned their number.[70] At first, confusing orders prevented our cavalrymen from acting more forcefully. Were we to "delay" the marchers or actually "block" them? In military jargon, these terms meant two different things. We repositioned several times in order to stay in front of the mob.

Quarterhorse finally established a strong blocking position where a railroad overpass intersected the road. With high banks on both sides and Bradleys and up-armored Humvees in the road behind a human wall of cavalrymen and engineers, we halted the mob. Angry Serbs threw rocks, spat, and taunted our men. Some even attempted to grab our weapons. We countered their lunges and grabs with buttstrokes from our rifles. All weapons were locked and loaded and triggers were set to fire. Some cavalrymen aimed their weapons into the crowd, hoping to convince the Serbs to back off.

Our self-discipline prevailed. No shots were fired, although the temptation was great. Civil affairs teams rushed in with Bosnian Serb leaders to inform the mob of what had happened in the town. They told them about the ongoing negotiations. Eventually, the Serbs settled down and headed back to Zvornik.[71]

Interestingly, in this situation where fixed bayonets would have enabled our cavalrymen to better defend themselves without the threat of deadly force, none were fixed. Quarterhorse never gained an appreciation for the bayonet as a crowd control weapon. Consequently, our cavalrymen were untrained in its use. Bayonets were merely an adornment on our belts or just another pain in the ass to account for in our arms rooms.

Our blocking action gave LTG Walker uninterrupted time to compel the RS Minister of the Interior to turn over his MUPs' weapons. It also allowed him to secure the release of the IPTF in Zvornik. Throughout the daylong episode, Quarterhorse kept the senior IFOR leaders fully aware of what was going on around them. According to LTC Harriman, LTG Walker developed a sudden affection for the U.S. cavalry.[72]

In Mahala, our cavalrymen confiscated three AK-47 assault rifles and one tear gas grenade. They also gathered 240 expended 7.62mm rounds for use in documenting what had happened. We permitted the regular RS police-men to keep their sidearms, which they were authorized to carry. Both entities claimed that the confiscated automatic weapons belonged to the other side. Anything to cause more trouble.[73]

LTC Harriman instructed the Chief of Staff of the ABiH 28th Division to personally reclaim his soldiers and to get them back across the ZOS. Quar-terhorse had plenty of clear evidence of multiple Federation violations of the GFAP. Soon afterwards, LTG Walker presented Federation President Alia Itzetbegovic with five confiscated weapons and evidence of Muslim civilian attacks on RS police. Likewise, he also presented RS President Plavsic with twenty confiscated weapons and evidence of RS police misconduct in the ZOS.[74]

After the incident was quelled, Quarterhorse kept a platoon in Mahala overnight to maintain force presence. LTC Harriman appeared on the ABC evening news in a story about the incident, which he later dubbed the "Maha-laday Madness."[75]

The day afterward, Quarterhorse conducted an area reconnaissance around Mahala.[76] We sent tank platoons on patrol to increase force presence. We added more checkpoints and employed REMBASS motion detection equipment to better control access to the area. MAJ Tubbs explained to a *Stars and Stripes* reporter that our mission was to maintain the ZOS as a demil-itarized, weapons-free zone.

Two days after the incident, the Muslims seemed undeterred by the possibility of renewed RS police harassment. A group of about seventy-five

Muslims crossed the IEBL towards Mahala. Our cavalrymen at Checkpoint Charlie confiscated some axes and knives from them in accordance with GFAP provisions. We detained some of the men, including the commander of the ABiH 281st Brigade. No incidents occurred in the village that day.[77]

Quarterhorse chalked the incident up to experience. Very quickly after things settled down, our officers conducted an after-action review on our performance. LTC Harriman led the discussion, which included a look at video footage shot from our AWTs.

Our NCOs and junior enlisted cavalrymen also talked it over at length. Their consensus was that it had been a confusing day. Radios kept our scattered elements in contact with the Squadron TAC and each other, but cavalrymen at the lowest levels had a hard time understanding the many, revised instructions that came down. LTC Harriman had been very quiet on the squadron command net, while Majors Tubbs and Elias and our troop commanders had all been very vocal. Cavalrymen monitoring the radios in the Squadron and Troop TOCs had difficulty understanding the frantic spot reports coming in. Consequently, their overall picture of the action was confused.[78] Such is the state of command and control under combat conditions.

MAJ Dixon, the 2 BCT Operations Officer, later wrote of the incident:

> The Quarterhorse soldiers demonstrated a significant degree of restraint and control ultimately preventing a very explosive situation from becoming any more dangerous. What began as a movement of self-acclaimed former Muslim residents of Mahala, quickly transitioned into a physical confrontation between Serbs and Muslims. Only the cool-headed approach by the entire squadron, plus the unified actions on the part of 2 BCT units themselves, kept this situation from escalating or getting out of control.[79]

LTC Harriman added, "In other words, you stopped three riots directly, one indirectly, helped the COMARRC advance the peace, and generally impressed all observers.... You did better than either faction expected: very, very well indeed."[80]

Thus far in Operation Joint Endeavor, all IFOR soldiers had shown tremendous self-discipline under threatening situations. The fact that we had always kept our cool and had yet to resort to use of deadly force probably had a significant, deterring affect on the FWFs. The degree of self-restraint that we had exercised thus far was surprising, and yet it had been essential to the successful continuation of the Bosnian peace process.

In stability operations, the decisions of young officers and NCOs under pressure have the potential to shape the entire operation and even the destiny of the nation itself. An excellent illustration of this fact was given by radio news commentator Paul Harvey. He reported on a young British NCO manning a checkpoint in the center of a hostile city. This corporal and his eight men were confronted by an angry, stone-throwing mob. Unable to contact any reinforcements, the corporal panicked and ordered his men to open fire. Several civilians were killed and a great outrage poured forth from the population against the peacekeepers. "The rest of the story," as Mr. Harvey revealed, was that this incident had not recently occurred in Bosnia as listeners probably assumed, but that it had occurred in Boston, Massachusetts, in 1770. Famously known as the Boston Massacre, it was a key event leading to the American Revolution.[81]

LTC Harriman was hopeful that the Mahaladay Madness might have prompted local officials to ensure that the upcoming national elections would be successful. He also felt that the publicity around the incident might have backfired on a possible BiH plan meant to cause the cancellation of elections in our sector due to (provoked) Serb misbehavior.

The incident hastened United Nations High Commission on Refugees (UNHCR) efforts to establish a mechanism for the peaceful resettlement of Muslim refugees in RS territory.[82] The mechanism did not finally go into effect, however, until a month later when another potentially violent episode occurred in a different ZOS village.

By coincidence, the commander of the American task force slated to relieve Quarterhorse of its sector in the fall was present to observe the Mahaladay Madness. What a perfect introduction to the complexities of Bosnian stability operations!

It was also quite an introduction for the MPs who had been recently attached to Quarterhorse. As LTC Harriman later wrote, "When the bullets started to fly in Mahala, the 64th and 536th [MP Companies] decided Quarterhorse country was their kind of place and signed on. Personally, I like having the MPs around."[83]

# 11

## SHIFT FOCUS

### *The September Elections*

At the beginning of September, it seemed that someone had flipped a big switch. The oppressive Bosnian heat, humidity, and dust suddenly turned to incessant rain, fog, and mud. Sunny days became a rarity. When the sun did come out again for short bouts, it had a visibly uplifting effect on our spirits.

The wooden-floored tents that Quarterhorse occupied had been oppressively hot during the summer. The interiors were open bays that provided little privacy. Policy permitted us to use scrounged materials to make low walls to compartmentalize our tents into individual spaces. Plywood was like gold. Practically anything could be crafted from it — shelves, chairs, desks, and even a four-poster double bed for our command sergeant major. The U.S. Army would not spend money on such luxuries, so what we wanted we had to make ourselves.

HHT was fortunate to count Specialist Koen among its ranks. With extensive civilian carpentry skills, Specialist Koen did much to improve the quality of life for Workhorse Troop. After finishing more basic amenities, he constructed a railed deck off the back of the HHT Command Post. Captain Wawro, the HHT Commander, was delighted with it, although he was only able to enjoy it for about six weeks before the weather turned.[1]

Just as the weather signaled a change of seasons, so too did a major political event offer hope for a brighter future in Bosnia. On September 14, the Bosnian people voted in the first free and fair elections since the outbreak of civil war. Quarterhorse played a major role in making them a success.

The newly drafted Constitution of Bosnia-Herzegovina declared the nation as a democratic state operating under the rule of law with free and democratic elections. As agreed upon in the Dayton Accord, the country was composed of two entities — the Muslim-Croat Federation of BiH and the Bosnian Serb Republika Srpska. The Federation controlled 51 percent of the territory. The Serbs controlled the remainder.[2]

The accord also stipulated a national government with limited powers. Bosnia-Herzegovina would have a three-member presidency of one Croat, one Muslim, and one Serb. The chairman of this presidency would rotate among the factions.

There would also be a two-chamber legislature: an appointed fifteen-member Upper House divided equally among Muslims, Croats, and Serbs, and a Lower House with twenty-eight members from the Federation and fourteen from Republika Srpska.

Likewise, the entities would each have their own president and legislature subordinate to the national government.

In the September 14 elections, votes were cast in several races: for the national presidency and House of Representatives, for the Federation House of Representatives, and for the National Assembly and presidency of Republika Srpska. Ballots were also cast for various canton legislatures and municipal governing authorities.[3]

These elections almost never happened. In late August, some international organizations called for a postponement. They claimed that conditions for a free and fair election did not yet exist. Too many people were still refugees, freedom of movement across the IEBL was still not assured in some places, and the media were unable to report freely on the issues.

Further and more ominously, nationalists like senior Bosnian Serbs indicted for war crimes were still in political power. Some groups argued that premature elections would only validate the ethnic cleansing that had purged areas of certain ethnic residents. Even Senator Bob Dole, the Republican presidential nominee, called for the postponement of Bosnian elections for these same reasons.[4]

But Carl Bildt, the NATO High Representative for Bosnia, explained:

> Elections are not important only for their own sake. It is of course vital that people have the opportunity to choose their own representatives if we are to create a new legitimacy. But even more pressing is the task of creating the joint institutions which will be the only way of bringing the country together again after the years of war.[5]

Despite the international chorus that cited elections as the only hope for peace, it would take a long time to heal the pain and despair felt across Bosnia. Ethnic hatred still simmered. Many Bosnians were doubtful, divided in opinion, and pessimistic about the upcoming elections.[6]

One Muslim man grumbled, "The Croats are no better than the Serbs.

I won't vote." Another said, "These elections are not Bosnian, they are American." He thought the United States was only involved in Bosnia in order to erase its shame for having allowed the war to continue for so long.[7]

A Muslim refugee said, "It's too early [to have elections] because I am not in my home. If all of us are in our homes, it would be a good time for elections."[8] But another Muslim countered, "It's not too early. Everyone should vote."[9]

A Muslim businessman suggested that the election may be too soon, but that it would probably lead towards solving some of Bosnia's many problems.

A Croat man said:

> The elections are cementing ethnic cleansing. People who never lived in a town can vote in that town. That's not logical.... This voting is just a thing for the Americans. Clinton needs it for his own re-election. It's political, and after the elections, everything will be the same as before.... This Dayton Accord is no peace agreement. Why don't you leave us alone? You have power only because you have weapons. Leave us alone and let us butcher each other until the end.[10]

International commentators felt that elections would provide two important insights into the progress of Bosnian peace. The nation's 2.9 million voters would demonstrate their level of concern for the political status of their own ethnic groups, as well as the degree of popular support for a new national government.[11]

Regardless of local and international debate, Quarterhorse began our election preparations in July. We had our own selfish reasons for wanting them to succeed as scheduled. "If the elections go well, we get to leave," observed Captain Glen Graham, our squadron communications officer. "If the elections go smoothly, we can focus on redeployment."[12]

Quarterhorse and other IFOR units were not tasked to administer the September elections. Rather, our critical role would be to provide security for the OSCE, the agency that would actually run them.[13]

Having been renamed in 1990, the Organization for Security and Cooperation in Europe (OSCE) was composed of fifty-four member nations. The United States, Canada, and all the states of Europe and the former Soviet Union were members. The OSCE's charter was to "consolidate common values and build societies, prevent local conflicts, restore stability and bring peace to war-torn areas, and to overcome real and perceived security deficits and avoid creation of hostilities by promoting a cooperative system of security."[14]

After the entities agreed to the Dayton Accord, the OSCE formed a Bosnian mission on December 8, 1995. This mission was the largest OSCE undertaking to date. Forty-six percent of the annual OSCE budget for 1996 (almost $530 million) was earmarked for Bosnia.

The OSCE established the following tasks for itself in support of the September elections:

- Certify that conditions exist in BiH to permit free and fair elections. (This was done in June.)
- Provide assistance to entities in creating the conditions for free and fair elections.
- Adopt and implement an elections program.
- Supervise preparation and conduct of elections.
- Extend invitations to other international organizations to take part in supervising the preparation and conduct of elections.[15]

Assisting the OSCE were nearly 150 observers from another nongovernmental organization, the Commission of International Monitors (CIM). Observers were needed to prevent vote fraud and tampering. The OSCE invited many international dignitaries to come to Bosnia as independent judges on the success of the elections. Several U.S. congressmen participated. On Election Day, OSCE personnel were distinguished from the remainder of these officials by their OSCE T-shirts, hats, and vehicle identifiers. Since IFOR was responsible for their security, we had to be able to readily identify them in a crowd.[16]

The Bosnian elections were big news all around the world. Hordes of journalists descended on the region to observe and render their own judgments.

Local entity police forces were responsible for maintaining civil order, ensuring freedom of movement for voters and candidates, and for providing security at polling stations. In other words, they had to ensure an unhindered voting process. Soldiers from the entities' military forces were permitted to travel to vote as individuals, but not as units. We did not want them to interfere with the electoral process or freedom of movement.

NATO officials were concerned about the commitment of some local officials to the elections. NATO vowed not to let them plead ignorance as a means of circumventing election rules. The senior leader of each of the three ethnic groups was issued a copy of the regulations in late August. NATO held them personally accountable for disseminating the rules down to local levels.[17]

On August 9, LTC Harriman told our assembled troop commanders and the Quarterhorse staff that the elections would proceed. He suggested that the factions would probably try to use the elections for their own political gain or to inflame the freedom of movement issue. LTC Harriman said the Bosnian Serbs did not want Muslims to cross the IEBL to vote. They wanted them to vote by absentee ballot instead.[18]

LTC Harriman felt it likely that Quarterhorse would have to contend with large-scale armed confrontation along the IEBL at the crossing sites. (Correctly, he made this prediction twenty days before the Mahaladay Madness incident.) He also anticipated the potential for incidents involving the transportation of ballots, as well as during the announcement of winners and the seating of the new governments.

LTC Harriman instructed our civil affairs, counterintelligence, and psy-ops teams to figure out what would happen. We would allocate our assets accordingly. LTC Harriman said the key was to keep all parties (the OSCE, voters, police, etc.) situationally aware. "Tell them what's going to happen, and what is happening," he said. "We will provide the parties with information for them to make their own intelligent decisions. And then we'll document their actions since they'll have to live with their decisions."[19]

In the ten weeks prior to the September elections, our civil affairs and psyops guys spent a good portion of their time talking with the residents of Kalesija, Zvornik, and Dugi Dio to gauge trends and any shifts in public opinion. They also took time to explain how IFOR would assist the OSCE on Election Day. By September 14, our teams also helped to produce more than seventy-five radio spots and twelve television broadcasts covering election issues. IFOR's *The Herald of Peace* newspaper published sixty articles about the upcoming elections.[20]

In mid–August, Quarterhorse focused a small group of staff officers on planning our redeployment while the rest of us geared up for the elections. MAJ Tubbs headed the redeployment cell, although we still did not know when we would depart.

The bulk of Quarterhorse intensified preparations to predict and counter potential election-related violence that might erupt. The Quarterhorse staff issued an operations order covering our critical reconnaissance and security missions. Later, we conducted numerous rehearsals and intelligence-gathering patrols.

Our cavalrymen and attachments were excited about the September elections. We knew that something big was in the works, something of historical proportions for the people of Bosnia. We would be right in the middle of it. Election support would be our capstone mission, the fruit of nine long months of forging the peace. A reporter asked Sergeant Barber, a scout from Bravo Troop, if he was ready to go home yet. SGT Barber spoke for many of us when he replied, "I want to stay for the elections."[21]

As Election Day loomed nearer, Quarterhorse continuously refined our intelligence estimate and revised our plans. LTC Harriman had already cautioned us to anticipate violence once Muslims began to cross the IEBL to vote in their former towns in RS territory. We also predicted that Bosnian Serbs in Zvornik would drive up the number of Serb votes cast by bringing in up to 6,000 fellow Serbs from Sarajevo. Before the civil war, Zvornik had a large Muslim population that eventually displaced towards Tuzla. If these Muslims cast ballots in Zvornik en masse, a Muslim-led local government could be elected.[22]

The OSCE and IFOR identified eleven other areas where tensions were likely to lead to violence. Among the list were Brcko, Doboj, and Srebrenica in the American sector. LTG Walker told the media that all 52,000 IFOR soldiers would be involved in supporting the elections.[23]

Late in August, COL Batiste clarified 2 BCT's role in the elections. He said that IFOR would support the agencies responsible for overseeing the elections, but would not encroach on local police authority. IFOR soldiers would not be responsible for the security of civilians — only for those agencies running the election. We would deliver and pick up voting materials to and from the polling stations. We would also provide logistical support to the nongovernmental organizations involved.[24]

With input from IFOR commanders like LTC Harriman, the OSCE designated specific routes for voters to cross the IEBL in order to vote in their former hometowns. IFOR soldiers would search vehicles and confiscate any weapons or political posters that might incite violence.

COL Batiste insisted, "I don't guard polling sites. That is the responsibility of the local police, the Ministry of Interior's police, and the International Police Task Force.... I will not put my Soldiers between factions in a fight."[25] Local police were responsible for controlling civil disturbances, but IFOR was prepared to assist as Quarterhorse had done during the recent Mahaladay Madness.

LTC Harriman specified some additional tasks as part of the Quarterhorse mission. We would make recommendations to the OSCE to adjust the Election Day plan in order to reduce the threat of incidents. We would also provide all organizations and the factions with information to allow them to make their own rational, informed decisions. Quarterhorse would then observe and document the results lest any post-incident accusations arise.[26]

As if we did not already have enough to contend with, on the night of August 9, Quarterhorse received a classified message with firm information that a terrorist attack against IFOR was imminent. This message prompted us to put all of our lodgment areas on heightened alert for nearly a month. What really concerned us were specific references in the message that seemed to match certain terrain features around the Dawg Pound.[27] A truck bomb (later to become known in GWOT parlance as a vehicle-borne improvised explosive device) seemed a very real possibility. Our cavalrymen maintained their vigilance. Fortunately, an attack never materialized.

By August 24, Quarterhorse had finished helping 2 BCT inspect all 291 polling stations scattered all over the 4,300-square-kilometer brigade sector.[28] One hundred and eight of them were within the Quarterhorse sector alone.[29] We also helped to coordinate election officials' activities and procedures. Squadron leaders coordinated for the security, delivery, and pickup of balloting materials.[30]

On September 13, the entities' special police and military personnel voted without incident. This was encouraging. But several international organizations and American presidential candidate Senator Bob Dole still called for a postponement. The White House issued a statement that conceded, "Conditions for free and fair elections — including freedom of movement and access to media — are far from perfect.... The elections are likely to be uneven; there may be some incidents."[31]

The Dayton Accord specified national and municipal elections be held once certain conditions were met. By anyone's measure, the conditions had not been met. Why proceed with the elections, then? "What's going on is an effort to complete the deal that the Clinton administration and NATO allies set up with the Dayton agreement so we can get the hell out," said Dan Gray, Deputy Director for Political-Military Studies at the Center for International and Strategic Studies, a Washington-based think tank.[32]

According to Mr. Gray, elections allowed the West to check the box. He said the elections and IFOR's deployment were two parts of a short-term fix to a long-term problem. One of the things that drove the national election timetable was the American presidential election in November. For political purposes, the troops had to be started home. Dayton had to be seen as a success.[33]

Task Force Eagle published the following guidelines for the success of Operation Mercury, as the election support mission was called[34]:

*Focus* — *Remove physical obstacles (to include human) that prevent freedom of movement to vote, and protect IFOR, OSCE, IPTF and other special status personnel.*

1. Press civil and police authorities to contain violence and support FOM (freedom of movement). IFOR involved as last resort.

2. Deny movement to groups intending to impede FOM or committing violence. No demonstrating or gathering is permitted on voter routes.

3. Take appropriate action to divert voters likely to become victims of violence.

4. Don't interpose troops between two hostile crowds.

5. Only visit Polling Stations in the course of official duties.

6. Right to search vehicles in the zone of separation still exists; outside the ZOS, search if reasonable cause exists.

7. No political paraphernalia or weapons of any type authorized on vehicles crossing the ZOS.

8. Right to regulate traffic flow still applies. Eight-passenger and above vehicles will have priority on voter routes.

9. Appropriate force authorized to protect IFOR, IPTF, OSCE & special status personnel to prevent serious crimes. Principles of self defense and minimum force always apply.

10. Timely, accurate, complete reporting and cross-talk at all levels is essential to successful conflict resolution.

11. Remember: isolate, dominate, situational awareness, multi-echelon/multidimensional response.

12. The Soldiers and units of Task Force Eagle will display at all times the characteristics of a tough, disciplined, competent and professional military force.[35]

The 2 BCT OPORD for Operation Mercury designated Quarterhorse as the brigade's main effort. We would concentrate our reconnaissance and security efforts on the four *opstinas,* or counties, of Osmaci, Banovici, Kalesija, and Zvornik. The other two task forces in 2 BCT were responsible for two just *opstinas* each.[36]

Under the Dayton Accord, a person's polling station depended on where he lived in 1991, the year of the last Bosnian census. However, all eligible voters — residents and refugees alike — had the option of voting in either their present location or in their prewar homes. Votes could be cast by absentee ballot or in person. Those voting in person could vote in any city simply by declaring it as their current or future home. Before the election, many Muslim and Croatian refugees were concerned about what LTC Harriman later described as a Serb "tactical voting" plan.[37] Their fear was the Serbs had organized voters to use the "future home" clause to obtain Serb majorities in former Muslim and Croat areas within Republika Srpska. This would effectively cement Serb control.

Part of the Election Day plan included the busing of refugees to polling stations in their former towns. Estimates were that between 30,000 to 150,000 refugees would cross the IEBL to exercise this option. In order to support this mass movement, Quarterhorse established a bus transload point at a vacant fuel compound about 500 meters west of the Dawg Pound. Captain Conor Cusick, our squadron supply officer, led the detachment that set up and ran this site. An engineer platoon from "Alpha Fortieth" erected concertina wire and tents and provided an onsite security force. A military police canine unit provided two dogs, which were used to inspect all buses for any explosives onboard.[38]

Over the course of the day, local Muslim police shepherded twenty-eight busloads of voters through the site. Several members of the IPTF observed their actions. After unloading the buses, the Muslims were ushered into tents

Quarterhorse cavalrymen and IPTF officers observe Muslim police searching voters at bus transload point, Election Day, September 14, 1996 (photograph: Mark Viney).

where Quarterhorse provided them with refreshments while they waited to be searched for weapons or other contraband. The Muslim police used pat-downs and metal detectors to search everyone before allowing them to reload the buses. No firearms or explosives were found on any of the nearly 1,450 people who passed through our site. Significantly, only a handful of pocketknives were discovered.[39] This suggested that Quarterhorse efforts to build local trust and confidence in IFOR had been successful.

Several American and European journalists visited our bus transload site early in the morning. They may have been disappointed to find no juicy story to report on. Everything ran smoothly with good cooperation from the Muslim police and the voters. Without delay, the reporters all scurried off in search of a better story.

Prior to the elections, both entities had agreed upon nineteen designated routes that cross–IEBL voters would take. Chartered buses were mandatory for extra security and control.[40] Quarterhorse elements patrolled all designated voter routes in order to stem any disturbances. We also established temporary checkpoints on other routes voters might have tried to use.[41] Bravo Troop reported a group of Muslims intent on disrupting the election process by refusing to go to their designated polling station. LTC Harriman informed them that they had two choices. They could either march and not vote, or they could vote and not march. They had to decide which was more important to them. They opted to vote.[42]

In the air and on the ground, our cavalry troops patrolled and maintained an imposing force presence. We kept a sharp lookout for unauthorized weapons and election propaganda materials, effectively creating a secure environment for the local populace and all international participants to do their thing unhindered. Every member of Quarterhorse supported the elections in some manner or other. Regular activities stopped. Everyone went to a checkpoint, polling station, or bus stop, or just stood by on call. It was a total team effort. Mechanics provided Quick Reaction Forces, while support platoon cavalrymen, cooks, and attached engineers manned the bus transload point and checkpoints.

Below Kula hill along the Spreca River, an elderly Muslim woman was overheard to say, "If only we could have voted at the top of the hill. I could have seen my house from the top of the hill."[43]

At about 10:00 A.M., we received an initial report from the Russian sector about a disturbance outside a polling station. There were several casualties. Several Quarterhorse officers assumed that it marked the beginning of a dangerous and exciting day. We sent an AWT up to the scene to check out the situation. There were no signs of pandemonium to be found. Apparently, the original message had been distorted in its translation from Russian to English.

Quarterhorse anticipated that the Bosnian Serbs would "play it cool" on Election Day. We did not think that they would harass the Muslims or cause any sort of trouble. By the Serbs' reasoning, clean elections would benefit their position of self-stated legitimacy. Besides, they thought, the Muslims could never move enough people across the IEBL to seriously affect voting in the Serbs' own territory.[44] Our prediction was validated over the course of the day. Dzevad Tosunbegovic, the Muslim mayor of Kalesija, reported to us, "The people [returning from voting in RS] said that the Serb police treated them well."[45]

At around 1:00 P.M., Quarterhorse reacted to a sniper scare near a Kalesija polling station. A sharp crack caused cavalrymen from Charlie Troop to duck behind their vehicles and ready their weapons. A Bradley was brought in and an AWT flew over. Our cavalrymen assumed that the noise had come from a gun. They dispatched a patrol to look for evidence of a sniper. Nothing was found. A NATO spokesman confirmed later that the noise was from an overheated water container that burst.[46] By the end of the day, this incident proved the closest thing to violence within the whole American sector.

Later in the afternoon, an AWT from Delta Troop reported observing "thirty civilians at Carparde, waving a Serbian flag."[47] Such displays of political propaganda, whether meant to intimidate voters from the other entity or just a promotional gimmick for a particular party, were strictly forbidden by the election rules. Quarterhorse ground elements dispersed the group peaceably.

The biggest problems encountered were mostly related to slow voting procedures at the polls. Voting hours were extended to allow all voters to cast their ballots and to make up for confusion earlier in the day with voter registration lists.[48]

At a refugee polling site named Zvornik 53, Quarterhorse provided cookies and coffee to Muslim voters while they waited in line to vote. The hungry Muslims did not refuse the free food. One cavalryman exclaimed, "These people can eat some damn cookies!"[49] Cavalry cooks at our bus transload point had similar difficulty keeping the refreshment tent stocked. Each busload passing through cleaned it out. Our interpreters encouraged Muslims carting off armfuls of cookies to consider the other voters who would follow after them.

Down in Alpha Troop's sector, Election Day was notably quiet. Securing an area that was a Serb stronghold, Alpha reported that only one man crossed the IEBL to vote. He was a Serb.

Our attached psyops teams positioned themselves near selected polling sites to help defuse any potential problems. Their presence gave voters an extra sense of security.

It started to rain around 5:30 P.M. at the bus transload point. By the time the message went out thirty minutes later to shut the point down, the rain had stopped. A beautiful double rainbow appeared in the eastern sky above Mahala, Carparde, and the other contentious ZOS villages. Its brilliant hues were superimposed on a backdrop of black clouds.

The symbolism of the rainbow was not lost on CPT Viney, who voiced that it was a message from God about the future of Bosnia. Captain Downey scoffed. Ever the pessimist, he suggested that the Muslims would interpret it to mean that the land to the Drina River was rightfully theirs and would be again someday. They should forget about the elections and go reclaim their "pot of gold" at the end of the rainbow![50]

Carol Schlitt, a human rights observer with the OSCE, said later that despite the decent weather, voter participation was less than expected.[51] The nearly 1,450 voters who passed through the Quarterhorse sector were among a total of only 13,500 throughout Bosnia who made the journey. Only 1,200 Serbs crossed over into BiH territory. These numbers were considerably less than expected.[52] Some people were fearful to return. Others stayed put because of inadequate transportation, although this was not the case in Kalesija. "Our" city kept nearly twenty empty buses on standby. Nevertheless, Muslim voters cast the most votes to give their leader, Alia Izetbegovic, the chairmanship of the three-seat national presidency.

In a final act of the historic, yet uneventful and somehow anticlimactic day, MAJ Roberts told a group of forty Muslim police in Kalesija, "Take the rest of the day off."[53] By 7:30 P.M., the much-anticipated, widely-hyped Election Day was over.

The smooth execution of Election Day amazed many military and political leaders. Quarterhorse received several messages of congratulations and thanks. One OSCE official said, "This would not have been possible without the organization and communications infrastructure of IFOR."[54]

"*Hvala* [Thank you]"—Dzevad Tosunbegovic, mayor of Kalesija, BiH.[55]

"*Hvala*"—Dragomir Vasic, police chief of Zvornik, RS.[56]

LTG Walker sent a message to all IFOR units on the evening of September 14. The following morning, LTC Harriman had gotten word of it and told the Quarterhorse staff, "The COMARRC has written some kind of letter. Haven't seen it yet. But it's British for 'You done good.'"[57]

COMARRC'S MESSAGE TO COMMANDERS AND TROOPS:

At the end of what has been a remarkable day in the history of Bosnia and Herzegovina, in which you have helped the people of this country exercise their democratic rights, I would like to send my personal thanks to all Commanders and Soldiers in the corps for all that you have done to make this day a success.

The eyes of the world have been focused on the corps operation and you have not been found wanting. Today, we have seen the birth of democracy in this country. Today, people went to vote: many to cast a secret ballot for the first time in their lives. Today, the vast majority of those who chose to vote were able to do so. None of that could have happened without the planning, preparation, and operations conducted by your Commanders and troops in whichever part of the country or the corps that you are. There has been no doctrine for what you have achieved today, but it has, nonetheless, been just as much a feat of arms.

All of the troops from the thirty-five contributing nations can be justifiably proud of the part that they have played in helping the people of Bosnia and Herzegovina take a step closer to a lasting peace. There is still much to be done and we must stay focused, but that should not prevent you from taking satisfaction in a job brilliantly done, and one in which you and your Soldiers can take great pride.[58]

Major General Nash published his own message a week after the elections:

To the Soldiers, Sailors, Airmen, Marines and Civilians of Task Force Eagle—

Congratulations on your magnificent performance in supporting the general elections of Bosnia-Herzegovina. You have shown the world that there is no mission too great, no challenge too tough for you to overcome. Saturday's achievement — of which you can be justifiably proud — is historic in scope and provides hope for the people of this troubled region.

Over the last several months, you have endured hardship and sacrificed much to do what many thought impossible — you have stopped the killing and given the Bosnian people a chance for peace. Today, the leaders of the world stand in awe of what you have accomplished.

Your nations are extremely proud of you and so am I. Working together, you have earned the respect of those you came to help. I am truly honored to serve with you. You are a great credit to the profession of arms.

Well done — and thank you.[59]

LTC Harriman sent his own message of thanks in his unmistakable prose:

On Election Day I listened and heard echoes of the complex political issues here, of pain, joy, humor, and continued tension. But I heard most the deep, bass Quarterhorse hoof beat, echoes of the unmatched quality of its NCO Corps, of our desire for home, of concern from family members, of the absolute excellence of the Task Force Quarterhorse Soldier. You did yesterday what nobody thought possible. You changed political reality here. Listen with me. You'll hear your hoof beat. You'll hear you done good.[60]

Amid all this backslapping, Captain Brown, our squadron chaplain, reminded us, "We should thank our heroes at home. [Our families] are the real heroes.[61]

IFOR anticipated possible violence once the OSCE announced the results of the election at the end of September, so Quarterhorse maintained its stepped-up patrols. Our psyops team conducted a post-election assessment to determine how the people felt the election went and how they perceived the process. They also continued to spread our message of hope, goodwill, and peace.

## The Municipal Elections

What did the September elections mean for Bosnia's future? Their historical impact could not be assessed immediately. At the time, no one could say for sure whether they had been a meaningful step towards inter-ethnic peace or, as most observers feared, towards a formalization of divisions between ethnic groups. Critics grumbled that the Bosnian people voted for ethnic nationalistic parties. They interpreted the low cross–IEBL traffic as evidence that the Bosnians had resigned themselves to the reality of a country permanently split into separate ethnic sub-states.[62]

Ambassador Richard Holbrooke, the architect of the Dayton Peace Accord, was in Bosnia to observe Election Day. Accompanying him was a delegation of U.S. State Department officials and legislators. Ambassador Holbrooke's delegation visited nearly eighty of the 4,600 polling stations across the country. That night, Ambassador Holbrooke told a press conference, "We all know this is a day historians will write about in the future. But whether they will write that it led to peace or was simply an interlude in the war is too soon to say."[63]

He noted that just one year earlier, the United States had been firing cruise missiles and dropping bombs on Bosnia. Sarajevo was then under siege, and fighting raged in several areas of the country. "We've come a long way," he said. "Every person we saw today in the field — Muslim, Serb, Croat — said they thought this was a historic day and that it would lead to peace."[64]

He added, "What we saw was, by and large, an election in which we did not see things that would disqualify [it, rendering it illegitimate]."[65] Several U.S. Congressmen compared the election favorably to ones they had seen elsewhere.[66]

But the OSCE soon uncovered much voting fraud, especially on the part of Bosnian Serbs. One week after the national election, discrepancies in the vote count were so troubling that the OSCE admitted that none of the election results were certain. The OSCE took remedial measures to guarantee an accurate count.[67] Regardless of these difficulties, the OSCE announced that municipal elections would proceed as scheduled on November 22.[68]

In mid–October, Ambassador Robert H. Frowick, the head the OSCE mission in Bosnia, made a public statement defending his decision against a barrage of criticism:

> The Provisional Election Commission met recently to review and make a final decision of the feasibility of adhering to the previously announced November timeframe for holding municipal elections.
>
> After a lengthy discussion centering on major administrative as well as substantive challenges that must be met, I made a Chairman's decision to proceed with these elections.
>
> This decision, ultimately supported by each of the three members representing the Parties but opposed by one of the three international members, was taken in full knowledge that we will be engaged in a high-risk operation.... My principal reason for staying on track with municipal elections before the end of the year is to take full advantage of the strength of the international community's presence, in both its civil and military dimensions, before that international presence is significantly diminished in 1997.
>
> It is essential to continue to overcome pernicious effects of the centrifugal political forces across the country through the electoral process while the international community retains the strength to do so.[69]

Throughout September, Quarterhorse continued to support 2 BCT missions, which COL Batiste described as setting "the preconditions for success" for the upcoming municipal elections in November. This meant our usual compliance missions like weapons storage site inspections, mounted and aerial reconnaissance, observation post duty, ZOS checkpoint operations, and lodgment area security.

On September 23, LTC Harriman gave a current events update to our troop commanders and the Quarterhorse staff. He said IFOR was entering a period of change with municipal election support and the change of control from the 1st Armored Division to the 1st Infantry Division. Overall command and control for the elections was still up in the air. Quarterhorse knew some of the dates for upcoming events, but nothing was certain. Our sector would see an influx of new units. We would eventually depart the Dawg Pound and take up temporary residence at LA Steel Castle prior to redeploying. LTC Harriman was worried about problems in maintaining our squadron's uniquely high standards once we came into close contact with other units there. He predicted more problems in Mahala. LTC Harriman mentioned the importance of the many personal relationships we had developed with the locals. He praised everyone for a job well done thus far. LTC Harriman concluded his comments with a reminder of the need for quality recovery following our eventual redeployment.[70]

On September 30, the Fifth Corps Aviation Standardization Detachment (CASD) arrived at LA Molly to conduct an in-depth inspection of our air cavalry troops. This was a big event for our aviators and crews. The CASD team applauded us for having applied the standards to which we had trained in Germany to the conditions in Bosnia rather than just throwing them out. Our air cavalrymen believed in doing things right. Inspectors noticed this in our aircraft engine compartments, in our night vision goggles (NVGs), and in our armament. Records-keeping and flight operations showed consistent high quality as well.

LTC Harriman praised our air cavalry troops for their outstanding overall performance: "Come to think of it, you didn't do anything different than what I saw you do [during aerial gunnery training] at Glamoc: conduct smooth, efficient, safe, to-standard operations. My hat's off to you."[71]

On the same day as the CASD inspection, elements from Bravo and Charlie Troops defused a minor incident near Mahala. Muslims were attempting to move truckloads of lumber and plywood to Mahala via different routes. Four times, our cavalrymen turned them around since refugee resettlement procedures were still under discussion between faction leaders and international mediators. We identified one of the Muslim truck drivers as a soldier in the ABiH 245th Brigade.[72] A Bosnian Serb punched him to the ground right in front of us. We detained the Serb. Captain Jeff Erron, the Charlie

Troop commander, gave him a stern dressing-down for his inappropriate behavior. This must have been memorable for the Serb, since CPT Erron was an imposing ex–football player. MAJ Roberts was also on hand and turned the Serb man over to RS police for them to deal with. CPT Ivy's Bravo Troop beefed up its checkpoints with MPs and Bradleys just in case there were any repercussions between the factions. None resulted.[73]

In early October, a Rumanian engineer unit learned from local Muslims that a Mujahadeen terrorist group planned to attack an American IFOR unit on October 5. Once again, we braced ourselves, and once again nothing happened.[74]

Local events conspired to prevent the municipal elections from happening in November. On October 22, Quarterhorse received word that the elections had been postponed. Diplomats needed more time to build a consensus that was seen as vital for Bosnia's long-term prospects for peace. Ambassador Frowick was forced to make another statement conceding that the Provisional Election Commission "decided today to postpone the exceptionally complex election because of continuing political problems in municipalities across Bosnia."[75] The OSCE had ongoing disputes with all parties, particularly the Serbs, over how local polling would take place.

The OSCE hoped to conduct the elections sometime between April and June 1997.[76] They were later postponed yet again. Bosnian municipal elections were not actually held until September 1997, much to the great relief of Quarterhorse. By early spring 1997, we were put on standby to return to Bosnia for the tentative summer election period. However, our packed training schedule that fall effectively kept us off the Election Force (EFOR) slate.

## Force Reshaping

Immediately after the national elections, senior NATO leaders announced that IFOR would not significantly draw down its forces in Bosnia until after the municipal elections, which were originally projected for November. Their postponement allowed IFOR to adjust the redeployment timetable.[77]

The good news for Quarterhorse was that our redeployment no longer depended on the elections. We would leave in time to allow President Clinton to keep his disingenuous promise of having American peacekeepers out of Bosnia within a year. Under the revised timeline, IFOR units would continue trickling out as the lead elements of a covering force entered the country.

The headquarters of the Allied Land Forces Central Europe (LAND-CENT) was ordered to deploy to the region in early November to replace the

Allied Rapid Reaction Corps (ARRC). NATO Secretary General Javier Solana said this change in headquarters opened the final phase of the Dayton Accord — "the redeployment of IFOR forces following completion of their mission." It was too soon to predict whether LANDCENT's covering force would eventually become a follow-on force after IFOR's one-year mandate expired on December 20.[78]

The covering force was the 2nd Brigade Combat Team of the famed 1st Infantry Division (Mechanized). This BCT was Quarterhorse's old neighbor back on Conn Barracks in Schweinfurt. Its soldiers had helped us to deploy almost a year earlier. Now it was their turn to experience the joys of Bosnian stability operations.

The covering force would enter Bosnia less heavily armed than the original IFOR. Although incidents continued to arise, conditions were stable enough to allow the operation to continue with forces using up-armored Humvees, which did far less damage to roads than did our tracked vehicles. They also required fewer support personnel to maintain them.[79]

The 1st Infantry Division planned on deploying 5,000 soldiers to replace the 1st Armored Division. By late October, 1,300 had arrived in Bosnia. Another 1,800 were en route. The remaining 1,900 had not yet begun to deploy.

At the same time, the bulk of 1st Armored Division units (12,600 soldiers) were still in Bosnia. Nearly 1,000 had already returned to Germany and 1,000 more were en route.[80]

Within Quarterhorse's parent brigade, TF 2-68 AR had already begun redeploying in mid–August. This task force had been the last combat element of 2 BCT to enter Bosnia, and now it was the first to leave.

Throughout the month of October, the covering force arrived in the Quarterhorse sector and began a transition period with us. Some officers of Task Force 1-26 Infantry gave us the impression that they were not much interested in learning all we had to teach them. We had a lot of valuable information from our ten months in sector that we wanted to share. We thought these new guys seemed overly self-assured. This concerned us because we knew firsthand that considerable finesse rather than brute force was the key to successful stability operations. (A few years later, CPT Viney learned from an officer of this task force that they soon regretted not having heeded more closely our advice. Once Quarterhorse departed, their learning curve was a steep and uncomfortable one.)

With municipal elections tentatively postponed until the spring of 1997, a NATO spokesman announced that IFOR's focus in Bosnia "now shifts from election support" to four main tasks:

- Maintain a stable security environment.
- Assist in the stabilization in the zone of separation for returning refugees.
- Take determined action to prevent further destruction of unoccupied homes or homes under repair in the areas where refugees may wish to return.
- Complete a full round of weapons inspections by early November.[81]

In the month after the September elections, tensions flared between the factions. In one twelve-day period in mid–October, at least seventy vacant houses were blown up. Most were in areas where Muslims intended to or had begun to move back.[82] Quarterhorse and other IFOR units maintained an increased presence in these areas throughout the fall. Our attached civil affairs team provided continuing assistance to the UNHCR and OHR on refugee resettlement issues.

## Letters to the Editor

American IFOR soldiers had few amenities to make life more bearable. One perk we enjoyed was free daily copies of the *Stars and Stripes* newspaper. This paper was a vital part of our life. It kept us in touch with the rest of the world, and it allowed us to read about the events and issues that we were directly involved in.

The opinion page of the *Stars and Stripes* became an unofficial bulletin board for deployed American soldiers to air their gripes and complaints. Some soldiers even wrote letters complaining about all the complaints that were printed. Several Quarterhorse cavalrymen wrote letters to the editor. Their messages were for the most part upbeat and proud. They provide insight into our collective mindset. While indicative of our frustrations, they also reflect the esprit de corps that sustained Quarterhorse throughout our year in Bosnia.

One such letter, from Echo Troop's Private First Class Christina D. Hampsten, was printed on October 6. PFC Hampsten was one of our few female cavalrymen. (While our ground cavalry troops were strictly all-male units, our air cavalry troops did include some female ground crewmen among their ranks.) She wrote:

> I am a Soldier with the air troops of 1/4 Cavalry that was deployed to Bosnia in late December.... This is not to complain or find humor but to praise the Soldiers of the mighty 1/4 Cavalry Squadron. The six months that I was deployed and the four months I have been on rear detachment I was very impressed with the professionalism that these Soldiers displayed. No one said it was a joy, but the mission was there and had to be carried out.
>
> The feelings of loneliness, home sickness, confusion and discouragement that everyone else felt existed. But with teamwork and support from families and

friends back home, it was much more bearable. Not once was there a complaint of living conditions or praise that was not deserved. Some people say it's because we have low standards, that we don't mind not having showers or undesirable food. But the fact is that we just know what it is to be a Soldier and to do it right, no matter what the conditions.[83]

In the fall of 1996, it bothered us in Quarterhorse that the *Star and Stripes* lavished so much attention on the deployment of the 1st Infantry Division to Bosnia. Sergeant Michael Long wrote to the editor:

> I beg to differ with the article "Big Red One Ready to Cover." The writer reports that the Big Red One officially became part of Operation Joint Endeavor on Oct. 13. Unfortunately, he was only about 10 months off the mark.
> The 1st Squadron, 4th Cavalry of the 1st Infantry Division has been deployed with the 1st Armored Division in Bosnia since December 1995. For our efforts, being allowed to remain in Bosnia to work with our parent unit while the 1st Armored Division redeploys rewarded us. Not exactly first in, first out. But I, for one, wouldn't have it any other way.[84]

The matter of end-of-tour awards was one of great contention within Quarterhorse. Everyone worked hard and wanted to be recognized in some fitting and equitable way. A big part of the problem was that neither LTC Harriman nor our squadron command sergeant major had disseminated much guidance to clarify the criteria for achievement awards. Widespread misunderstanding resulted. Many thought a cavalryman's rank automatically determined what award he would get. Understandably, many of our junior cavalrymen were incensed.

Corporal David Hjelm wrote to the *Stars and Stripes* to complain about the de facto awards policy within Quarterhorse:

> An issue has arisen that has many a Soldier thinking twice about the job that they have done here in Bosnia. That issue is the fact that almost all the enlisted members of 1st Squadron, 4th Cavalry Regiment are getting nothing but Army Achievement Medals (AAMs) for their drawn-out and tedious deployment here.... In addition to the enlisted are the E-5s and E-6s who have done their jobs exceptionally and are not receiving their due recognition. Very few of the Soldiers are not complaining about this issue. When you hear of some of the few people who are receiving ARCOMs for only being out here for a total of four to six months, it brings down the morale of Soldiers — especially if these people did nothing other than what they were trained for and the tasks given them for their level of work.[85]
> This may sound like a gripe, and we hope it does, because that is exactly what it is supposed to be. All that we are asking for is the correct recognition for the job that we did here. Many of the Soldiers who have gone on leave to the states from here have come back to tell of the many people back there who do not remember or know that we have Soldiers in Bosnia. Some of the Soldiers think

the higher chain of command may be in the same state of mind. It is as if we were not putting our lives on the line during this deployment.

From day one, we were patrolling areas that were known to be heavily mined and confronting many of the military factions from both sides. We are proud that we could accomplish something for the country of Bosnia — something that our country asked us to do. However, it seems that we are being rewarded as though we accomplished nothing.[86]

CPL Hjelm was one of many Quarterhorse cavalrymen who felt that they deserved higher recognition because they had performed their jobs under the difficult and dangerous Bosnian conditions. But the Army had already recognized these conditions. Prior to our redeployment, every American IFOR Soldier who had served more than thirty days in-country was presented the newly-instituted Armed Forces Service Medal. NATO awarded us its NATO Service Medal with Former Yugoslavia campaign bar. All units serving in the original Task Force Eagle, including Quarterhorse, received additional recognition through the award of the Army Superior Unit Award.

Many of our cavalrymen did not understand what all of these awards recognized. They wanted to get their share of the inflated achievement awards

As Captain Joe Wawro looks on, Lieutenant Colonel Anthony Harriman presents the NATO Medal to cavalrymen from Headquarters Troop in the Thunderdome, November 1996 (photograph: Mark Viney).

that they perceived being presented to others. Not satisfied with Army Achievement Medals, many appealed for the more coveted Army Commendation Medal. One troop commander boasted about the incredibly high number of ARCOMs that he managed to win for his cavalrymen by way of effusive recommendations. Other troop commanders were less successful because their award recommendations simply did not demonstrate exceptional performance beyond normal expectations.

It was unfortunate that Quarterhorse received such negative publicity over awards. Only after the issue blew up in our faces were awards criteria clearly enunciated.

As our squadron commander, LTC Harriman usually did not provide detailed guidance to his subordinates. He granted us tremendous latitude in the performance of our duties. That was a good thing, since cavalry leaders must be conditioned to act with great initiative and independence. In a practical sense, however, some troop commanders and staff officers occasionally found LTC Harriman's lack of clear guidance disconcerting.

After Quarterhorse redeployed to Germany, we learned that Congress had recently authorized the award of the Armed Forces Expeditionary Medal (AFEM) to the original units of IFOR. This presented a quandary for the Army since the Armed Forces Service Medal had already been distributed. Were we to receive two service medals for the same operation? Some commentators believed that the gesture was to placate lobbyists from the Veterans of Foreign Wars (VFW). Combat service was a criterion for VFW membership. If Congress awarded the AFEM to IFOR, it would make several thousand more service members eligible for membership.[87] A final decision over service medals was not announced until the spring of 1999. The Army decided that members of the original IFOR units could keep and wear both the AFEM and the AFSM. Members of subsequent rotations to Bosnia could choose to wear either the AFEM or the AFSM, but not both.

# 12

# FINAL OPERATIONS

## *The Jusici Impasse*

In early October, Quarterhorse refocused on the issue of the resettlement of refugees into their prewar homes. We applied lessons learned from previous incidents to contend with situations that developed in Mahala and in the Russian-sector villages of Dugi Dio and Jusici. Our human intelligence network had improved considerably since August's Mahaladay Madness. We knew that each of these ZOS villages was a stepping stone in the Muslim SDA Party's strategy for the resettlement of refugees in RS territory. Both the SDA and the ABiH 281st Brigade intended to repopulate these towns before ultimately reoccupying Kozluk on the Drina River. This would effectively cut Republika Srpska in half.[1] The Bosnian Serbs correctly interpreted these initial Muslim resettlement efforts as military incursions into their territory, although the Dayton Accord did stipulate freedom for the resettlement of prewar homes.[2]

Besides the need to uphold provisions of the Dayton Accord, the international community had another reason for their pressing desire for resettlement to succeed. During the Bosnian Civil War, thousands of refugees fled other to European nations, including Germany. Now, the cost of supporting their prolonged stay was straining national budgets.

Task Force Eagle had been working to bring all parties involved — the Federation and RS governments, the United Nations High Commission for Refugees (UNHCR), and the United Nations Office of the High Representative for Bosnia (OHR) — together to create a practical solution. Thus far, unconstructive posturing by the entities had been the norm.[3]

The UNHCR developed a procedure for certifying refugee claims of property ownership. Federation and RS leaders had agreed upon the plan, but late on the night before it went into effect, the Muslims acted in contravention.

On September 20, a group of 117 armed Muslim families unexpectedly returned to Jusici to reclaim their bombed-out homes. Most in the group were elderly men and women. Accompanying them was an officer and several soldiers of the ABiH 28th Division. They were armed with AK-47s, a pistol, and several grenades.[4]

The Muslims had not cleared their move with international refugee agencies. They had not given advance notice of their intended move to IFOR. And they had not submitted any paperwork proving ownership of the homes. The UNHCR was angry with the Muslims' clear affront to the agreed-upon resettlement plan. IFOR was concerned about the presence of armed ABiH soldiers in the ZOS — a blatant violation of the GFAP.[5] "There are certain procedures that must be followed," said Rosanna San of the UNHCR. "We cannot allow the people of Jusici to derail the process we implemented in September."[6] Ms. San credited RS officials for cooperating and not trying to prevent the Muslims from returning home. "All the Bosnian Serb government wants is for the refugees to follow the procedures established."[7]

Initially, the Muslims were unmoved by UNHCR complaints. The refugees had grown impatient waiting for someone to give them permission to go home. They contended that the Dayton Accord provided them and other refugees all the authority they needed to return. One Muslim man told IFOR officers that the group would only leave when carried out in caskets.[8]

A message released jointly by IFOR, the UNHCR, and other international agencies involved said, "Government leaders must take responsibility for the actions of their ... citizens.... The International Community will strictly enforce the provisions of the peace agreement, and will act swiftly and decisively against any violations."[9]

Local entity police — in this case from Republika Srpska — were responsible for enforcing GFAP provisions. "IFOR stands ready to provide assistance if requested," the statement read. So far, RS policemen had shown "welcome restraint and confidence in established procedures."[10]

Small, vacant, and isolated, Jusici lay about one mile inside RS territory. The village was about twenty miles east of Tuzla in a remote mountainous area. Bosnian Serbs had driven the previous Muslim residents from their homes there in 1992.[11] RS police quietly established an OP nearby to observe the village. Russian and American IFOR soldiers came in to observe the UNHCR as it attempted to persuade the Muslims to leave. Quarterhorse AWTs flew aerial reconnaissance missions and kept IFOR leaders informed.

Major John Kershaw, the American liaison officer to the Russian airborne brigade, was on the ground in Jusici. He made it clear to reporters that IFOR had no intention of getting involved in the negotiations. "IFOR's primary role is that of a facilitator."[12]

The following day, a conference between both entity interior ministers was held at the Dawg Pound to discuss housing and resettlement issues. The UNHCR sponsored the meeting, which was also attended by LTG Walker and BG Casey. The discussion focused on refugee resettlement procedures, the means to formalize refugee claims of home ownership, and the means for notifying entity governments of refugee returns. The participating BiH leaders dragged their feet for strategic political reasons.

The negotiations were suspended so that the BiH interior minister and local officials could accompany BG Casey, the Russian brigade commander, and IPTF officers to Jusici. An IFOR spokesman reported that the BiH interior minister "was given the opportunity to rectify the situation and to stress the serious nature of the Muslim's actions.... In the end he did not attempt to persuade the Muslims to leave the village."[13]

IFOR soldiers searched the Muslims and confiscated fifteen grenades, three rifles, and a pistol. The following day, September 22, IFOR Soldiers searched the Muslims again. This time, they confiscated and photographed an assault rifle and five more grenades. IFOR then ordered the Muslims to leave.[14]

BG Casey led daily negotiations, which initially fell flat. The Muslims were told that they could not begin to rebuild their homes until after they had registered with RS officials and proven their ownership of the houses.[15] Russian IFOR soldiers then blockaded the village to prevent building materials from reaching it. Only food, water, and medicine were allowed in. Relations between the Muslims and the Russians had been fragile since the beginning of Operation Joint Endeavor.[16] The Russians were historical allies of the Serbs. Their blockade of Jusici only exacerbated the strain. Accordingly, senior IFOR leaders ensured that American soldiers were also on the ground in Jusici. Quarterhorse elements were among them.

As a further disincentive to the Muslims, IFOR punished the ABiH 28th Division for its involved foot-dragging by suspending approval of all ABiH training and military movements.[17]

By the first week of October, both sides were weakening. Lacking adequate shelter, some of the Muslim refugees became sick. Up to this point in Operation Joint Endeavor, the international community had always spoken with a unified voice. Now a rift developed. Members of the UNHCR were uncomfortable with the military situation. One representative complained that the blockade was punishing old women and children. Apparently, the measure conflicted with the representative's ideal of nonconfrontational humanitarian relief.[18]

On October 3, a compromise was reached between the Muslim mayor, the Serb canton leader, and the UNHCR. The agreement upheld refugees' rights to go home, while protecting entity governments from having to receive disruptive persons without legitimate claim to be there.[19]

The Muslim villagers then departed Jusici, but not without incident. Nekir Islamovic, the Muslim mayor, told his people about the agreement that was forcing them to leave. A man later identified as an ABiH officer incited the villagers to resist. They eventually left without further incident. IFOR dismissed the charade as a propaganda effort orchestrated by the Federation government.[20]

BG Casey was relieved that a compromise had been reached. "In order to get this situation resolved peacefully, it took a lot of effort from many people from all the international organizations, the Republika Srpska, and the Governor's office all working together.... I think it is important that the first instance of conflict here since the September elections has been resolved peacefully. That is a big step forward for everybody."

BG Casey also praised the professionalism of the Russians. "The determination and perseverance of Russian Brigade soldiers kept control of the situation here. I think we wouldn't be here today if it weren't for the great job the Russian Brigade soldiers did."[21] But BG Casey's congratulations were premature. The Jusici impasse was far from over. It was merely entering a new phase.

At this point in the drama, Quarterhorse reported:

> The [squadron] continues to focus on cross boundary excursions by the Muslims and the expected or anticipated responses by the Republika Srpska. To date, only the towns of Mahala, Dugi Dio, and Jusici have been occupied by the Muslims in a manner that contradicts the Dayton Peace Accords. To help solve this, the squadron has been working many hours with the Joint Commission and patrolling all of the towns. We currently have troopers assigned to Bravo, Charlie, and Headquarters Troop[s] observing the various towns with Delta and Echo Troop aerial assets on standby in case things get out of hand.[22]

When the Muslim villagers departed Jusici, they moved into a tent city in Federation territory. They had agreed to occupy the UNHCR tents for three days while their claims of ownership were processed. Officials from the UNHCR and other international agencies formed the above-mentioned Joint Commission, which worked day and night to process at least fifty percent of the paperwork submitted by the villagers. The marathon session ended on October 6. Sixty of the 117 families were certified as legal owners or heirs to homes in Jusici. That afternoon, the approved Muslim families were allowed to return.[23]

Prior to their arrival, an explosion echoed through Jusici at around 4:05 P.M. American and Russian soldiers immediately fanned out to investigate. It turned out that a small bomb had been wired to a Russian generator. The bomb exploded when a soldier attempted to start the generator. Fortunately, the charge was only large enough to cause a disturbance. Initial fears that the Serbs might have tampered with the generator were soon discounted. The Russians had only recently unloaded it from one of their own trucks. BG Casey suggested that a Russian soldier may have played an untimely prank on his comrades.[24]

At 5:00 P.M., Russian IFOR soldiers escorted Muslim families back into the village. BG Casey was on hand to witness their return. The Russians checked for identification and required the villagers to sign in. RS police watched quietly nearby.

Mumin Islamovic, a relative of the mayor, proceeded up the hill to his old house. Suddenly, a commotion started and villagers picked up sticks and rocks and ran to his location. Mr. Islamovic claimed that a Russian soldier had beaten him to the ground. His unfounded allegation was yet another propaganda ploy. BG Casey told reporters, "I think there is a little hyperbole going around up here."[25]

As part of the agreement reached on October 3, IFOR invited RS police to conduct joint patrols through Jusici, Dugi Dio, and Mahala with Quarterhorse and the Russians. IFOR and UN leaders saw the joint patrols as a way to ease tensions. They were intended to show Bosnian Serbs that Muslim villagers were willing to live under RS law and to show the Muslims that RS police would protect them just as they would any Serb citizen.[26]

During joint patrols of Jusici and Dugi Dio on October 9, RS police took the opportunity to post Republika Srpska flags on several telephone poles. In both locations, Muslims tore them down and burned them.[27] Dragan Kijac, the RS interior minister, said the missing flags were evidence of the Muslims' unwillingness to live under RS law. Mr. Kijac said that because of the flag-burning and other incidents, he would halt attempts to normalize relations between RS police and Muslim villagers. Referring to the emblems on the BiH flag, he said, "Lilies cannot exist on our soil."[28]

The Serbs refused to continue our joint patrols until the sixty Muslim families in Jusici were expelled. BiH leaders insisted that they stay.

On October 10, a Muslim crowd in Dugi Dio interrupted RS police attempts to arrest a Muslim man in illegal possession of two rifles, two grenades, and two magazines of ammo. Muslim women and children screamed, cried, and rushed between the Serb police and the man.[29] IFOR soldiers, including elements from Quarterhorse, stopped the arrest. We needed to calm and contain the situation. It was no wonder, though, after this incident and our perceived partiality in September's Mahaladay Madness that many Serbs concluded that IFOR had become an ally of the Muslims. This was a dangerous perception that needed to be corrected.

On the morning of October 11, ethnic tensions in the ZOS turned violent. At about 3:00 A.M., five houses in Jusici were mysteriously blown up. On the next night, four more were destroyed. Similar blasts occurred simultaneously in other Muslim villages within the ZOS. The explosions continued over several nights. Initially, IFOR did not know who had perpetrated the bombings or what methods had been used. We suspected that the Serbs intended to destroy habitable houses to prevent the Muslims from reoccupying them. An IFOR spokesman said it appeared that antitank mines had been detonated inside houses under reconstruction. No Muslim casualties had resulted thus far.[30]

On October 12, an AWT from our Echo Troop gathered video footage confirming that the houses in Jusici had been blown apart from within. They had not been struck from the outside by rocket-propelled grenades or other means. The houses were completely reduced to rubble.

At mid-morning on the day of the first explosions, ten to fifteen RS policemen swarmed into Jusici. In full battle gear with AK-47s and one machine gun, the Serbs roughed up an American journalist and took his camera. They seized three Muslims while holding American and Russian IFOR soldiers at gunpoint. The police dragged the three Muslims into a truck. MAJ Kershaw attempted to block the vehicle with his body, but was forced out of the way. The Muslims were taken to the Zvornik police station, where they were reportedly beaten. IFOR responded in force. Ten RS automatic weapons used in the incident were confiscated.[31]

The need for increased dialog was clear. Otherwise, the cycle of violence would spiral out of control. IFOR and agencies from the international community acted with resolve to finalize the resettlement issue. In Sarajevo, officials pressured faction leaders to end the series of house bombings. In the ZOS, Quarterhorse and other IFOR elements pressed local leaders to cooperate.

"The international community will not be satisfied only with diplomatic statements and signatures at high levels while at the village level the mining of houses is exploding the hopes of ordinary people for a return to peace and normalcy," said Colum Murphy, a spokesman for Carl Bildt, the UN High Representative for Bosnia. "Each destroyed home is an explosion of someone's hopes and dreams and a direct attack on the spirit of Dayton," said Mr. Murphy.[32]

The explosions in Jusici were not isolated, locally sponsored incidents. On one mid–October night alone, explosions destroyed ninety homes in Prijedor, a village over in the British sector that was patrolled by Czech troops. About eight mines per house were used in Prijedor. "Somewhere between 700 and 800 mines were laid," Mr. Murphy said. "So any notion that this was not a highly organized sabotage is dispelled."[33] Clearly, the RS government was waging a large, covert military operation.

In the third week of October, MAJ Dixon, the 2 BCT Operations Officer, wrote about the dangerous situation we faced:

> [During ongoing] Federation attempts to achieve resettlement in the Republika Srpska, specifically at Mahala, Dugi Dio, and a town called Jusici.... The Saber element [Quarterhorse] has continued an outstanding effort to peacefully accomplish this task, actually laying the foundation for procedures, which the UNHCR and the Office of the High Representative now use. However, the [Bosnian Serbs] view the Federation resettlement attempts as simple aggression and continued encroachment to reach the Drina River and split RS; therefore, they refuse to cooperate. With the international community and IFOR unable to actually get both sides together, this situation definitely has the potential to ignite. Recently in Jusici, both the Bosniaks and the RS police have clashed. Both sides have either voiced or demonstrated threats directly towards IFOR forces. As the resettlement dilemma continues to unfold, many outcomes are possible — most could result in violence. To avoid surprise, 2 BCT has executed a coordinated reconnaissance effort with Task Force Eagle. Saber also continues to pursue resolving resettlement using procedures and dialogue. As always, stay vigilant and do not let your guard down.[34]

By the sixth week of the Jusici impasse, a local RS official continued to insist that the Muslim resettlements were premature and that the national government should first approve reparations for all those whose homes were destroyed during the war. Serb leaders also renewed their charges that Muslim villagers were hiding illegal weapons in their homes. RS officials demanded repeatedly that Serb police be allowed to search for them. IFOR recognized that we could not sanction such a search at the present time. The potential for violence was just too overwhelming. We reached a compromise to placate Serb fears.

On October 31, Quarterhorse led a multinational search for illegal weapons in Jusici. Our cavalrymen formed the bulk of the 200-man IFOR search force. Elements from the Russian airborne brigade, the Nordic-Polish brigade, and IFOR units from Turkey and three other nations also participated. BG Casey, the Russian brigade commander, and RS police from Zvornik observed. Our no-notice inspection of 109 houses and buildings failed to produce any contraband supporting Serb claims.[35]

Meanwhile, tensions were growing down in Mahala again. RS officials warned IFOR that they might not be able to control growing resentment over the presence of Muslim settlers there.[36] LTC Harriman ordered the Quarterhorse staff to develop an operation plan to control possible mob violence in Mahala. We feared a repeat of August's Mahaladay Madness. LTC Harriman specified the need to clarify how we would respond to certain situations. It was key for our cavalrymen and attachments to understand exactly what we were supposed to do in such actions as delaying mobs.[37]

Our squadron's operations in the ZOS villages of Dugi Dio, Mahala, Jusici, and Osmaci were among the most intensive air-ground, military-political actions of our tour in Bosnia. LTC Harriman recognized that tensions would linger in these villages for quite some time. He told us, "Keep a sharp eye out. Keep your reports rolling in. Keep up with the detail."[38] We did, and our leaders continued to play a vital part in negotiations to resolve the resettlement issue. However, by the date Quarterhorse was relieved of responsibility for our sector, the issue remained unresolved.

While most of Quarterhorse was focused on events in the Russian sector, as well as in our own, Alpha Troop maintained its watch over the southern half of the 2 BCT sector. Once the TF 2-68 AR headquarters redeployed, the troop operated in support of TF 4-12 IN.

## Scare in the Air

Training was a central element of our routine in Bosnia, even while Quarterhorse was heavily engaged in major events like the ongoing Jusici impasse. A flight training accident on November 1 nearly cost us the first casualties among our air cavalry troops.

Our Kiowa Warrior pilots were required to conduct night training flights as part of their annual certification. On this particular night, Echo Troop's Chief Warrant Officer Three Paul Pedersen evaluated Chief Warrant Officer Two Dave Wilson in artillery targeting tasks. Their aircraft hovered over a wooded ridgeline south of LA Molly while CW2 Wilson practiced identifying targets and simulated calling indirect fires on them.

As in all night flights, our pilots wore night vision goggles. Our NVGs were top-of-the-line equipment, but the existing technology still created a dangerous tunnel-vision affect and a significant reduction in depth perception. Night flight was exponentially more dangerous than daylight flight. Our low-level reconnaissance tactics brought our aircraft into close contact with power lines, towers, and other obstacles on the ground.[39]

The Kiowa Warrior has a complex array of optical sights, cameras, and flight controls that keep pilots very busy in flight. Concentrating on their illuminated controls and the thermal image of their designated target, CW3 Pedersen and CW2 Wilson did not realize that their hovering Kiowa had actually drifted away from the ridge underneath them. Their aircraft slowly drifted backwards across a narrow valley and towards a higher ridgeline. The Kiowa was too high for the pilots to get their bearings off any trees out either side of the aircraft. Suddenly, a loud, very irregular noise shook the aircraft. The tail rotor thrashed through the branches of a tree. In this type of accident, either the tail rotor or the entire rear boom could have easily snapped off. The aircraft would then have gone into an immediate, uncontrollable spin to the ground.[40]

The Lord saved our pilots. They reacted quickly and averted disaster. CW3 Pedersen was one of our most experienced pilots. His quiet demeanor gave no indication of his considerable combat record flying Kiowa Warriors in the Persian Gulf in the early 1990s. He and CW2 Wilson were able to make an emergency landing nearby.

Upon inspection, the damage proved to be not too severe. The tail rotor sustained several thousand dollars' worth of damage, yet it had not disintegrated. The accident drove home to everyone in Quarterhorse why U.S. Army aviators are paid so well. The chances of surviving a major in-flight accident or battle damage while flying an aluminum and plastic aircraft were very low.

LTC Harriman wrote soon afterwards, "Friday, God plucked two of our pilots out of the trees. God couldn't have given us a better gift.... This lesson I pass to you from them: work to keep aware of events around you. Work hard to keep focused as reunion nears."[41]

This was the most serious flight accident Quarterhorse had experienced to date. It also turned out to be our last. By the time we ceased stability operations in November, our two air cavalry troops logged a combined total of 4,580.5 operational flight hours under dangerous combat flying conditions.[42] With no fatalities or casualties, this was truly a feat to be proud of.

## Hot APCs

The U.S. Army cavalry doctrine that stressed initiative and decentralized execution made Quarterhorse well-suited for the Bosnian stability operations environment. To say that we were going in a hundred different directions at once would not have been an overstatement.

While a good portion of our assets were involved up in Jusici, other Quarterhorse elements trained, manned checkpoints and OPs, inspected weapons storage sites, and performed regular maintenance and security duties. Civil affairs missions, intelligence gathering, and planning and preparing for redeployment also kept us busy.

In late October, a patrol from Bravo Troop made an unusual find. While in RS territory, Captain Bob Ivy's scouts located a suspicious pair of armored personnel carriers (APCs). CPT Ivy said, "As soon as we saw them, we knew they didn't belong."[43]

Most VRS armored vehicles were obsolete Soviet models, some of which dated back to World War II. The variant model M113 APCs discovered by Bravo Troop were unlike any other VRS vehicles we had seen all year. An investigation into their origin revealed that they had been captured from Dutch UN peacekeepers during the fall of Srebrenica in July 1995.

CPT Ivy radioed his find back to the Squadron TAC, who in turn passed the report on to Task Force Eagle Headquarters. Naturally, the Dutch Army wanted their APCs back. Quarterhorse soon dispatched a hastily-assembled recovery mission. We provided a section of Bradleys from Bravo Troop, a squad of military police, and an AWT to deter possible VRS resistance. U.S. Air Force ground liaison and fire support personnel from 2 BCT were also on hand in case greater firepower was needed.

The Dutch Army sent out an explosive ordnance disposal team to examine the vehicles for any trip wires, booby traps, or mines. They also brought along two Heavy Equipment Trailers (HETs) to cart off their APCs. No problems arose during the recovery. The vehicles were later sent back to Holland for refurbishing.[44]

## Spurs

On the evening of October 26, Quarterhorse assembled our scattered and busy leaders for a special ceremony in the Dawg Pound. The occasion was our long-awaited Spur Dinner, an old cavalry tradition in which spurs — vestigial symbols of the cavalry's horse-mounted days — were awarded to deserving officers and NCOs.[45]

Under normal garrison circumstances, U.S. cavalry squadrons conduct annual or semi-annual Spur Rides. These are esprit-building events in which candidates complete a series of individual cavalry skills tests in a rigorous field environment. Spur Rides are an important activity for the indoctrination of new cavalry leaders. History, customs, and standards are all reinforced for candidates and spur holders alike. A certain level of well-intentioned hazing is thrown in for good measure. Spur Rides typically end with a Spur Dinner, a rowdy, full-dress dining-in.

Since Quarterhorse was completely involved in stability tasks, it was impractical to conduct a traditional Spur Ride. Many eligible spur candidates did not think we needed one. Hadn't we already earned our spurs by forging a path into the Bosnian war zone, securing the entire 2 BCT sector, and establishing and maintaining the peace for nearly eleven months?[46]

LTC Harriman and our squadron command sergeant major agreed. The criteria for the award of spurs were that an officer or NCO must have served with Quarterhorse in Bosnia for at least six months, or have crossed the Sava River in January. Even officers and NCOs from our attached engineer, civil affairs, military police, psyops, and counterintelligence elements were eligible for spurs. This was a big honor for them, since all of our attachments were proud of "being in the Cav."

On the special evening, the Dawg Pound mess hall was decked out in cavalry regalia. The national colors, squadron colors, and troop guidons were all displayed proudly. Large hand-painted insignias of the 4th Cavalry Regiment and our parent divisions hung around the room.[47]

Many cavalrymen wore Stetsons. These broad-brimmed, black felt hats typified the popular image of the Wild West cavalryman. As late as the 1970s, some cavalry squadrons wore Stetsons as their daily headgear, but by 1996 Stetsons had been relegated to social and ceremonial occasions. Officers wore a gold bullion cord around the crown of their Stetsons. Warrant officers had silver cords. NCOs wore yellow wool cords. Everyone wore his rank and the crossed-sabers insignia of the cavalry on front. Some added an individual touch by lining the base of the crown with the insignias of their previous units. Some officers had not brought their Stetsons with them to Bosnia. Captain Wawro wore a "field Stetson"—a dyed-black jungle hat with the appropriate cavalry insignia. CPT Viney wore a reproduction cavalry officer's kepi of American Civil War design, similar in shape to a baseball cap. He found it easier to stow away than a Stetson.

Our guests of honor were Colonel Webb, the commander of the 1st Armored Division's 4th (Aviation) Brigade, and our own brigade commander, COL Batiste.[48]

The evening began with the squadron command sergeant major leading the color guard in posting the colors. Our seven troop commanders then performed our traditional punch-bowl ceremony in which each commander poured a different beverage into the punch to commemorate particular phases of our regiment's long and illustrious history. Because we were bound to the "no alcohol rule" of General Order Number One, we had to substitute non-alcoholic drinks into the normally potent concoction.

Quarterhorse cooks prepared a fine dinner of grilled steak and fried shrimp. As we enjoyed our meal, CPT Viney recited a lengthy history of the 4th U.S. Cavalry Regiment. (Earlier, LTC Harriman confided to him his uneasiness over our regiment's record during the Indian Wars period. It was too much like ethnic cleansing. We didn't want to call attention to that.[49])

After dinner, a group of lieutenants and captains performed several hilarious skits parodying the Quarterhorse leadership. First Lieutenant Elrod then read a poem about a fictitious cavalryman that he'd composed for the occasion. LTC Harriman and COL Batiste both gave speeches tying together Quarterhorse's past with the current chapter of its history that we were writing. By this point, the smoking lamp had been lit, and the air was cloudy with dense cigar smoke. (During our tour in Bosnia, many Quarterhorse cavalrymen joined the new fad of smoking cigars.)

The main event of the evening was the presentation of 250 sets of spurs to deserving officers and NCOs. The seven troop commanders and MAJ Elias each presented spurs to their subordinates. This was done by having the individual stand on a chair while the presenter affixed the spurs to his boots.[50]

We then recited "Fiddler's Green" — the traditional poem of the U.S. cavalry — in unison. One of our lieutenants delivered a benediction, and then the colors were retired. As the color party marched out, one of our NCOs beat a drum roll. The evening was rich with camaraderie, pride, tradition, and history. After a thunderous cavalry cheer, the party adjourned. Many cavalrymen removed their new spurs before departing the mess hall since the ground outside was muddy as ever.

The evening of our Spur Dinner was the first night in almost seven months that temperatures dropped below freezing. Fall had definitely returned to Bosnia.[51]

# 13

# CHANGE OF MISSION

Into mid–October, the Clinton administration continued to dance around the question of how long American forces would remain in Bosnia. President Clinton had promised in December 1995 that we would be out in less than a year.[1] During hearings of the House National Security Committee on September 25, Deputy Secretary of Defense John White insisted to lawmakers, "The Implementation Force mission will be completed in December and the implementation force will be withdrawn."[2]

But the following day, Secretary of Defense William Perry added that Washington would consider keeping U.S. troops in Bosnia through 1997 if NATO deemed their presence a necessity. "The United States is not prepared to make a commitment at this time," Secretary Perry said, "but we are prepared to consider participating if the NATO study shows that our involvement is necessary and appropriate."[3] House Republicans blasted the Clinton administration for betraying its earlier and oft-repeated pledge to limit the mission to one year.

Stephen Stedman, a Visiting Research Fellow at Stanford University who authored a recent study of the Clinton administration's Bosnia exit strategy for the Council on Foreign Relations, said, "This is a very nice semantic game. [The Implementation Force] will leave Bosnia, but we will still have troops there under some other name. It assumes that the American people have the intelligence of a six-year-old."[4]

It was widely expected that NATO would approve another peacekeeping force after the American presidential election. Of course, NATO could not have sustained its course without the continued involvement and leadership of the U.S. military. Sure enough, following President Clinton's reelection in November, his administration agreed to participate in the follow-on force. President Clinton was unwilling to risk a renewal of the civil war. Besides, his argument went, the stakes went far beyond Bosnia. There were issues of

U.S. prestige and the cohesion of NATO. To leave Bosnia at this point would have meant throwing away NATO's investment of over $6 billion.[5]

The follow-on force was conveniently titled the Sustainment Force (SFOR) to distinguish it from IFOR. This name change may have duped some Americans into believing that President Clinton had actually honored his politically expedient pledge.

On October 19, the 2 BCT Headquarters reported:

> The [brigade] continues to execute operations in sector to monitor compliance with the D+120 GFAP requirement, while concurrently preparing to conduct an area relief with 2 BCT from 1ID, then withdraw to Central Region [Germany]. As the scouts and Tactical Command Post from TF 2-68 (AR) returned back to Germany, 2 BCT force reshaping was completed and the BCT now has shifted focus to transition operations and withdrawal. Even though the operation for 2 BCT might be winding to a close, much remains to do while still operating in a very dangerous environment, which could suddenly change at any moment. Force protection remains the number one priority and a task all leaders must ruthlessly enforce.[6]

With 2 BCT headquarters already busy managing the redeployment of other brigade elements, Quarterhorse did not shift gears until the end of October. As the second IFOR unit to enter Bosnia back in January, we had been the first to occupy the 2 BCT sector. Now, Quarterhorse would be the last 2 BCT element out.

Quarterhorse completed its transition from peacekeeping to redeployment during the first week of November. We didn't simply end the former mission and assume the latter. For a two-week period, our activities redoubled. We secured more fixed sites than ever before. With Alpha Troop covering all of the former TF 2-68 AR sector, Bravo and Charlie Troops were stretched very thin.[7] On October 28, TF 1-26 IN finally relieved Quarterhorse of Sierra 10, Rock OP, and Mount Vis.[8] LTC Harriman admitted that he was "looking forward to becoming a visitor in my own sector."[9] All of us agreed.

COL Batiste wrote in one of his last columns for the brigade newspaper:

> It's D+304 and the mission continues to a very high standard. Take pride in your accomplishments. You have had a dramatic impact on Bosnia-Herzegovina. Continue to focus on the mission. Force protection remains my number one priority.[10]
>
> Planning for the 23 and 24 NOV 96 municipal elections continues as the balance of the Iron Brigade continues redeployment operations. The 1ID's 2nd Brigade and TF 1-26 (IN) are closing into sector. Insist on safe and deliberate operations—whether conducting a tactical road march or compelling compliance. It is not over until it's over.

The success of the 2 BCT is due in large measure to teamwork, competent NCOs, and great Soldiers. We will keep a good thing going in Central Region. Teamwork is everything. It has been an honor to serve with great units such as the 1-4 Cavalry and 720 MP Battalion.[11]

As the original NATO peacekeeping forces redeployed and were replaced by smaller elements, several IFOR lodgment areas were either consolidated or closed down. Only seven or eight of the more than twenty camps would remain. Among those to endure was the Dawg Pound.

LA Linda down in Olovo was slated to be closed down. Our Alpha Troop had established it back in January, and now it took the place apart after TF 2-68 AR completed its withdrawal. Once the job was done, Alpha Troop and local officials held a ceremony to mark the occasion.[12]

Alpha Troop physically rejoined the rest of Quarterhorse on November 2. The troop established a temporary home at LA Bedrock in the middle of "the quarry." LTC Harriman wrote:

Alpha Troop ... took down the checkpoints that protected (LA) Linda. Alpha Troop tore down (LA) Linda. I'm not certain Alpha Troop ever got to enjoy (LA) Linda (with its cantina patio restaurant and the second-best PX in Bosnia). But, I am certain that Alpha Troop set standards of performance, discipline, and can do attitude that nobody else there could match.[13]

At 12:00 P.M. on November 3, an announcement went out to all Quarterhorse elements that transfer of authority for our sector had gone into effect.[14] Hurrah! It was an anxious moment for many of us. And somewhat anticlimactic. Bosnia had been our home and our purpose for nearly a year. The unknown of the redeployment and our reunion with loved ones now loomed before us. We were tired, yet proud. Happy to be going home, but anxious that those who were relieving us would get it right and not screw up all of our hard work. We felt a profound sense of ownership for our sector and for our portion of the Bosnian peace. As easy as it was to leave, it was hard for many of us to let go inside.

The afternoon of November 3 was unusually sunny and warm. COL Batiste presided over a ceremony at the Dawg Pound to mark the transfer of authority from 2 BCT to TF 1-26 IN.[15] In testament to the level of security we had established, it was now safe for one lightly armed battalion to take over the entire huge 2 BCT sector. COL Batiste addressed our ground cavalry troops one last time:

While peace rests squarely in the hands of the Parties to the Agreement, we have given them a start — only a start. We have pointed them in the right direction. Our collective efforts are all but a chapter in the book. It will say in that chapter that [we] separated the Former Warring Factions and established a two-kilometer-wide Zone of Separation along the former confrontation line. For the first time in four years, roads were open to civilian traffic as obstacles and mines were removed and unauthorized checkpoints were dismantled.

We stood firmly on the moral high ground and stared the factions down. We accomplished what many said was impossible over a 4,300-square-kilometer sector. We occupied the sector in the dead of winter. We separated factions — forced weapons into approved storage sites and compelled habitual compliance.[16]

In all, 2 BCT confiscated 342 illegal weapons and destroyed 195 of them. It monitored the clearance of more than 388 minefields and the destruction of 299 bunkers.[17] COL Batiste continued:

Operations were deliberate, synchronized, rehearsed, and well-executed then and remain so today. You young officers and NCOs remember that standard twenty years from now. Have the moral courage to do the harder right than the easier wrong.... The Lord has a plan for Bosnia, and we have played a small role in that effort. We put our trust in the Lord....

Addressing the Blue Spaders of TF 1-26 IN, he said, "Remember, we are only a phone call away!"[18]

Later that day, COL Batiste reflected with a reporter on his brigade's 318-day operation. We had faced rugged mountains and frequent resistance from the Bosnian Serb army to comply with the Dayton Peace Accord. But by this point, the VRS was "largely complying with the military aspects of Dayton.... We check them all the time.[19]

"Our ability to synchronize combat power the old-fashioned way was the reason we were successful here in Bosnia," COL Batiste insisted. Our displays of military power earned "the respect of the factions."[20]

COL Batiste also visited LA Molly, where he made similar congratulatory remarks to our assembled air cavalrymen and squadron headquarters personnel. Afterwards, he posed for photographs with LTC Harriman and our seven troop commanders.

Immediately after the transfer of authority (TOA), LTC Harriman wrote:

Today the squadron became the division reserve, with the mission to go home. It's my kind of mission.[21]

TOA changes our mission, not our responsibilities. In other words, if a Bosniac asks you to provide armed escort for his goat so it can eat greener grass in Srpska, a Blue Spader gets to tell him no. On the other hand if a faction member lights a Molotov cocktail within throwing range while giving you the evil eye you still shoot him. You still have the responsibility to protect your force. Besides, asking a Blue Spader would take too long. Let me lay out responsibilities for you.

• Force protection is Job #1; we don't work for FORD.
• Safety.

• Take time to do it to standard.

• Thieves watch you; are you watching for them?

• Maintenance is Job #2; get parts on order. Put it away right.

• Preliminary gunnery is Job #3; TTA provides a great opportunity to shoot.[22]

Prepare for reunion with families as well. You have changed. Those you left in Schweinfurt have changed. Work through the Personal Redeployment Readiness Guide that you will get as you redeploy.

Finally, TOA does not end our mission here. OPERATION JOINT ENDEAVOR ends when your 1st Sergeant releases you for block leave.

About ten years ago, I lost a knife fight with an unarmed watermelon. Took my eyes off it for an instant and sliced my hand. Since then I go carefully around watermelons, especially melons that look ornery. I just forgot what I was doing for a moment; thinking about other things I was.... The safety fat lady never sings.[23]

Colonel John Batiste, the 2 BCT Commander, addresses cavalrymen from Delta, Echo, Fox, and Headquarters Troops in LA Molly, November 1996 (photograph: Mark Viney).

On November 5, LTC Harriman made a final round of visits to the civilian and military leaders in Kalesija, Zvornik, and Osmaci. Lieutenant Colonel Swan, the commander of TF 1-26 IN, accompanied him. LTC Harriman wished them well and offered his hope that they would continue on the path towards a lasting peace that we had led them along for the past eleven months.[24] With this final act, Quarterhorse concluded our stability operations in Bosnia.

Charlie Troop moved from the Dawg Pound to LA Molly to help tear down our headquarters camp. The Dawg Pound had already begun to transform before our eyes. The infantrymen of TF 1-26 IN had their own standards and ways of running things, and they weren't at all like our well-established routines. They even renamed the place Camp Dobol. It was definitely time for Quarterhorse to get the hell out of there. On November 7, the Squadron TAC departed the Dawg Pound.

Fittingly, Bravo Troop was the last Quarterhorse element to leave the

Dawg Pound. Its final departure on November 8 occurred just one day short of the ten-month mark from its arrival at that once desolate, snow-covered battlefield. Bravo Troop moved to LA Bedrock for a stay that was supposed to last almost two weeks, but IFOR planners had other things in store for the troop.

The newly arrived 1st Infantry Division provided the headquarters for the covering force with the nominal mission of protecting the 1st Armored Division as we redeployed. The outgoing and incoming Task Force Eagle (TFE) commanders held a high-level meeting with senior FWF leaders on November 1.[25] Major General Montgomery C. Meigs, the commanding general of IID and the new TFE commander, said, "We have reorganized the force so that a smaller number of units can cover the same amount of ground. Given that the military threat has become such a small one, we do not have the same requirement for overmatch that existed one year ago."[26]

When Quarterhorse and the other original IFOR units first entered Bosnia, we came prepared to fight. But fighting had proven unnecessary, and so we became diplomats, mediators, and crowd control specialists. Planners hoped that MG Meigs' force would be able to forego many of those tasks because of its reduced size and the realization that Bosnia would eventually have to be weaned from dependence on international players if the peace were to last.

MG Nash, the outgoing TFE commander, recalled, "Over the past year, we've had the cessation of hostilities, the breaking up of the armies.... A large part of the armies has been demobilized.... But there's still a lot of work for others to do to bring a long-lasting peace. A military force can only give you an absence of war — not peace. Peace will come from political, economic, and social change. Peace cannot be delivered by an outside agent."[27]

"The Soldiers and Commanders of Task Force Eagle have been privileged to work so hard to try to bring about peace," MG Nash told the faction leaders. "But, ultimately, the responsibility for peace rests on the shoulders of the people and the leaders of Bosnia-Herzegovina."[28]

VRS Major General Novica Simic complemented MG Nash with an important observation: "IFOR and the U.S. and the former opponents — four armies in place and several different nations within this group — and not a single unresolved incident, not a single use of force on any side. I have to admit that's a great thing."[29]

The transfer of authority between the two American divisions went into effect on November 10. The formal end of the Implementation Force (IFOR) occurred on December 20. On that date, the number of American troops in Bosnia was about 20,000. Planners anticipated the number to shrink to around 8,500 in 1997.[30]

## Under Fire in the Thunderdome

By mid–November, Quarterhorse had been in Bosnia for over ten months and had not received any direct fire from any FWF or terrorist element. Rounds had been fired past our cavalrymen during the Mahaladay Madness, however. We had come close to opening fire during the several physical altercations we had had with angry rioters, but we had yet to be the intended target of enemy fire.

Throughout the year, Quarterhorse received occasional intelligence reports of expected terrorist attacks against IFOR camps. Over the fall, an added concern was the increased susceptibility of our lodgment areas as we tore them down. Our worries were well founded.

At about 4:30 P.M. on November 14, CPT Viney watched the sun set behind the mountains south of the Thunderdome for the final time. This was his last night in Bosnia before departing for the Intermediate Staging Base (ISB) early the next morning. The peaceful calm was suddenly interrupted by a series of fifteen to twenty loud pops. The sound, like a string of firecrackers, echoed through the camp from the vicinity of the southern gate.

CPT Viney watched and waited. It was too many rounds to have been an accidental discharge at one of our clearing points. It had obviously been incoming fire, but there was no answering fire in return. Minutes passed and he could detect no unusual movement from his location in the HHT motor pool. The situation did not appear critical, so he simply noted the time and went back to work.[31]

But elsewhere, Captain Wawro was in action. He had heard the firing and observed several tracer rounds entering the camp. He immediately dispatched HHT's Quick Reaction Force to move to the south gate. CPT Wawro then personally directed all other troop elements to man their assigned sectors of the perimeter. He called our Squadron TOC, which was a couple of miles away at LA Molly, and requested an AWT to fly over and help figure out what was going on. To his mind, the firing may have been the premature signal of an imminent attack. Quarterhorse had been warned of the possibility for so long.

MAJ Robert Elias, our unflappable squadron deputy commander, was in the TOC and heard CPT Wawro's call for help. He calmly asked CPT Wawro what was going on at the moment. The perimeter was manned but all was quiet. There had been no more fire. How long had it been since the rounds were heard? Twenty minutes. MAJ Elias told him, "Joe, I'm not gonna send any Kiowas over for that. You handle it yourself, and if anything else happens let me know."[32]

HHT was denied its long-anticipated opportunity to defend the Thunderdome. Word soon spread about what had happened. Apparently, two Muslim opportunists had concocted a half-baked scheme to sneak off with construction materials while we were eating dinner. One of the duo opened fire into the camp from near the giant earth-moving conveyor machine by the south gate. His mission had been to draw our attention while his buddy snuck through the wire on the north side and carted off as much plywood as he could manage.

The American soldiers guarding the south gate were from another unit within 2 BCT. When fired upon, they took cover but did not overreact. Sensing that the gunman was a lone perpetrator, they captured him and took his AK-47 away. By the time his partner attempted to infiltrate the wire, the whole camp had been alerted. He was unarmed, and the guards easily detained him.

The "hostile fire" had been inaccurate and desultory. The two Muslims had not intended to shoot anyone or to destroy any IFOR equipment. They did not want to get into any serious trouble. We found no damage from their fire. The incident was comical, but it reminded us to stay on our toes. Even as Quarterhorse began its slow march towards home, Bosnia remained a land of dangerous surprises.

## *The Long Road Home*

On November 10, Quarterhorse was detached from the 1st Armored Division and reassigned to our parent unit, the 1st Infantry Division. We then turned our full attention toward preparations for redeployment. The Squadron Operations Section was already planning the training that we would conduct in Germany after a forty-five-day leave period.

For reasons that baffled us, USAREUR decided to keep Quarterhorse so busy after we got home that we would have little opportunity to dwell on the lingering hardships of our year-long tour in Bosnia. We would return to Germany just before Christmas, thank God. Many of us were stunned to learn that we would leave home again in April for nearly two months of training. There was nothing we could think of at this point but being at home with our families.

Some of our officers predicted that we would begin to see the negative repercussions from our year-long operation as early as the spring. They predicted a drop in retention levels and an increased number of divorces, officer resignations, and alcohol-related incidents. Over the next year, Quarterhorse did experience many of these problems, but not to the degree some feared. Cavalry pride and discipline carried us a long way.

Considering the huge funds spent to refurbish the old Soviet base at Taborfalva, U.S. lawmakers grumbled about the limited training actually conducted there during Operation Joint Endeavor. In order to justify our expenditures, the U.S. Army required all redeploying combat units, including Quarterhorse, to rotate through the TTA ranges on their way home.[33]

At first, our cavalrymen did not receive this news very well at all. What else were they planning to challenge our morale? We were ready to "get home to mama." Eventually, we resigned ourselves to the fact that whatever it was going to take to get home, we would do it, and do it well. This meant that in addition to tearing down lodgment areas, repositioning our elements, and preparing our vehicles for the long road march north, we would also have to conduct TCPC and BCPC training. The closer we got to home, the more complicated and hectic things seemed to become.

A few days after Quarterhorse learned of the TTA gunnery requirement, Bravo Troop received additional orders to move to Slavonski Brod to secure the bridge that all NATO units would cross when exiting Bosnia.[34] This was a traditional cavalry mission, but we wondered why some other unit with less time in country couldn't take the job. Bravo Troop road-marched its vehicles out of LA Bedrock on November 8. It established a temporary camp at the Redeployment Staging Base (RSB) on the south bank of the Sava River. Beginning the next day, the troop rotated platoons up to the bridge, which was located in the heart of the devastated city.

Slavonski Brod was a mid-size city that had been destroyed in the latter phases of the Bosnian Civil War. Urban fighting between Bosnian Serbs and Croats had reduced entire city blocks to rubble. U.S. Army engineers built a temporary span over the ruined bridge to support the continual NATO convoys leaving Bosnia. Bravo Troop guarded the bridge without incident until November 26, when it too crossed the Sava and headed north.[35]

The Task Force Eagle redeployment plan specified that all vehicles had to be fully mission-capable for the long road march through Bosnia, Croatia, and Hungary. Consequently, in the late fall maintenance became a much higher priority for us.

Chief Warrant Officer Three Sayan Saevivat, our outstanding squadron maintenance technician, and Second Lieutenant John Adams, the platoon leader of our attached "Team Cav" Maintenance Support Team, were up to the challenge. This pair journeyed all over the American sector to requisition needed parts. Some of their forays took them through the 2,400-square-mile NORDPOL sector. Centered on Doboj, this sector was about twice the size of Rhode Island and was considered the most heavily mined area in all of Bosnia.[36]

Deploying and redeploying NATO units followed separate routes. IFOR units departing Bosnia crossed the bridge in Slavonski Brod. Incoming SFOR units traversed Route Arizona through Zupanja. This was the same route on which Quarterhorse had entered Bosnia over ten months earlier.

Brigadier General O'Neal, Task Force Eagle's senior logistician, stressed repeatedly that we would conduct the redeployment in an orchestrated, orderly, and deliberate manner. There would be no mad rush for the barn door. The intent was to have soldiers and equipment feasibly ready for another deployment upon returning to garrison. The entire process from Bosnia to home station in Germany was scheduled to take twelve days.[37]

So long as the weather cooperated, TFE planners estimated that it would take redeploying units about a day to reach the Redeployment Staging Base (RSB) at Slavonski Brod. There, units would spend four days processing through the RSB. The first day included the tactical road march from our current lodgment areas, then washing and refueling our vehicles. Wheeled vehicles would then drive over the Sava into Croatia. Day Two activities included maintenance and downloading all vehicle ammunition. On the third day, units' heavy equipment, including tanks and Bradleys, would be ferried across the Sava by barge since the temporary span on the main bridge could not support such weight. Once across the Sava, all tracked vehicles would be loaded on Heavy Equipment Trailers (HETs) for transport to the Intermediate Staging Base (ISB) at Taszar, Hungary. On Day Four, our wheeled vehicles would drive to the ISB in convoys.

While at Taszar, units would turn in special equipment and all remaining ammunition, perform maintenance, inventory their equipment, and complete several personnel readiness checks. From the ISB, all vehicles would be shipped by rail to Germany.[38]

Safety was continually stressed during our redeployment. In late October, MAJ Dixon, the 2 BCT operations officer, wrote:

> Although the movement north may seem relatively non-threatening, no unit or leader should approach this essential task in that manner. The route is not only dangerous because a long portion runs through the ZOS, but the route is congested with both civilian and military traffic. Leaders must enforce the following measures: conduct proper risk assessments, maintain designated speeds, keep windshields and lights clean, stop at designated locations using TCPs which are visible, and if unscheduled stops develop — establish visible TCPs.[39]

Unfortunately, MAJ Dixon's warning proved well justified. As our fellow cavalrymen of the 1st Squadron, 1st Cavalry (1-1 CAV) processed through Slavon-

**Typical Bosnian wagon passes halted Quarterhorse convoy north of Olovo, October 21, 1996 (photograph: Mark Viney).**

ski Brod, one of their trucks overturned into a water-filled ditch. An Alpha Troop NCO was trapped inside underwater and drowned. The incident was a sad, strange coincidence. Alpha Troop, 1-1 CAV had the inglorious distinction of having both the first and last American soldiers killed during Operation Joint Endeavor.[40]

During the week of October 14–21, Quarterhorse sent a small party of officers to recon the route to Taszar. Led by MAJ Tubbs, the group spent the night at the RSB, which was located in a former Croatian tank factory. After making the necessary coordinations there, the officers then drove another six hours to Taszar. They spent several days at the ISB confirming the details of the redeployment plan and making useful contacts with support unit personnel. Our officers gained valuable information that was later disseminated throughout the squadron.

The highlight of this reconnaissance mission was the rare opportunity to enjoy the ISB's legendary beer tent, which was the only location where deployed Task Force Eagle Soldiers could legally consume alcohol. Having been dry for over ten months, it was only natural that some of our officers overdid it. At least it was in a controlled environment, which was the whole purpose of the beer tent anyway.

In the pre-dawn hours of November 15, the first redeploying Quarterhorse element departed Bosnia. Led by MAJ Elias, this element included several squadron staff officers and troop executive officers. Their mission now was to conduct follow-up coordinations with support units at Slavonski Brod and Taszar. The rest of Quarterhorse began moving north on November 18. Our redeployment timeline extended to mid–December because our ground cavalry troops had to shoot gunnery at TTA.

Upon reaching the ISB, our cavalrymen who had not seen the airfield in almost a year could not believe their eyes. The runway was no longer blocked with columns of vehicles and supply stores. Now, American intelligence and cargo planes came and went, along with occasional Hungarian Air Force MIGs. The base now had an air of order, routine, and permanence to it.

Redeploying units spent seven days at the ISB. One of the first orders of business was to download and turn in all remaining ammunition. Our cavalrymen removed all equipment from vehicles, cleaned and inventoried it, and then packed it into containers for shipment home. We verified that we still had all of our sensitive items like weapons and NVGs.[41] Generators, floodlights, and all other equipment that had been issued to Quarterhorse just for the operation were turned in on an "as-is" basis. This was a good thing since nearly all of it was inoperable. Having received no manuals, parts, or maintenance support, there was nothing we could have done to keep the stuff serviceable.

Despite temperatures hovering in the mid-thirties, we were required to thoroughly wash all of our vehicles before they were accepted for rail-loading. For those support vehicles that had remained stationary for most of the operation, this was their first washing in a year!

Quarterhorse also completed several important maintenance activities at the ISB. Crewmen performed their own Preventive Maintenance Checks and Services (PMCS).[42] Any vehicles requiring direct support maintenance were worked on by supporting Army National Guard and U.S. Army Reserve maintenance companies. Required parts were put on order for shipment to our home station. Unfortunately, we later discovered that when Quarterhorse was reassigned from 1AD to 1ID, all of our requisitions were lost and had to be reordered.

Finally, Quarterhorse passed through a series of personnel out-processing stations. Our pay was adjusted to remove the special benefits of service in Bosnia.[43] Eleven months of Hostile Fire Pay and Combat Zone Tax Exclusion meant that our cavalrymen would have plenty of extra cash for our upcoming block leave.

One criticism of the U.S. Army in the Gulf War was its failure to conduct thorough health inspections to detect symptoms of diseases or long-term illnesses that soldiers may have contracted during the war. Having learned its lesson, the Department of Defense required all personnel serving in Operation Joint Endeavor to undergo a three-phase medical screening as they departed the theater of operations. Our cavalrymen completed the first phase in the ISB. We saw the dentist, had blood samples taken, and received whatever immunizations were needed. We even met with psychologists to diagnose any cases of post-traumatic stress disorder or other mental illnesses. The second and third phases of the screening were completed at our home station in Schweinfurt.[44]

Our eagerness to go home rose with every minute spent in the ISB. According to CPT Ivy, only the "endless amounts of *bureaurocrity*" stood in our way.[45] For eleven months, we'd lived an isolated, Spartan, stress-filled existence without many options for relief. We needed to decompress in a major way.

One amenity in the ISB purposefully intended to facilitate our decompression was the beer tent. For many of our cavalrymen, this was their first opportunity to consume alcohol in many months. Needless to say, the beer tent was a happening place.

Early on in the operation, senior IFOR leaders had discussed the propriety of allowing stressed-out soldiers to drink on their way home. Some feared massive drunken brawls or other serious misconduct. Wisely, they concluded that no matter what happened in the beer tent, it was better for us to decompress in that relatively controlled environment than to have alcohol-related incidents spring up all over Germany.

The first redeploying Quarterhorse elements to enjoy Taszar's beer tent were the pilots and ground crewmen of our three air cavalry troops. Our warrant officer aviators were mostly an older, mature, and proud group of professionals. They took great pride as cavalrymen, and wore their distinctive Stetsons to the beer tent on their first evening off. Their drinking was low-key until they mounted their seats to do a traditional cavalry cheer. "If you ain't Cav, you ain't shit!" they called. Guards broke up their fun and told them to remove their Stetsons. Our pilots were insulted but did nothing more than complain loudly to the officer-in-charge.

Another night, one of our single officers chatted up an unattractive female officer. The good-natured ribbing he received from his fellow officers prompted him to escort her outside to the smoking patio where they could be left alone. He asked her to wait for him while he used the nearby Porta-Potty, promising to be right back. Instead, he passed out inside the Porta-Potty. Oblivious to the smell, the sub-freezing temperature, and the frequent pounding on the latrine door, the officer didn't wake up until 5:00 A.M. Cold and embarrassed, he slinked back to his tent.

At least he made it back, which was more than one of our pilots could say. After drinking his fill, this aviator returned to his tent, zipped up his sleeping bag, and promptly fell asleep. He was roughly awakened several hours later by an annoyed soldier who informed him that he had fallen asleep in *his* bunk! The pilot eventually found his own bunk in the correct tent.

Another Quarterhorse officer really wanted to dance with someone. He knew that his chances of finding a willing female officer were limited as most of the women present were enlisted. He traded BDU shirts with a private first class and had a great time on the dance floor.

Our enlisted cavalrymen had their share of fun, too. Two PAC clerks from HHT were in a contest to out-drink each other. CPT Viney observed them making their way through the crowd, each with a stack of fifteen empty 16-ounce cups. Another cavalryman from HHT had them beat at twenty-eight cups, but he soon lost his fill and had to be carried out.

As juvenile and unprofessional as this conduct was, this was the extent of it. None of our cavalrymen got into any fights or other serious trouble. Some members of other units did not behave so well. The beer tent was an authorized place to let our hair down. Having been dry for so long, our cavalrymen deserved credit for behaving themselves as well as they did. Although Quarterhorse did have some alcohol-related incidents after our return to Schweinfurt, the number was remarkably small.

The pilots and aircrews of Delta and Echo Troops were the first Quarterhorse elements to process through the ISB. When they departed, they flew their Kiowa Warriors through Austria and around the Alps, arriving home on November 22. Fox Troop spent the week of November 21–27 in the ISB. HHT arrived the day Fox Troop left. HHT departed for Germany on December 3. Alpha and Charlie Troops both fired gunnery at Taborfalva before arriving at the ISB. They processed through between November 30 and December 6. Bravo Troop sent its support vehicles and some cavalrymen to the ISB on November 29 to begin processing while the troop's tank and Bradley crews fired gunnery at TTA. Bravo Troop reconsolidated at Taszar on December 8 and departed for Germany on December 14.[46]

At the same time Quarterhorse was scattered across Hungary, slowly making our way through each of the redeployment gates, one of our wives wrote an irate letter to the *Stars and Stripes*. Mrs. Kara Hill complained about all the publicity heaped on units already home while we remained downrange — one of the last original IFOR units to leave the theater.[47] Our cavalrymen shared her ire:

> 1st Squadron, 4th Cavalry Regiment was deployed Dec. 31. 1/4 who? Yeah, we here in Schweinfurt, Germany, don't know who 1/4 Cav is either since we never

hear about the role they have been playing in Operation Joint Endeavor.

In the year 1/4 Cav has been deployed, the great job they have done has been overshadowed by everybody and everything under the sun.

We know you are probably thinking, "Oh, those whiny wives," but we are the ones who get the letters from all those 1/4 Cav Soldiers who neither read nor hear anything about the work they have done, only of the work of others (Want to talk about low morale?).

Will 1/4 Cav's redeployment in December be forgotten as their part in Operation Joint Endeavor has throughout the year? Even though 1/4 Cav has been forgotten by the media, their loved ones here in Schweinfurt want them to know the great job they have done will never be forgotten by us.[48]

## Reunion

Delta and Echo Troops were the first Quarterhorse elements to return home to Schweinfurt. Early on the morning of November 22, their fifteen

Pilots and support personnel from Delta and Echo Troops return to Quarterhorse airfield at Conn Barracks in Schweinfurt, Germany, November 22, 1996. From left, CW2 Dave Wilson, CW2 Phil Nusbaum, CW2 Randy Parent, CPT Russ DeMartino, and 1LT Chon Taylor (photograph: 1st Infantry Division Public Affairs Office).

Kiowa Warriors and two attached UH-60 Black Hawks departed Taszar. After a long flight around the Alps and a two-hour delay due to bad weather in Hungary, they touched down that evening at our own airfield on Conn Barracks. Forty Quarterhorse cavalrymen were finally home. Ecstatic families and friends greeted our air cavalry troops with cheers and waves.[49]

The Quarterhorse Rear Detachment and the Family Support Group (FSG) had worked together to develop an excellent reception program for us. Immediately upon return, our cavalrymen completed several quick out-processing stations at an undisturbed site in the motor pool. We needed to keep the families at bay in order to finish our mandatory tasks as quickly as possible. After receiving a warm, welcoming hug from volunteer huggers, our cavalrymen turned in their weapons, received keys to their new barracks rooms, signed out on leave, and then waited for the group to finish while looking over recreational information provided.

Once complete, the group then formed up and marched the short distance to the Finney Community Center gym. A formation was held in front of giddy wives. A few (fortunately) brief speeches were made. With a great cheer, the soldiers were released into the arms of loved ones. Tears of joy fell openly. Everyone was moved by the emotion of the moment.

Our single cavalrymen were not forgotten. Far from it. The Rear Detachment had provided barracks room assignments to the Family Support Group, whose volunteers made up the beds, turned them down, and placed yellow ribbons and big bows on each one.

"Each pillow is topped with a little chocolate mint, and a large grocery bag of cookies, gum, candy, instant soups, and food is placed at the foot of the bed," said Captain Rich Spiegel, the squadron Rear Detachment commander.[50] The same process was repeated several more times as other troop-size elements returned.

Fox Troop's buses arrived on November 27. The bulk of HHT returned on December 3. Alpha and Charlie Troops both arrived on December 6. Bravo Troop returned on December 14. The last Quarterhorse element to return from Operation Joint Endeavor, a small headquarters detachment led by MAJ Elias, arrived at Conn Barracks on December 15. Our squadron had been gone a total of 351 days.[51]

LTC Harriman immediately sent a message to our families:

Without you the old oak tree would have been just an old oak tree. You put the ribbon around the tree. Without you the faces of the crowd would just be so many faces in a crowd. Your face we strained to see. Without you the greetings of well wishers might cheer us for a moment, but the cheer would pass. Your "welcome home!" we most needed to hear. This year away we spent without you.

And when you have been away as long as we have, the yellow ribbon makes all the difference. It means we are welcome at home.[52]

In his Christmas message to Quarterhorse, LTC Harriman wrote:

While events in Bosnia separated us for almost all of 1996, all Quarterhorse families can take pride in their contributions to humanity. Those of you who served in Bosnia and Herzegovina, and those of you who bore the sacrifices associated with life in Schweinfurt without their marriage partner, all of you acted in the spirit of Christmas this year. This year you helped establish the Peace on Earth of the Christmas Season. You helped bring Good Will Toward Others closer to reality. The peace wish inherent in Christmas will come this year to Sarajevo, to Mostar, to Banja Luka. You helped make it so. Thanks for your Christmas gift.[53]

# 14

# NO RESPITE

The story of Quarterhorse in Operation Joint Endeavor would be incomplete without an examination of what transpired in the year following our redeployment from Bosnia. We were granted no respite.

Immediately upon our return, we were granted forty-five days of well-deserved and much-needed block leave.[1] It meant so much to be with loved ones for the holidays. We recalled the painful memory of the previous Christmas, just before we deployed.

The leave period passed much too quickly and did not erase the lingering exhaustion and hardships that our cavalrymen and their families would feel for quite some time. (In retrospect, the forty-five days of block leave that Quarterhorse received seems generous in comparison to the fifteen to thirty days of leave that U.S. Army units redeploying from Iraq or Afghanistan typically receive nowadays.)

Before the block leave period was even half over, Quarterhorse was alerted that we might return to Bosnia to support the next round of municipal elections. We were staggered by this news. Our families took it even worse. It just didn't seem right that Quarterhorse would have to return so soon, or ever, for that matter. The U.S. Army still had eight other divisions not yet involved in Bosnia.

LTC Harriman explained:

> [Just because] the Implementation Force folded its flag and left Bosnia does not change an important truth. The NATO commitment to implement the General Framework for Peace has not gone away. 1st Infantry Division will deploy the 3rd BDE (including a battalion from FT Riley) as the SFOR to continue supporting national policy in Bosnia. SFOR has a mission similar to the IFOR mission we did so well. The SFOR mission is a duration mission — roughly 179 days.[2]
>
> EFOR stands for Election Force. Planners feel that we need more force in country to run the election. My experience leads me to agree. I expect Quarter-

horse to deploy to help conduct the election. Unlike SFOR, EFOR is an Event Force. Expect our deployment to last only as long as the time needed to go to Bosnia, the time needed to conduct the election, and the time needed to return to Schweinfurt. I figure the mission will last between six weeks and ninety days.

YFOR — Why for indeed? Quarterhorse is part of the force pool planners have made available for the Election Support Mission. I figure they reasoned this way:

- we're close
- we're good
- we're Big Red One
- and we can go there and get back quick.

When — I think the election will occur in July. I think we will deploy in June. I think we will return in August. Remember that the EFOR is an event force. Postpone the election date and you postpone the EFOR deployment.[3]

To our great relief, Quarterhorse was later told to disregard the warning order. The municipal elections had been postponed until September. By that time, we would be heavily involved in home station pre-gunnery training. But Bosnia lingered in the background for more than a year. Prospects of a return haunted us every so often.

On February 13, 1997, the day after our block leave ended, the 1st Infantry Division held an official welcome-home ceremony for Quarterhorse at our airfield on Conn Barracks. Numerous individual achievement awards were presented. Armed Forces Service Medals and NATO Service Medals were also presented to those who had not already received them in troop-level ceremonies in Bosnia back in November.[4]

Now back on duty, Quarterhorse focused on reestablishing garrison systems and conducting much-needed vehicle services. All twelve of the tanks that we'd left behind in Schweinfurt were non-mission capable even though we had left their crews with them and had made a deal with another unit to provide maintenance support while Quarterhorse was deployed. The tasks of cleaning up, setting up, and moving in were difficult and compounded by the need to rapidly prepare for upcoming major training events.[5]

All of our vehicles were in dire need of quality services. During Operation Joint Endeavor, our 409 vehicles and ground equipment items operated at nearly two and a half times their normal annual rate. Quarterhorse drove a combined total of 785,117 miles. In spite of this usage, Quarterhorse mechanics sustained an operational readiness rate of 92 percent for pacing items (tanks and Bradleys) and 93 percent overall during the last nine months.[6] This was a remarkable achievement, considering that the U.S. Army standard for units in garrison was only 90 percent.

In Bosnia, our sixteen Kiowa Warriors flew at nearly four times their normal annual rate. Air crews and mechanics sustained a mission capable rate above 80 percent for the year. Nearly one-third of all flight hours were flown at night with night vision goggles.[7] Our air cavalry troops deserved further praise for having sustained only one major flight accident during the entire year.

Quarterhorse officers were informed that U.S. Army Europe (USAREUR) headquarters wanted to assess how badly our conventional warfighting abilities had atrophied during our year-long stability operation. USAREUR also needed to gauge how long it would take to get units back into fighting condition. Operation Joint Endeavor had been the longest operational deployment conducted by heavy U.S. Army combat forces since the Vietnam War. Quarterhorse was the designated guinea pig. Having been back on duty a mere six weeks, we were deployed again for two months of combat training at Grafenwoehr and Hohenfels.[8]

Thanks to the Army's personnel management system (the proverbial tail that wagged the dog), our veteran squadron essentially ceased to exist within ninety days of our redeployment from Bosnia. Quarterhorse underwent a massive turnover of leadership at all levels. MAJ Elias departed immediately for the Fifth Corps Headquarters. MAJ John Keraus, his replacement as squadron executive officer, had joined us in Bosnia in the fall. MAJ Roberts soon departed as well. All seven cavalry troops changed commanders within an eight-week period. Captain Jeff Erron left Charlie Troop in late January and was replaced by Captain Conor Cusick, our squadron supply officer. Captain Rich Spiegel, the squadron Rear Detachment commander, assumed command of Alpha Troop from Captain Semuel Shaw. Captain Brian McFadden departed Delta Troop and was replaced by Captain Tim MacDonald, a new arrival to Quarterhorse. Captain Joe Wawro relinquished command of HHT to Captain Bryan Denny, who had served as an assistant operations officer in Bosnia. Captain Mark Viney replaced Captain Bob Ivy as commander of Bravo Troop. Another newcomer, Captain Tom Voneschenbach, assumed command of Echo Troop from Captain Kerry Brunson, who moved over to replace Fox Troop's Commander, Captain Gary Stevens.[9] Simultaneously, Quarterhorse lost a large number of lieutenants and NCOs to normal personnel rotation. Those who remained were reshuffled into new duty positions.

Thus, it was an entirely green Quarterhorse that deployed to Grafenwoehr Training Area (GTA) in late March 1997 to conduct our first complete gunnery since October 1995. Tank and Bradley crews completed individual vehicle qualifications, as did our Kiowa Warrior crews. Despite protests from some of the new troop commanders over the lack of available train-up time, our scout and tank platoons received external evaluations on their maneuver proficiency during a "Three Day War" Situational Training Exercise (STX).[10]

After less than a week of rest at home, Quarterhorse deployed to Hohenfels Training Area (HTA) in the first week of May. After a few days in garrison there, our ground cavalry troops spent a week on troop-level STX lanes that replicated our conventional combat missions. Kiowa Warriors from both air cavalry troops flew in direct support, permitting us to hone our air-ground coordination measures.

Quarterhorse then "went to war" against the excellent Opposing Force (OPFOR) in a series of ostensible cavalry missions. The reality was, however, that our assigned missions were nothing more than the same mock battles of annihilation typically fought by armor and infantry task forces at HTA. Most of our officers, some Observer/Controllers (OCs), and even Major General Meigs, the commanding general of the 1st Infantry Division, all complained that the missions we were assigned were completely inappropriate for a division cavalry squadron.[11]

Our training at HTA was unsatisfactory for two reasons. The missions that Quarterhorse was evaluated on were quantifiable against the performances of regular line units, but they did not support our primary combat mission of providing reconnaissance and security to our parent division. Secondly, the training was conducted far too soon. While the OCs and our own officers marveled at how well Quarterhorse managed to perform, all were in concurrence that our proficiency was far below what it should have been by the end of our multi-million-dollar training rotation. Brigadier General Reginald Clemmons, the 1st Infantry Division's assistant division commander for maneuver, said Quarterhorse "had attained baseline proficiency in conventional warfighting operations."[12] Had we invested the same $15 million on this training a few months later, we could have achieved far more.

During our final after-action review at Hohenfels, Quarterhorse officers brainstormed our training needs and suggested many creative ways to achieve them. We implemented a few of them over the subsequent months, but the majority were simply unfeasible due to inadequate training time, money, ammunition, and maneuver area. Besides, our hands were full with the multitude of administrative duties that typically bog units down in garrison.

Immediately upon Quarterhorse's return to Schweinfurt in the last week of May, we conducted recovery activities for two weeks. Our mechanics then resumed conducting much-needed annual services on our vehicles.

On June 13, the night before Quarterhorse began its second much-needed block leave period of the year, we held an all-ranks formal ball in the beautiful medieval castle over the Main River in Mainberg.[13] Everyone had a great time and drunkenly continued our process of decompression.

Earlier, in mid–June, MAJ Gregory Tubbs, the new squadron operations officer, convened a meeting with all seven troop commanders. He had been on the phone with his buddies in USAREUR headquarters. Reportedly, USAREUR regretted putting Quarterhorse through our recent breakneck schedule. MAJ Tubbs told us that USAREUR planners admitted to him the error of sending us to Grafenwoehr and Hohenfels when we were nowhere near ready to train there.[14]

USAEUR also supposedly admitted its mistake of keeping the original Task Force Eagle in Bosnia for too long. It had been an experiment, but the strain on our soldiers and their families was recognized as too severe. (LTC Harriman had recently briefed BG Clemmons on the family life of a typical Quarterhorse pilot who had been home less than two months out of the previous eighteen.) From here on out, subsequent Sustainment Force (SFOR) deployments to Bosnia would last only six months.[15]

Our troop commanders were much relieved by all this great news. Our higher-ups had finally come to their senses! Our elation was cut short when the door to the meeting room burst open and a panting runner announced that the squadron commander wanted to see MAJ Tubbs and all three air cavalry troop commanders in his office immediately.

About an hour later, CPT Tim MacDonald emerged from LTC Harriman's office with an ashen face. He looked like he had been punched in the gut. We could not believe what he'd been told. The substance of our meeting with MAJ Tubbs turned out to be rubbish. Our three air cavalry troops had just been alerted that they would return to Bosnia for up to three months and that they had less than a week to prepare.[16]

Our anticipated and badly needed two-week block leave was only days away. The impact of this bad news was staggering to the morale of all Quarterhorse families. Those directly affected by the announcement also had to stomach the waste of money already spent on travel arrangements for block leave.

Just a week later, Quarterhorse received even worse news. A tasking had come down requiring a number of our NCOs to run tank ranges at Taborfalva for two months. Incredibly, those selected had less than twenty-four hours' notice to depart.[17]

Upon receipt of these orders, CPTs Cusick and Viney both immediately phoned their protests to LTC Harriman, but to no avail. Neither relished having to call one of their platoon sergeants in the middle of a four-day weekend to spring this news on him. One NCO from Bravo Troop was literally walking out the door with his five kids to go on a camping trip when he got the call. His dismayed reaction was predictable (and preventable, had staff officers at higher echelons acted in a more timely fashion.)

A small team of irate Quarterhorse NCOs was sent to Hungary in accordance with the short suspense. This tasking, along with the deployment of one of our air cavalry troops, exacerbated the general weariness that pervaded our squadron. Morale dropped considerably. By mid–June 1997, Quarterhorse was exhausted.

Some good news that month was that Specialist Kyle Wren was finally awarded the Soldiers Medal he had earned back in February 1996. SPC Wren was the Humvee driver who had saved his fellow cavalryman's life during the rollover accident on Mount Vis. He was the fourth Bravo Troop cavalryman to receive the award. Specialist Alcantar from "Alpha Fortieth" was the fifth member of Quarterhorse to receive the Soldiers Medal. To our knowledge, these five cavalrymen were the only American soldiers within the 20,000-strong Task Force Eagle to receive the nation's highest peacetime award for gallantry during Operation Joint Endeavor.[18] SPC Wren's award ceremony could have been an occasion for celebration for Quarterhorse, but LTC Harriman opted to keep it low-key. The ceremony was conducted with little fanfare before a small audience.

During July through September, we devoted our attention once again to restoring our garrison operating systems. Quarterhorse also conducted more home station pre-gunnery training at Conn Barracks. Platoon-level STX training at the Area Mike local training area was another event added to our already full calendar. In early October, Quarterhorse returned to Grafenwoehr for more gunnery training.

On October 11, we returned to Schweinfurt for a squadron change of command ceremony. Like clockwork, the duration of battalion-level command tours was two years. LTC Harriman's time was up. On October 13, he relinquished command and departed for the division staff.[19] During the ceremony, mention was made that Quarterhorse had been awarded the Army Superior Unit Award for our distinguished service in Bosnia.

LTC Harriman had the following final words for us:

> I ask you do what you have always done: soldier.... We went through rough times, exciting times, sad times, and boring times together. We went through deployment. We went through redeployment.... I'll go proud to say that I served among you.... You are prepared. You are loyal. You are cavalry. You are the best of Soldiers. You are Quarterhorse.[20]

LTC Harriman's successor was Lieutenant Colonel James W. Shufelt, Jr. Like LTC Harriman, LTC Shufelt was a West Pointer with a considerable cavalry background. His arrival breathed new life into Quarterhorse, as did that of the new 1st Infantry Division commanding general, Major General David L. Grange. LTC Shufelt reintroduced basic unit activities that LTC

Harriman had eschewed — squadron runs, awards ceremonies, newcomer briefings, and farewell breakfasts for departing cavalrymen. Under LTC Shufelt, Family Support Groups rose to the fore of importance as well.

MG Grange confirmed that conventional warfighting, not stability operations, was our new training focus.[21] We spent November and December preparing troop areas and activities for the external inspections that were later conducted in January 1998.

In December, our ground and air cavalry troops implemented MG Grange's instructions to develop air assault capabilities. Troop commanders led a series of aerial insertions, air assaults, aerial zone recons, and screens. A JAAT exercise was also conducted with the 1st Battalion, 1st Aviation (1-1 AV), 2nd Battalion, 1st Aviation (2-1 AV), and 6th Squadron, 6th Cavalry (6-6 CAV).

Several Quarterhorse cavalry troops concluded the year with troop-level Christmas parties. Many of our officers attended a winter ball hosted by our neighbor, the 2nd Brigade, 1st Infantry Division.[22] A new year dawned for the weary cavalrymen of Quarterhorse, and with it came the prospect of adding yet another chapter to our squadron's distinguished history.

# CONCLUSION

Several factors contributed to the remarkable success achieved by Quarterhorse within the unique constraints of the Bosnian operational environment. Thorough planning enabled our squadron to anticipate major events or incidents and then to act quickly and decisively when they occurred. Effective use of available intelligence gathering assets resulted in good situational awareness. Active force protection measures sustained combat strength. Information operations effectively managed factions' expectations. Versatile and agile application of overwhelming combat power enabled Quarterhorse to overcome operational challenges and to deter or defuse confrontations with and among the factions. These means were facilitated by the high quality of our soldiers; the caring, communicative nature of our chain of command; and the high esprit de corps that Quarterhorse enjoyed. An appropriate level of concern for and communications with our families indirectly influenced the success of our mission.

In 1996, it was commonly understood that American commanders must contend with the issue of domestic support for military operations. This requirement had its roots in the Vietnam experience, the massacre of U.S. Marines in Beirut in 1983, and most recently in the horrifying images of dead American soldiers being dragged through the streets of Mogadishu just over two years before Operation Joint Endeavor commenced. The relatively bloodless 1991 Persian Gulf War and combat operations in Grenada and Panama fostered a false expectation that modern military campaigns can, and therefore *must*, be waged with minimal loss of American lives. Deepening concern over the growing number of American soldiers killed in Iraq and Afghanistan is a constant reminder that the Achilles' heel of American foreign policy is our national aversion to casualties.

This constraint necessitated two priorities in Bosnia, the first being to manage expectations of the American public. The second was to adopt active force protection measures to minimize losses to U.S. forces.

As for managing public expectations for the amount of time, money, and materiel required to achieve NATO's objectives in Bosnia, the Clinton administration set itself up for increasing criticism by sticking with its politically expedient but disingenuous assertions from the outset of the operation that American troops would be withdrawn in a year. As the months passed, the reality loomed ever more apparent that enduring success would require a much longer commitment. Force reshaping sustained the American presence in Bosnia, albeit at ever lower numbers. American soldiers did not finally leave Bosnia until NATO officially concluded its peacekeeping operations there nine years later! As of December 2011, the American military commitment in the Balkans continues, with 750 soldiers still serving in Kosovo.[1] President Clinton invited the criticisms hurled at his administration for not setting expectations upfront with the press, the Congress, and the American people.

The imperative of minimizing losses to U.S. forces manifested itself two ways in Bosnia: in the centralization of planning and execution, and in a host of active force protection measures.

As a division cavalry squadron, Quarterhorse was doctrinally geared towards the decentralized execution of tactical missions. Decentralization required trust and confidence in junior leaders to act within the stated parameters of the commander's intent and the rules of engagement. We intended for our junior leaders to act with appropriate latitude, tempered with a degree of control reflecting an appreciation for the potential strategic impact of tactical actions in stability operations.

Yet, in the opinion of many Quarterhorse junior officers, tactical actions in Bosnia were more centrally planned, executed, and controlled than was warranted. To their mind, senior commanders and their staffs possessed an apparently insatiable appetite for minute tactical information. Their hunger was fueled by the capabilities of modern information technology to provide them with ever-more-detailed and timely information. The fear was that senior commanders would accustom themselves to becoming directly involved in the most minor of actions, as some battalion and brigade commanders had done in Vietnam. Illustrating this trend was the direct involvement on the scene by LTG Walker, Brigadier Weedy, and COL Batiste in the Han Pijesak incidents, by LTG Walker in the second Mahala incident, and by BG Cherrie in the Zvornik Seven incident, as well as by BG Casey in the Jusici standoff.

Our junior officers noted the dichotomy between the centralized command and control exercised in stability operations and our Army's *warfighting* doctrine — the doctrine we were imbued with. Our cavalrymen understood very well that junior leader initiative and decentralized execution within the commander's broad intent are essential to success *on the battlefield*. Stability operations, on the other hand, evidenced a great deal more personal action by senior commanders at the tactical level than many in our ranks had anticipated or could appreciate.

Their resentment was warranted, but not fully. The centralized command and control exercised by our senior commanders in Bosnia was heavily influenced by the reality that in stability operations tactical decisions made under duress by junior officers and NCOs have the potential to spawn unforeseen strategic results. Radio commentator Paul Harvey illustrated this point magnificently with his tale about the British corporal ordering the Boston Massacre. Other facts bearing consideration were that most of us were novices in our roles as peacekeepers, and that this was our first "real world" operational deployment. On these grounds, the direct involvement of senior IFOR leaders in sensitive major incidents was justifiable. But to many of our young leaders, their involvement was taken as a general lack of faith in our abilities and reflected a cover-your-ass mentality that also seemed to inspire our force protection measures.

The second manifestation of the imperative to minimize American losses in Bosnia was the host of active force protection measures adopted by Task Force Eagle to reduce the threat from potential enemies, accidents, and illnesses.

In his commander's intent for the operation, MG Nash admitted, "Ultimately, we will be judged by our ability to protect our forces in this highly uncertain, difficult, and lethal environment. Therefore, I expect commanders and leaders to take the required measures to care for, secure, and protect their Soldiers and organizations."[2]

Quarterhorse did not know with certainty whether any of the former warring factions would engage us as we entered sector and then acted to contain their forces. We assumed that they would, and so prepared for the possibility. We were also aware that foreign militant groups had hostile intentions towards IFOR. Communications intercepted in Bosnia between Muslim extremists from Iran and other Middle East countries suggested that the ideological war against the West that came to full light in September 2001 was, in fact, already underway five years earlier.

Our combat forces and lodgment areas were fully prepared for any attack, as was evidenced by Workhorse Troop's rapid response to the small arms fire incident in the Thunderdome in November. The same could not be said of Quarterhorse logistical convoys. Just as vulnerable then in Bosnia as they were in Iraq and are in Afghanistan today, logistics convoys were IFOR's soft underbelly. Unarmored vehicles with only one crew-served weapon per convoy would have made easy targets for terrorists intent on exploiting America's limited tolerance for casualties.

Up-armored Humvees were a new development in 1996, and Quarter-horse received but a few. Measures such as the armoring of some truck cabs and the issue of Kevlar blankets as protection against mine strikes were steps in the right direction.

Another protective measure that Quarterhorse should have implemented but did not was the provision of armored gun shields for our machine gunners standing half-exposed out the top of our Humvees. When this suggestion was made to the Quarterhorse chain of command, it was dismissed as unwarranted and an impediment to turning in the vehicles at the end of our tour. The first reason cited was defensible. The second was egregious.

True, no ambushes on IFOR convoys had yet occurred. Therefore, the *probability* of attack was assumed to be low. But U.S. Army experience in Somalia just two years earlier had already demonstrated the catastrophic *severity* of small arms fire against Humvee gunners who were not afforded any means of armor protection. Thus, it was in the second and third steps of the Army's Risk Management Process — those of assessing the hazards and developing controls — that Quarterhorse was deficient.[3] Subsequent experience in Iraq and Afghanistan, where the vast preponderance of American casualties has resulted from ambushes and improvised explosive device attacks on our convoys, confirms the need to control the severity of such attacks through better crew protection.

Had our ground cavalry troops mounted improvised gun shields atop their vehicles as our predecessors did upon their arrival in Vietnam in 1965, then perhaps the same measure would have been implemented by Quarterhorse three years after Operation Join Endeavor. Had that occurred, the near ambush of a lone Bravo Troop Humvee by Serb forces in Macedonia might not have resulted in the capture of three cavalrymen. Instead, the gunner likely would have manned his weapon in self-defense instead of merely dropping down into the relative safety of the vehicle without returning fire.[4]

Given that IFOR convoys were such easy targets, why then were they never attacked? To some degree, because of our force protection measures. American soldiers wearing full "battle rattle" everywhere, all the time, created a perception of readiness. The appearance of strength was an important deterrent. The ubiquitous presence of our armored vehicles and armed helicopters certainly helped in the Han Pijesak incidents, which illustrated the intransigence of some faction military leaders and the latent animosity extant toward foreign peacekeepers. But potential adversaries were unwilling to challenge IFOR's resolve to the point of provoking our wrath. This had less to do with our force protection measures and overwhelming combat power and more with the fact that the Bosnians were simply tired of fighting. After three and a half years of civil war, the factions were militarily spent. Peace suited each entity's objectives. They grudgingly accepted IFOR's presence as a means to securing the peace.

When it comes to protecting one's force, there is a fine line between prudence and paranoia. Many Quarterhorse junior leaders were convinced that Task Force Eagle had stepped way over that line. They perceived that the Clinton administration's hypersensitivity to incurring casualties trickled down the chain of command. A zero-defects culture seemed to be contaminating our Army. Proof was in the collective overreaction to the death of the first American soldier in Bosnia. Quarterhorse observed it firsthand when "the circus" descended on the scene of our first mine-strike incident.

On the contrary, our senior military leaders understood that minimizing casualties was a measure of success, like it or not. Force protection was a specified task from the Department of Defense. Therefore, a considerable, even startling, level of attention was indeed lavished on casualty-producing incidents. They were examined in detail and probed for lessons to be applied in subsequent policies and procedures so that no other soldiers would be lost for the same reasons. What was there to complain about that?

Whether force protection was prudence or just covering one's ass depended largely on the rank of the observer. Most Quarterhorse junior leaders and cavalrymen accepted the stated rationale. We also understood how our general confinement to lodgment areas protected us from numerous health hazards that exposure to the Bosnian population would likely induce, not that we enjoyed being "prisoners for peace."

A much harder policy to appreciate was the total restriction on the consumption of alcohol for all American soldiers in Bosnia. We were fully and enviously aware that our IFOR allies drank beer on their bases and in towns among the locals. Why couldn't we? Weren't we much better soldiers than those of our allied nations? Everything we witnessed convinced us that this was so. If our leaders trusted us enough to operate multi-million-dollar vehicles and aircraft under dangerous operational conditions, then why couldn't they trust us to drink responsibly within reasonable limitations? The bottom line, confirmed by veterans of the Korean and Vietnam Wars, is that the consumption of alcohol in a combat environment, no matter how tightly controlled, has a debilitating effect upon good order, readiness, and discipline.

A legitimate criticism that could be leveled against Task Force Eagle headquarters was its failure to ensure that the rationale for such a controversial policy was understood all the way down the chain of command. Our junior leaders could hardly defend it and help our soldiers appreciate that the restriction was in their best interest if all they knew was that "the Commanding General said so." Inspector General sensing sessions might have uncovered and helped rectify the disconnect and source of great resentment.

Another deficiency regarding the policy banning alcohol consumption was that it was not attuned to the cultural reality in Bosnia. Our junior leaders engaging local civilian and military leaders were initially torn over the propriety of partaking in customary toasts of *slivovitz* before getting down to business. It wasn't long before many simply ignored the prohibition. This prompted murmurings of hypocrisy and double standards within Quarterhorse. The general order should have been amended accordingly.

Quarterhorse confirmed in Bosnia that the structure of the heavy division cavalry squadron adopted following Operation Desert Storm provided for a lethal, versatile, and agile organization capable of achieving great depth and synchronization for the retention of the initiative. The structure proved as suitable for stability operations as for combat. Fielding of the OH-58D Kiowa Warrior in 1995 gave Quarterhorse a highly valued intelligence-gathering capability unique within Task Force Eagle and unavailable to 1-1 CAV with its 1960s-vintage OH-58Cs.

Units operating in an austere environment require certain mission-specific, non-organic equipment. Light sets, generators, and Small Unit Snow Vehicles (SUSVs) were all critical to Quarterhorse in Bosnia. Severely limiting their impact, however, this equipment was issued on the eve of our deployment and with limited operator training and no parts or maintenance support. New equipment must be fielded in a timely manner along with a system for maintaining it. Otherwise, it soon becomes useless.

Quarterhorse observed that the requirement for maintaining overwhelming combat power applies as much in stability operations as it does in combat. Tanks and other armored vehicles played a vital role in force presence and deterrence in Bosnia. Task Force Eagle got this right down there, and we were successful. Yet, just three years later, the U.S. Army committed the same blunder that contributed to the debacle in Somalia in 1993.

In early 1999, when the Quarterhorse mission in Macedonia changed from one of United Nations peacekeeping to NATO deterrence, our squadron did not have its armored vehicles and armed helicopters to perform our new, more dangerous screen mission along the rugged Serbian border. Quarterhorse remained largely dismounted and understrength, and had limited wheeled and tracked vehicle support for our widely dispersed elements. The result was the humiliating capture of three Quarterhorse cavalrymen in March 1999 by Serb forces who penetrated the squadron's ineffectual screen line.[5]

In Bosnia in 1996, Quarterhorse and Task Force Eagle brought superior firepower and protection to bear. Overwhelming combat power was persuasive in compelling VRS submission to inspections of its headquarters at Han Pijesak on several occasions, quelling riots in the two Mahala incidents, and deterring any serious attacks on our lodgment areas. On the other hand, our lack of adequate combat power on the scene during the Zvornik Seven incident emboldened the Serb mob surrounding the IPTF compound and jeopardized the security of MAJ Roberts's patrol.

In Bosnia, Quarterhorse demonstrated the hallmarks of a disciplined unit. While performing myriad missions pursuant to enforcing the peace, we also continued to train, perform routine maintenance, and plan for future missions. Joint, combined-arms, live-fire training events like those conducted at Resolute Barbara range sustained our conventional warfighting skills and our ability to respond rapidly with overwhelming force to incidents such as those at Han Pijesak and Mahala. They also signaled a strong warning to the faction leaders who observed them.

COL Batiste attributed the success of his brigade combat team to the fact that our operations were deliberate, synchronized, rehearsed, and well-executed.[6] Task Force Eagle's relatively smooth occupation of its sector and the immediate assumption of stability tasks by combat units like Quarterhorse demonstrated the value of good planning, realistic training, and deliberate execution of the operations order (OPORD).

On the other hand, strategic and operational planners failed to adequately synchronize logistical support with the maneuver aspect of the operation. This compelled Quarterhorse to assume the unusual mission of providing logistical support to the rest of 2 BCT for nearly two months until the 47th FSB became fully functional. Why this task devolved to our cavalry squadron baffled us, especially given that the 1st Armored Division had ostensibly had three years to refine its plan for the occupation of Bosnia. The truth was more complex.[7] Quarterhorse later boasted of our success as logisticians during the most active and dangerous portion of the operation, but we would much rather have preferred that combat service support units were better integrated into the flow of Task Force Eagle elements deploying into Bosnia.

Agility and versatility were required of units and leaders at all levels in Bosnia. Quarterhorse embodied these attributes, which are as essential in stability operations as they are in combat. We demonstrated laudable agility by rapidly shifting our forces from other missions to contain and defuse the two Mahala incidents. Our ad hoc logistics support to 2 BCT testified to the versatility of Quarterhorse and to the resourcefulness of our cavalrymen. Quarterhorse mechanics served as combat engineers when situations required it, such as when HHT welders disassembled and removed a derelict bus from a roadway in Kalesija, and when Alpha Troop mechanics employed their M88 recovery vehicle as a bulldozer to clear obstacles from the road between Kladanj and Vlasenica.

IFOR was responsible for accomplishing the military objectives of the General Framework Agreement for Peace (GFAP). With the exception of the removal of land mines, these military objectives were achievable within a matter of months. Most Quarterhorse officers seemed to comprehend IFOR's intrinsic obligation to also provide certain, limited support for the accomplishment of the GFAP's political objectives as well. These sought no less than to overcome generations of ethnic animosity and to restructure Bosnian national institutions. They necessitated a long-term international commitment. Although certainly not keen for Quarterhorse to remain in Bosnia for a year, or even beyond six months for that matter, we did wish for our successes to be followed through and capitalized upon. We sensed that an enduring American military presence would be required in Bosnia if the United States was serious about our international commitments there.

At the outset of the operation, senior civilian and military leaders wrangled over how IFOR would support the political objectives of the GFAP. It was appropriate that American Secretary of Defense Perry refused in early January 1996 to allow IFOR to assume the primary function of the fledgling and still ineffectual International Police Task Force (IPTF).[8]

Later that month, Admiral Smith refused to provide the logistical support and security requested by the International Criminal Tribunal for War Crimes in the Former Yugoslavia (ICTY) to facilitate its investigations. The request was not for IFOR to supplant the ICTY, but merely to provide limited support that only IFOR could provide. Therefore, it was a legitimate request. Admiral Smith was corrected by American Assistant Secretary of State for Human Rights John H.F. Shattuck.[9]

This sort of wrangling over the proper use of military force in support of nonmilitary functions was a good and necessary discourse. IFOR's proper role was not to assume direct responsibility for nation-building tasks, but merely to provide logistical and security support to the various international and nongovernmental organizations (NGOs) whose legitimate purview they were.

IFOR's mission in support of the Bosnian national elections was appropriately defined. We did not run the polling stations nor secure them directly. Rather, we conducted an effective intelligence preparation of the battlefield (IPB), arrayed our forces accordingly, and established a secure climate for other election support organizations to do their jobs. Information operations constituted a huge part of this endeavor. Thus, IFOR enabled the Bosnian people to vote without fear of attack or harassment. That no weapons were discovered on Muslim voters at the Quarterhorse busload transload point spoke volumes about the level of trust and confidence we had engendered by our information operations.

Recalling the debilitative effect of the loss of neutrality on the United Nations mission in Somalia, IFOR strove to maintain the neutral, moral high ground among the three squabbling Bosnian factions. The mandated task of training and arming the Federation military was a potential pitfall that could have cost NATO its impartial status had it not been outsourced to an outside party. Rightly, this kept IFOR units focused on our stability tasks at hand.

During the resettlement confrontations in Jusici and Mahala, Quarterhorse was compelled to intercede in the middle of factional disputes in order to prevent or contain violence before it spiraled out of control. Playing umpire between the conniving, accusatory, and self-aggrandizing factions was a tricky business and always risked alienating one side or the other. The riot that ensued when Quarterhorse enquired into the treatment of the Zvornik Seven detainees by Bosnian Serb police well illustrated this point.

NATO's stated objectives of providing for a lasting peace in Bosnia did not seem to jibe with our senior civilian leaders' decision not to pursue indicted war criminals. To many within Quarterhorse, this stance was hypocritical, even cowardly. It announced the fragility of our resolve. With all the firepower at our disposal, it made little sense to allow indicted war criminals to remain free instead of bringing them to justice before an international war crimes tribunal. But the imperative of maintaining our neutral status weighed heavily upon our senior leaders' decisions. GEN Shalikashvili vowed that IFOR would not be drawn into the mission creep that had sunk the UN effort in Somalia three years earlier. In consequence, indicted Bosnian Serb political leader Radovan Karadzic remained free until July 2008. (Interestingly, his capture occurred twelve years to the day after his indictment for war crimes.[10]) Bosnian Serb General Ratko Mladic remained at large for fifteen years.

Having been surprised by the first Mahala incident in April, Quarterhorse soon became more adept at synchronizing our organic and attached intelligence gathering assets with those of higher headquarters. This flexible arrangement of complimentary sources provided highly valuable information that Quarterhorse employed to anticipate events, allocate assets, and prioritize tasks. Our achievement and sustainment of good situational awareness throughout our sector enabled us to take a more proactive approach to the difficult issues of freedom of movement and the resettlement of refugees. Such was the value of the amalgam of intelligence that we derived from multiple sources, including especially the human intelligence (humint) drawn from close, frequent contacts with local leaders, that LTC Harriman accurately predicted a second major confrontation brewing in Mahala weeks before it erupted in August.

Achieving a common operating picture (COP) with a high degree of accuracy during an unfolding incident is a difficult task, as was evidenced during the second Mahala incident. But a reasonably accurate COP developed among and communicated to all players involved that day permitted Quarterhorse to change mission focus and rapidly reallocate our forces.

Good situational awareness also enabled us to adjust force protection levels in our lodgment areas appropriate to the changing threat. HHT's rapid response to the small-arms fire incident in the Thunderdome in November was largely attributable to good crosstalk among junior leaders that facilitated a quick assessment of the situation.

Whether in combat or peacekeeping operations, leaders at every level must lead by example. The vast majority of Quarterhorse officers and NCOs were dedicated, competent, and caring leaders worthy of emulation. SFC Iacono epitomized the aggressive, courageous scout platoon sergeant. Aware of the danger as his section ventured into the mine-laden ZOS, he did not ask his subordinates to do what he himself was unwilling to do. For that reason, his Bradley assumed the lead and subsequently struck an antitank mine. In the second Quarterhorse mine-strike incident, SFC Iacono again endangered himself while coordinating efforts to evacuate the wounded from the minefield. Contrast his conspicuous efforts with the notable absence of the senior engineer officer on the scene, who quietly slipped away after the explosion.

The Quarterhorse chain of command dealt inappropriately with the young tank platoon leader from Bravo Troop who lost control of his dismounted patrol in June. His deficient leadership was already well-known. This incident, capping a pattern of mediocre performance, should have prompted his relief. In the midst of a fast-paced and dangerous operation with soldiers' lives on the line, he should have been swapped out with one of our lieutenants in the Rear Detachment as soon as possible. He was not.

Our leadership also failed to act upon subsequent recommendations to segregate living arrangements according to rank, an appropriate measure that should have been taken early in the operation when Quarterhorse moved out of its vehicles and into tents. This would have afforded a modicum of separation beneficial to all ranks. The convenience of billeting by organization was contrary to the time-honored traditions of the U.S. Army and not worth the debilitating effect on good order and discipline. Over an extended period, overfamiliarity bred contempt.

When Quarterhorse entered Bosnia in early 1996, we expected to engage in combat. This proved unnecessary, and so we became diplomats, mediators, and crowd control specialists. In these capacities, we employed an entirely different skill set than what we'd honed in training for combat. Our primary weapons became bluff, negotiation, arbitration, and restraint. Stability operations required our leaders to be multidimensional, to possess soft people skills and hard tactical and technical expertise.

LTC Harriman and MAJ Roberts both exemplified the successful stability operations officer. Both were competent cavalrymen. Both were adept negotiators and arbitrators. They understood when to draw a hard line and when to keep things casual. They also maintained a healthy degree of skepticism towards the self-aggrandizing claims of the competing factions. Quarterhorse leaders recognized from the duplicitous actions of Muslim "refugees" in the first Mahala incident and those of Serbs and Muslims alike during the Zvornik Seven incident that there were no truly good guys in Bosnia. This understanding enabled us to remain impartial. Just as U.S. Army leaders serving in Iraq and Afghanistan today understand the criticality of getting to know the local power players in their sectors, so too did our Quarterhorse leadership in 1996. Lauded by the OSCE official who couldn't believe the number of locals that we knew, Quarterhorse apparently grasped this imperative better than many Task Force Eagle units did.[11]

Abiding by public affairs guidance from higher up to afford open access to the press, Quarterhorse was surprised when stung by negative reporting that such access sometimes allows. From the sensational reporting of internal discord over the medical evacuation of the injured Muslim boy, Quarterhorse came to appreciate the maxim that the military cannot always trust the press to report in its favor. Sensationalism sells. Most often, however, we found that a certain level of friendly but guarded openness with reporters resulted in favorable reporting, such as the article about our Alpha Troop scouts on patrol, a good story that provided the public with an accurate picture of stability operations at our muddy-boots level. Quarterhorse knew well enough to avoid obfuscation or the deliberate withholding of information. We were proud of our work and eagerly shared our information with the press.

Another important aspect of leadership during operational deployments is maintaining effective communications with subordinates. Commanders at task force, brigade, and squadron level all made effective use of printed communications to impart their messages. Verbal communication not being his strong suit, LTC Harriman relied instead upon his considerable writing talent to communicate to Quarterhorse. His biweekly "Crosstalk" newsletters conveyed his understanding of the situation, his guidance on issues of command importance, prioritization of efforts, and warnings on safety and force protection issues, as well as his attaboys for accomplishments well performed. The newsletters fostered situational awareness and also assisted with internal expectation management too, but not as well. LTC Harriman addressed the important soldier issues of leave and redeployment squarely, yet failed to shape our cavalrymen's expectations on the highly charged issue of end-of-tour awards. The disappointment and frustration felt by many Quarterhorse cavalrymen, expressed rather embarrassingly in the *Stars and Stripes*, evidenced this particular deficiency.

As the spring of 1996 plodded into summer, our stability tasks grew increasingly mundane. Our operational security began to lag as the frequency of serious incidents diminished. Under such conditions, Quarterhorse leaders were obligated to keep our cavalrymen's heads in the game, to remind them of the ever-present threat, and to avoid complacency. Our chain of command responded fairly well with newsletters, pep talks, and on-the-spot corrections.

Particularly susceptible to boredom were our tower guards and occupants of vehicles on convoy. It was essential that they remain on their toes and alert for potential threats, not merely being physically ready to respond, but mentally engaged by constantly thinking through what they would do in certain, sudden situations. Our usual, boring pre-convoy briefings and talk-through rehearsals could have been spiced up with subordinate back-briefs and walk-through rehearsals of increasingly higher levels of detail to cover various contingencies. Members of our chain of command might also have visited our guard towers more often to quiz guards on how they would respond to hostile actions.

Leaders are supremely responsible for ensuring the safe conduct of their unit's missions. Effective planning among our air cavalry troop commanders succeeded in sustaining a high tempo of flight operations over an extended period. Our air cavalry troops' commitment to safety resulted in few aviation incidents. Blessedly, none of them were injury-sustaining.

Accidents that occurred, such as when the Bravo Troop cavalrymen attempted to jump free of their Humvee sliding on the ice, well illustrated the responsibility of junior leaders to reinforce safety directives issued by higher commanders. LTC Harriman's safety missive in April was a good reminder to all in Quarterhorse to stay alert for potential hazards and to take appropriate actions to prevent mishaps.

By and large, Quarterhorse cavalrymen were extremely intelligent. They wanted to know what was going on. They wanted to be treated as adults. They expected to be respected. Further reflecting our nation's democratic character, our cavalrymen were convinced that their opinions mattered. Smart Quarterhorse officers and NCOs listened to their subordinates. They exchanged information with them. Our leaders capitalized on good ideas readily shared by cavalrymen who were made to feel like valued members of the team. In Bosnia, Quarterhorse was blessed with such leaders and cavalrymen as these. This explained much of the high esprit de corps and camaraderie that we shared.

Indicative of the high quality of Quarterhorse enlisted men were our four cavalrymen and one attached engineer who earned the Soldiers Medal for individual acts of gallantry in Bosnia. They were not unique characters. Rather, they typified our rank and file. They were proud of their unit, felt a strong kinship with their buddies, knew that they could trust them with their own lives, and were disciplined enough to do the right thing when bad situations arose. Most other Quarterhorse cavalrymen would have acted in similar, laudable manners had other life-threatening incidents arisen.

Another ingredient to the high esprit de corps enjoyed by Quarterhorse, besides mutual trust and confidence both up and down the chain of command and laterally among peer groups, was the strong sense of identification that we felt with our squadron. To us, 1-4 CAV was not an abstract number on an organization chart. Rather, it was *Quarterhorse*, a team, an elite brotherhood that we were proud of and toward which we felt strong ownership and responsibility.

As with most American cavalry units, Quarterhorse fostered high esprit de corps by indoctrinating our members in the storied histories and traditions of our regiment and the mounted service. Vestigial accoutrements like Stetsons, spurs, sabers, and cavalry cheers went a long way toward building our cohesive and aggressive fighting spirit and our dedication to very high standards of performance. By incorporating unit history into our normal unit activities, our cavalrymen sensed the obligations inherent in the Quarterhorse legacy. They realized that our predecessors had set high standards of performance during incredibly trying circumstances, and that those of us currently embodying Quarterhorse must uphold their standards. Units of the British Army also accomplish this same effect very well. Therefore, the teambuilding events conducted by Quarterhorse in Bosnia, namely our Memorial Day ceremony and the Spur Dinner, were of great value and importance.

Unfortunately, Quarterhorse did not optimize every esprit-building event to its full advantage. It was regrettable that LTC Harriman chose not to make a big deal out of the award ceremony for SPC Wren following our redeployment. The Soldiers Medal is our nation's highest award for gallantry in noncombat situations. SPC Wren was the fifth member of Quarterhorse to receive this award. These heroes were the only American soldiers in the 20,000-man Task Force Eagle to receive the Soldiers Medal during Operation Joint Endeavor. This was a momentous occasion, not just for SPC Wren, but for all of Quarterhorse!

We should have held a squadron formation, invited the press and our families, and used the occasion to explain to our loved ones and to those Quarterhorse cavalrymen who had not served in Bosnia just what exactly we had accomplished down there. We also could have related our successful stability operation in Bosnia with those conducted by our predecessors in "Bleeding Kansas" in 1855, during Reconstruction in the post–Civil War South, the Indian Wars period, the Philippine Insurrection, and again during the post–World War II occupation of Germany. We had upheld the proud Quarterhorse legacy! It could have been a great esprit-building event. But it wasn't. LTC Harriman gave little explanation for his decision to keep the award ceremony low-key. Stress levels were high, and he probably wanted to minimize the number of activities on the Quarterhorse calendar.

LTC Harriman's successes far outweighed his shortcomings. To his great personal credit, he succeeded in making our attached engineer and military police companies, civil affairs, counterintel, psyops, and direct support maintenance teams all feel like they were equal partners in the Quarterhorse team. There was no "us and them" mentality. He also broke down the barriers that existed when our air cavalry troops rejoined our ground cavalry troops in the fall of 1995. In LTC Harriman's eyes, all of us were Quarterhorse cavalrymen. Awarding spurs to the leaders of our supporting units was just one of the effective measures he employed toward this end. He also credited their small units' contributions toward meeting our mission in his periodic "Crosstalk" newsletters.

Our caring Quarterhorse leadership recognized the importance of providing information and support to our families in Germany during our extended tour in Bosnia. We anticipated correctly that family-related incidents back at home station would become significant distractions to our deployed cavalrymen. Therefore, it was imperative that Quarterhorse form a Rear Detachment of capable, compassionate leaders who were trained and prepared to care for our families in our absence. Working hand-in-hand with the Rear Detachment was our active Family Support Group led by highly motivated spouses.

The negative incidents involving property accountability, equipment maintenance, drug use, and adultery that occurred at home station illustrated the need to select strong leaders to remain behind to form the Rear Detachment chain of command. This is often a difficult choice, as senior commanders want to deploy with their strongest officers. U.S. Army Garrison commands and nondeployed senior headquarters must provide considerable administrative, legal, supply, maintenance, and behavioral health support to sustain the good order and discipline of a deployed unit's Rear Detachment.

The years 1996 and 1997 were challenging times for Quarterhorse cavalrymen and our families. Our experiences typified the strain upon U.S. Army units between the end of the Cold War and the dawn of the Global War on Terrorism. Historians would later categorize this period of U.S. military history as the Age of Interventions.

In the late 1990s, the U.S. Army found it increasingly difficult to maintain morale. Some old-timers who remembered the 1970s, one of the lowest eras in U.S. Army history, said that challenges to morale weren't a hell of a lot worse back then. But that was an overstatement. Nevertheless, in the decade following the end of the Cold War, the U.S. armed forces were cut in half. The national defense budget was also slashed by fifty percent. Incredibly, the tempo of "real world" operations *increased* by 300 percent![12] Stress was high on soldiers and their families unaccustomed to the many lengthy separations that this new operational tempo entailed. Now eleven years into the Global War on Terrorism, this sustained pace has become an enduring fact of Army life.

Many fine young officers and seasoned NCOs left the U.S. Army at the dawn of the new millennium. The economy was good back then. Pastures looked much too green in the civilian world. Fewer young soldiers saw the benefits of reenlisting as outweighing the costs. Money for college just wouldn't cut it, and it was no wonder. More and more, U.S. Army units were being sent on peacekeeping and humanitarian deployments to forlorn, irrelevant nations around the globe. The average American didn't give a damn about most of these places. Many Americans felt that our nation had offered up our armed forces to be the world's rent-a-cops. The benefits associated with military service were not attractive for recent high school graduates or young people with families. Recruiting and retention suffered.

Indicative of the high operational tempo of the time, Quarterhorse returned to the Balkans little more than two years after our return from Bosnia. In February 1999, Quarterhorse secured the border of Macedonia from possible Serb incursions. Thankfully, this deployment lasted a relatively short four months.[13] Our squadron's reputation and laudable service were tarnished by the capture of three Bravo Troop cavalrymen in a Serb ambush within Macedonian territory. U.S. Army spokesmen remained purposefully vague about the details of the incident.[14] The unintended result was that both the 1st Infantry Division and Quarterhorse were humiliated by the erroneous and speculative reporting that was not rebutted with the facts, however sensitive or embarrassing.

A component of the Army's retention problem since the 1990s is the fact that the majority of our soldiers are married. In the long term, Army families do not withstand the strain of prolonged absences as readily as soldiers themselves do. This was as true for the families of Quarterhorse in 1996 as it is today for those Army families dealing with multiple, extended deployments in support of the ongoing Global War on Terrorism.

Many officers were embittered by U.S. Army personnel management policies in effect during the 1990s. These policies were perceived to favor the career progression of individual officers over the sustainment of units' combat readiness. Many in Quarterhorse considered it the epitome of dumb bureaucracy that LTC Chamales had to relinquish command on the eve of our deployment to Bosnia just because he'd reached the end of his mandated command tour length. This, after two years of training and molding Quarterhorse into a cohesive and aggressive team that was confident in its leadership.

Equally lamentable was the wholesale turnover of leadership within Quarterhorse immediately following our redeployment. Our veteran squadron, so expert in stability operations, virtually ceased to exist overnight. Had Quarterhorse returned to Bosnia as a squadron in 1997 as part of SFOR election support, it would have been a mere shadow of its former self. Our massive outflow of institutional knowledge was hugely lamentable. Our mediocre performance in simulated combat at Hohenfels five months after our return from Bosnia well illustrated our sorry state of readiness.

Early in the Global War on Terrorism, the U.S. Army adjusted its personnel management policies to better facilitate the deployment of units fully trained for combat. This meant bringing units up to full strength well before their deployment date so that training is conducted and equipment is fielded, and even more importantly, so that teams can gel and bonds can form. Units are kept together longer nowadays, yet there still exists considerable loss of institutional knowledge following redeployment. Given the continual need for officers and noncommissioned officers to attend professional military education schools following combat tours, there seems little else that can be done to mitigate the rapid decline in combat readiness of our units following their redeployment.

The story of how Operation Joint Endeavor was executed at the tactical level is highly relevant to the ongoing Global War on Terrorism. General George Casey, Chief of Staff of the Army, stated to the author in 2009, "I don't think we could have done what we are doing in Iraq and Afghanistan without having done what we did in Bosnia first."[15] The doctrine and tactics, techniques, and procedures (TTPs) for today's stability operations had their genesis in the stability operations of the 1990s. The lessons learned, or more correctly in some instances *rediscovered*, by our peacekeepers in Bosnia surely resonate with deployed soldiers today.

A primary motivation behind this book was to provide a useful case study of modern U.S. Army operational deployments for cadets and junior officers to study. Understanding the Quarterhorse experience before, during, and after its tour in Bosnia will better help young leaders to prepare and lead their soldiers through all four phases of the deployment cycle.

Another use for this story is in teaching or reinforcing U.S. Army doctrine. Just as doctrinal terms are applied to describe and analyze campaigns and battles fought centuries ago, so too can the campaign analysis methodology be applied to Operation Joint Endeavor. Suitable illustrations can be found of our Principles of War and Operations, the Additional Principles of Joint Operations, Warfighting Functions, and Tenets of Army Operations, as well as both positive and negative examples of our eleven Leadership Principles. No wonder, then, that the collective NATO and American experience in the Balkans influenced the reformulation of Army doctrine, ultimately resulting in the publication of *Field Manual 3-0, Operations*, in February 2008 and *Field Manual 3-07, Stability Operations*, in October of that year.

On August 10, 1996, COL Batiste prophesied to the soldiers of his 2nd Brigade Combat Team, "This is a defining moment in all of our lives; we will look back on it with enormous pride."[16] He was absolutely right.

Operation Joint Endeavor was a worthy introduction to the unique requirements of stability operations for our company-grade officers and junior NCOs, many of whom have since risen to field-grade officer and senior NCO status. Two Quarterhorse field-grade officers are now general officers today. Unquestionably, our experiences in Bosnia in 1996 have influenced our outlook and the performance of our duties in Iraq and Afghanistan. We certainly do reflect back on those experiences with gratefulness and pride.

No longer stationed in Schweinfurt, Germany, Quarterhorse rides on. Our venerable squadron serves once again at Fort Riley, Kansas, its home for most of the Cold War era. Cavalrymen continue to arrive and depart. They leave their mark and then rotate out. They take with them enormous pride in having served in one of the most illustrious combat units of the U.S. Army. Thus, the history of Quarterhorse is written in portions, one chapter at a time. Each cohort of cavalrymen adds another chapter, some more dramatic than others. Those of us who served in Bosnia added a major chapter to our squadron's history. Our accomplishments there reflected the enduring high standards of professional performance maintained by our predecessors in both combat and stability operations from 1855 through the Persian Gulf War. Since our time, equally proud, skilled, and well-led Quarterhorse cavalrymen have carried our squadron colors into Macedonia and Iraq. Surely, many chapters have yet to be written, and many laurels have yet to be added to the distinguished Quarterhorse legacy. *Paratus et fidelis*: Prepared and Loyal!

# GLOSSARY

*AAM*—Army Achievement Medal.

*AAR*—After action review.

*ABiH*—The military forces of the Muslim-Croat Federation of Bosnia-Herzegovina.

*Abrams*—American M1A1/A2 Main Battle Tank; the most lethal and survivable weapons system on the modern battlefield.

*ACFL*—Agreed Cease-Fire Line; the location of front lines when the Bosnian Civil War ended.

*ACFL ZOS*—Two-kilometer-wide Zone of Separation on either side of the ACFL.

*AC-130 Specter*—Slow-flying close air support aircraft used for concentrated, pinpoint fires against enemy ground targets.

*AFN*—Armed Forces Network television channel for American military viewers in Europe.

*AK-47*—Soviet-made automatic assault rifle.

*Alpha Fortieth*—Alpha Company, 40th Engineer Battalion; engineer asset attached to Quarterhorse.

*AOR*—Area of responsibility.

*AP*—Armor-piercing machine gun or cannon ammunition; also, anti-personnel mines.

*APC*—Armored Personnel Carrier.

*APOE*—Aerial Point of Entry.

*ARCOM*—Army Commendation Medal.

*Areas of Transfer*—Areas where the ACFL and IEBL did not match; resulted in transfer of control from one entity to another.

*ARRC*—The NATO Allied Rapid Reaction Corps.

*AT*—Anti-tank mines.

*Audie Murphy Board*—A selection board screening candidates for admission into the prestigious noncommissioned officer fraternity named for World War II hero Audie Murphy.

*AWT*—Aerial Weapons Team; two Kiowa Warriors operating as wingmen.

*BCPC*—Bradley Crew Proficiency Course.

*BCT*—Brigade Combat Team.

*BDU*—Battle Dress Uniform.

*BFV*—M2A2 Bradley Fighting Vehicle; the infantry version of the Bradley.

*BG*—Brigadier General; officer grade O-7.

*BGST*—Bradley Gunnery Skills Test.

*BICC*—Battlefield Intelligence Collection Cell.

*BiH*—The Muslim-Croat entity of the Federation of Bosnia-Herzegovina.

*Boresight*—Process in which the axis of a weapon is aligned to converge with the line of sight of its sighting instruments at some predetermined range.

*Box*—The maneuver area at CMTC where force-on-force training is conducted.

*BTR-50*—An obsolete Soviet-made Armored Personnel Carrier.

*CA*—Civil Affairs.

*CADST*—Civil Affairs Direct Support Team.

*Cantonment area*—Registered, nontactical garrisons for FWF military units; their only authorized location under terms of the GFAP.

*Cav*—Common reference to units of the United States cavalry.

*Cavalry*—An historically elite combat arms branch responsible for reconnaissance and security operations. Speed, shock effect, and the ability to rapidly maneuver over large distances are some of its attributes.

*Central Region*—The portion of Western Europe where American military forces are garrisoned.

*CFV*—M3A2 Cavalry Fighting Vehicle; the cavalry version of the Bradley.

*Chain of command*—The hierarchy of authority and control between echelons of military units.

*CI*—Counterintelligence.

*CID*—Criminal Investigation Division.

*CIM*—Commission of International Monitors.

*Claymore*—A type of directional, American-made anti-personnel mine.

*Cluster bomb*—A type of aerial bomb that explodes and releases a number of smaller high-explosive bomblets with devastating effect on troops and thin-skinned vehicles.

*CMTC*—The Combat Maneuver Training Center in Hohenfels, Germany. The area where most maneuver training by American and German NATO units is conducted.

*CNN*—Cable Network News.

*COL*—Colonel; officer grade O-6.

*COMARRC*—The Commander of NATO's Allied Rapid Reaction Corps.

*C-130 Hercules*—A 1960s-era, four-propeller transport aircraft used by the United States Air Force for theater-wide air mobility operations.

*CP*—Command post.

*CPT*—Captain; officer grade O-3.

*CS*—Chemical smoke; commonly referred to as tear gas.

*CSM*—Command Sergeant Major; enlisted grade E-9; the senior noncommissioned officer in units of battalion or larger size.

*CW4*—Chief Warrant Officer Four.

*CW3*—Chief Warrant Officer Three.

*CW2*—Chief Warrant Officer Two.

*Dayton Peace Accord*—The peace plan for Bosnia agreed upon in Dayton, Ohio, by leaders of the three warring factions; also, the GFAP.

*D-Day*—The first day of Operation Joint Endeavor in which military operations commenced.

*Delta Force*—A nonattributed American special operations unit.

*DEROS*—Date of eligibility for return from overseas.

*DFAC*—Dining facility; mess hall.

*DOD*—The U.S. Department of Defense.

*Downrange*—American military slang for any deployed location.

*ECMM*—European Community Monitoring Mission.

*ECWCS*—Extended Cold Weather Clothing System.

*EFOR*—Election Force; a NATO augmentation force to support IFOR.

*Ethnic cleansing*—The brutal use of terror and war crimes by ethnic groups to eradicate rival ethnic groups from contested areas.

*EUCOM*—European Command; the American joint military command in Europe.

*Exclusion Zone*—Ten-kilometer zone on either side of the IEBL in which entities could not position or move military forces.

*FAC*—Forward Air Controller.

*FARP*—Forward Air Refueling Point.

*Federation*—The Muslim-Croat entity comprising one-half of the state of Bosnia-Herzegovina.

*.50 caliber MG*—Heavy, air-cooled machine gun, normally mounted on vehicles; dating back to World War I, it is the oldest weapon in the American inventory.

*Fighter Management Pass*—Short rest and relaxation trips to Hungary for selected American IFOR Soldiers in Bosnia.

*FLE*—Forward Logistics Element.

*FMC*—Fully mission capable.

*FOM*—Freedom of movement.

*Force protection*—Active and passive risk reduction measures aimed at preserving the health, safety, and fighting condition of American forces.

*Force reshaping*—The restructuring of NATO peacekeeping forces in Bosnia in late 1996.

*40 EN*—The 40th Engineer Battalion.

*49 FSB*—The 49th Forward Support Battalion; provided logistical support to 2 BCT during Operation Joint Endeavor.

*Four-Duece*—The 1930s-era, 4.2-inch heavy mortar; remained in use with Quarterhorse until early 1998.

*4-29 FA*—The 4th Battalion, 29th Field Artillery; provided indirect fire support to 2 BCT during Operation Joint Endeavor.

*FRAGO*—Fragmentary order.

*Freedom Bird*—Chartered civilian airliner flying American IFOR soldiers on R&R out of Bosnia (and back).

*FSE*—Forward Security Element; a company-size echelon in Soviet attack doctrine.

*FSG*—Family Support Group.

*FSO*—Fire Support Officer.

*FWF*—Former Warring Factions — the Bosnian Serbs, Muslims, and Croats.

*General Order Number One*—A restrictive order that limited the activities of American IFOR soldiers in Bosnia, most notably banning consumption of alcohol and the collection of war trophies.

*GFAP*—General Framework Agreement for Peace; the Dayton Peace Accord.

*Ghostbusters*—Comprehensive, annual maintenance checks and services performed on U.S. Army tank turret systems prior to gunnery.

*GPS*—Global Positioning System device; uses a network of orbiting satellites to accurately pinpoint one's location anywhere in the world.

*GSR*—Ground Surveillance Radar; employed to detect movement of enemy vehicles.

*GTA*—Grafenwoehr Training Area in southeast Germany; site where most American and German NATO units conduct gunnery and live-fire training.

*Guidon*—The swallow-tailed flag for U.S. Army troops, companies, and batteries. The cavalry troop guidon is a red field bearing the regimental numeral in white above a white field with the troop letter in red. The squadron numeral appears centered at left.

*HE*—High-explosive ammunition for either direct or indirect fire weapons.

*Hellfire*—A highly effective, laser-guided antitank missile mounted on American attack and armed reconnaissance helicopters.

*HEMMT*—A family of American eight-wheeled heavy cargo trucks.

*Hesco bastions*—Durable, woven steel baskets that, when filled with dirt or gravel, provide protection from enemy weapons effects.

*HET*—Heavy Equipment Trailer, essentially a military version of a flatbed semi-trailer; used for transporting armored vehicles over long distances.

*HHT*—Headquarters and Headquarters Troop.

*HIND-D*—An armored, Soviet-made attack helicopter.

*HTA*—Hohenfels Training Area in southeast Germany; also known as CMTC.

*Humint*—Human intelligence; intelligence gathered from human sources.

*Humvee*—Slang for the American M998-series High Mobility, Multi-Purpose, Wheeled Vehicle (HMMWV) family of light utility trucks.

*HVO*—The Croatian Defense Forces.

*ICTY*—The International Criminal Tribunal for War Crimes in the Former Yugoslavia.

*IEBL*—The Inter-Entity Boundary Line.

*IFOR*—Implementation Force; the original NATO force that conducted peacekeeping operations in Bosnia during 1996.

*Intel*—Intelligence; the collection, analysis, and dissemination of essential information in support of military operations.

*IPTF*—The UN International Police Task Force.

*ISB*—Intermediate Staging Base; located in Tazsar, Hungary.

*JAAT*—Joint Air Attack Team.

*JMC*—Joint Military Commission.

*Kevlar*—The synthetic fiber material used in American combat helmets and flak vests.

*Kevlar blanket*—An add-on armored device offering enhanced mine strike survivability for Humvee passengers.

*LA*—Lodgment area; base camp.

*LARS Reps*—Civilian technical maintenance experts employed by the U.S. Army; many were retired mechanic NCOs or warrant officers.

*Load plan*—A standardized vehicle equipment stowage plan.

*LOGPAC*—Logistical Resupply Package.

*LRF/D*—Laser Range Finder/Designator on the OH-58D.

*LTC*—Lieutenant Colonel; officer grade O-5.

*LTG*—Lieutenant General; officer grade O-9.

*LZ*—Helicopter landing zone.

*MACS*—An American small arms marksmanship training device.

*MAJ*—Major; officer grade O-4.

*MASH*—Mobile Army Surgical Hospital.

*Master Gunner*—A specially trained NCO who is a technical expert on vehicle gunnery and weapons systems for the Bradley or Abrams.

*M88*—A tracked Armored Recovery Vehicle.

*Medevac*—Medical evacuation helicopter.

*METL*—Mission Essential Task List; a short list of critical tasks that units must be able to perform to standard to be successful in combat.

*MG*—Major General; officer grade O-8.

*Mk-19 AGL*—40mm Automatic Grenade Launcher; often mounted on Humvees.

*MKT*—Mobile Kitchen Trailer.

*MIG*—Family of Soviet-made fighter aircraft.

*Milvan*—Commercial shipping container.

*MLRS*—Multiple Launch Rocket System.

*MMS*—Mast-Mounted Sight on the OH-58D.

*M978*—An eight-wheeled fuel truck; member of the HEMMT family of trucks.

*M106A2*—Vietnam-era tracked armored carrier for the 4.2-inch heavy mortar.

*MP*—Military Police.

*MPRI*—Military Professional Resources, Incorporated.

*MRB*—Motorized Rifle Battalion, a unit echelon from Soviet doctrine.

*MRE*—Meal, Ready to Eat.

*MRUD*—A type of directional antipersonnel mine.

*MSG*—Master Sergeant; enlisted grade E-8.

*M60 MG*—Vietnam-era 7.62mm machine gun; can be fired from a bipod, tripod, or vehicle mount.

*MSRT*—Mobile Subscriber Radio Telephone.

*MST*—Maintenance Support Team; provides limited direct support maintenance to a battalion-size combat unit.

*M-36 tank*—An obsolete Soviet-made tank with additional upgrade features.

*M249 SAW*—5.56mm Squad Automatic Weapon; a light machine gun normally fired from the bipod configuration but can be mounted on a tripod or vehicle mount.

*Mujahadeen*—Islamic fundamentalist fighters supporting the ABiH during the Bosnian Civil War.

*MUPs*—Ministry of Interior police.

*MWR*—Morale, Welfare, and Recreation service.

*NATO*—North Atlantic Treaty Organization.

*NBC*—Nuclear, Biological, and Chemical.

*NCO*—Noncommissioned officer, the backbone of the U.S. Army; enlisted grades E-4 (Corporal) through E-9.

*NCOIC*—Noncommissioned Officer-in-Charge.

*Near beer*—Foul-tasting, unpopular, nonalcoholic brew available for purchase by U.S. Soldiers in Bosnia.

*NGO*—Non-governmental organization.

*NORDBAT*—The Norwegian battalion that served in Bosnia as part of the United Nations peacekeeping effort.

*NORDPOL*—An IFOR brigade comprising units from the Scandinavian countries and Poland.

*NVGs*—Night Vision Goggles; also known as NODs (Night Observation Devices).

*OC*—Observer Controller; an impartial training facilitator.

*OH-58C*—The "Slick 58" light reconnaissance helicopter; predecessor to the Kiowa Warrior.

*OH-58D (I)*—The Kiowa Warrior armed reconnaissance helicopter.

*OHR*—The United Nations Office of the High Representative for Bosnia.

*OIC*—Officer-in-Charge.

*1 AD*—The 1st Armored Division.

*1 BCT*—The 1st Brigade Combat Team, 1st Armored Division.

*1 ID*—The 1st Infantry Division (Mechanized).

*1LT*—First Lieutenant; officer grade O-2.

*1-1 AVN*—The 1st Battalion, 1st Aviation.

*1-1 CAV*—The 1st Squadron, 1st Cavalry.

*1-4 CAV*—The 1st Squadron, 4th Cavalry.

*1SG*—First Sergeant; enlisted grade E-8; the senior noncommissioned officer in a troop/company/battery.

*OP*—Observation post.

*OPFOR*—Opposing Force; the "enemy" aggressors at CMTC.

*OPORD*—Operations order.

*Opstina*—Bosnian term for county.

*OSCE*—Organization for Security and Cooperation in Europe.

*PAC*—Personnel Actions Center.

*PAKBAT*—The Pakistani battalion that served as part of United Nations peacekeeping efforts in Bosnia.

*Peace enforcement*—Military intervention operation in support of and in conjunction with diplomatic efforts to restore peace; implies use or threat of use of force to coerce factions to cease and desist from violent actions; the application of combat power to restore order, to separate warring factions, and to return environment to conditions more conducive to civil order and discipline.

*Peacekeeping*—Military operations that maintain peace already obtained through diplomatic efforts.

*PFC*—Private First Class; enlisted grade E-3.

*PGS*—Precision Gunnery System; a laser-based vehicle-mounted system that provides Bradley crews with feedback to do quality gunnery evaluations.

*Pioneer*—A type of unmanned aerial vehicle used for intelligence gathering.

*PLL*—Prescribed Load List; a quantity of common, high-use spare parts that units are allowed to keep on-hand for immediate use.

*PMCS*—Preventive Maintenance Checks and Services.

*Porta-Potty*—A commercial portable latrine; usually foul-smelling.

*Predator*—A type of unmanned aerial vehicle used for intelligence gathering.

*PROM-3*—A type of anti-personnel mine.

*Psyops*—Psychological Operations.

*PT*—Physical fitness training.

*Purple Heart*—Award presented to Americans killed or wounded by effects of enemy weapons or acts of fratricide.

*PV1*—Private; enlisted grade E-1.

*PV2*—Private; enlisted grade E-2.

*PX*—Post Exchange; a military store.

*Quarterhorse*—Nickname for the 1st Squadron, 4th Cavalry.

*QRF*—Quick Reaction Force.

*R&R*—Rest and relaxation.

*Rear D*—Rear Detachment; that element of a deploying unit that remains in home station to attend to administrative matters.

*Reconnaissance*—Cavalry mission to obtain information about the activities and resources of an enemy, or about the meteorological, hydrographic, or geographic characteristics of a particular area.

*REMBASS*—Remotely Monitored Battlefield Sensor System.

*Republika Srpska*—The Serb Republic; one half of the state Bosnia-Herzegovina.

*Retrans*—Radio retransmission site; allows distant units to communicate by relaying messages through a centrally located radio transmitter/receiver.

*ROE*—Rules of Engagement; certain rules stipulating the limits of combatant actions by an armed force.

*RS*—Republika Srpska.

*RSB*—Redeployment Staging Base; located in Slavonski Brod, Croatia.

*Safe haven*—A failed attempt by UN peacekeepers in Bosnia to provide safety and security for displaced persons against attack by rival ethnic forces.

*Sagger*—Soviet-made anti-tank missile system.

*SA-7*—Soviet-made anti-aircraft missile.

*SCO*—Squadron Commander.

*SDA*—Party for Democratic Action.

*SDS*—Serbian Democratic Party.

*Sector North*—The American-led IFOR sector in Bosnia.

*Sector Sarajevo*—The French-led IFOR sector in Bosnia.

*Sector West*—The British-led IFOR sector in Bosnia.

*Security*—Cavalry mission to provide information about the enemy and to provide reaction time, maneuver space, and protection to the main body force.

*720 MP BN (CBT)*—The 720th Military Police Battalion (Combat).

*SFC*—Sergeant First Class; enlisted grade E-7.

*SFOR*—Sustainment Force; the successor to IFOR.

*S-4*—Staff section responsible for coordinating logistics actions; found within squadrons, battalions, and brigades.

*SGT*—Sergeant; enlisted grade E-5.

*Shopette*—A small post exchange or convenience store.

*SIMNET*—A computer simulator in which armored and mechanized forces up to battalion size can train on tactical maneuver.

*SINCGARS*—Single Channel Ground/Airborne Radio Subsystem.

*Sitrep*—Situation report; rendered by one unit to advise another of its current tactical situation.

*6-6 CAV*—The 6th Squadron, 6th Air Cavalry.

*SKS*—A 1950s-era, Soviet-made semiautomatic rifle.

*SMO*—Squadron Maintenance Officer; staff officer responsible for coordinating all maintenance activities within a cavalry squadron.

*SMS*—Squadron Maintenance Sergeant; the senior enlisted mechanic in a cavalry squadron.

*SMT*—Squadron Maintenance Technician; a warrant officer providing maintenance management expertise for a cavalry squadron.

*Soldiers Medal*—America's highest peacetime award for gallantry.

*S-1*—Staff section responsible for all personnel actions; found within squadrons, battalions, and brigades.

*SPC*—Specialist; enlisted grade E-4.

*Spot Report*—A tactical report rendered to higher headquarters describing notable activity observed.

*SSG*—Staff Sergeant; enlisted grade E-6.

*Stability operations*—Operations that promote and protect U.S. national interests by influencing the threat, political, and information dimensions of the operational environment through a combination of peacetime developmental, cooperative activities and coercive actions in response to crisis.

*Stars and Stripes*—Commercial newspaper available to American service members in Europe.

*S-3*—Staff section responsible for all operations and training within squadrons, battalions, and brigades.

*Stinger*—American-made anti-aircraft missile; can be fired from man-portable, shoulder-fired configuration or mounted on rotary-wing aircraft.

*Stop Loss*—Personnel management decision issued in time of war or "real world" operations in which personnel transfers and temporary duty orders for professional development schools are suspended.

*S-2*—Staff section responsible for all intelligence gathering and analysis within squadrons, battalions, and brigades.

*STX*—Situational Training Exercise; a tactical scenario that allows units to train several unit, crew, and/or individual tasks simultaneously.

*Surveillance*—Systematic observation of airspace or surface areas by visual, aural, electronic, photographic, or other means.

*SUSV*—Small Unit Snow Vehicle.

*SXO*—Squadron Executive Officer.

*TAA*—Tactical Assembly Area.

*Table 8*—An individual vehicle gunnery qualification table in which stationary and moving Bradleys or tanks engage simulated stationary and moving enemy vehicles with live ammunition in realistic combat scenarios.

*TAC*—Tactical Command Post.

*TACP*—Tactical Air Control Party.

*Talon*—The command information newsletter of 2 BCT, 1AD.

*Task Force Eagle*—The American contingent of IFOR.

*TC*—Track Commander; also Truck Commander; the senior person on any military vehicle who is responsible for its safe operation.

*TCGST*—Tank Crew Gunnery Skills Test.

*TCP*—Traffic control point.

*TCPC*—Tank Crew Proficiency Course.

*Team Cav*—The maintenance support team providing direct support maintenance to Quarterhorse.

*TF 4-12 IN*—Task Force 4-12 Infantry.

*TF 1-26 IN*—Task Force 1-26 Infantry.

*TF 2-68 AR*—Task Force 2-68 Armor.

*TF 2-26 AR*—Task Force 2-26 Armor.

*3 ID*—The 3rd Infantry Division (Mechanized).

*TIS*—Thermal Image Sight.

*TMM-1*—A type of anti-tank mine.

*TOC*—Tactical Operations Center.

*TOW*—Tube-launched, Optically sighted, Wire-guided antitank missile system; mounted on the Bradley, Humvee, or ground-mount tripod.

*T-rats*—Heatable tray rations; provides eighteen servings of food; moderately better than MREs.

*Trip flare*—Wire-activated illumination device providing early warning of enemy movement during periods of limited visibility.

*TTA*—Taborfalva Training Area, Hungary.

*TVS*—Low-light Television Sensor on the OH-58D.

*TWGSS*—Tank Weapons Gunnery Simulation System.

*2 BCT*—The 2nd Brigade Combat Team, 1st Armored Division; also the 2nd Brigade Combat Team, 1st Infantry Division.

*2LT*—Second Lieutenant; officer grade O-1.

*2-1 AVN*—The 2nd Battalion, 1st Aviation.

*UAV*—Unmanned Aerial Vehicle.

*U/COFT*—Unit Conduct of Fire Trainer.

*UH-1 Huey*—Vietnam-era utility helicopter.

*UH-60 Black Hawk*—Current-day utility helicopter; successor to the Huey.

*UN*—The United Nations.

*UNHCR*—The United Nations High Commission for Refugees.

*UNPREDEP*—United Nations Preventive Deployment Force in the Former Yugoslav Republic of Macedonia.

*UNPROFOR*—United Nations Protection Force in Bosnia.

*USAR*—The United States Army Reserve.

*USAREUR*—The United States Army in Europe.

*V Corps*—The 5th U.S. Corps.

*VFW*—The Veterans of Foreign Wars.

*VRS*—The Bosnian Serb army of Republika Srpska.

*Warfighter*—A computer-based Tactical Exercise Without Troops that develops the planning and operations management skills of staffs from the battalion to corps level.

*Weaponeer*—A marksmanship training device for the M16A2 rifle.

*WO1*—Warrant Officer One.

*XM114*—Experimental up-armored Humvee.

*ZOS*—The Zone of Separation.

# CHAPTER NOTES

## *Chapter 1*

1. Captain Brian McFadden, interview with Mark Viney, 25 September 1996, Banovici, Bosnia.
2. First Lieutenant Scott Rutherford, interview with Mark Viney, 19 May 1996, Banovici, Bosnia. 1LT Rutherford was our Squadron Adjutant (S-1).
3. J.P Barham, "On the Borderline; GIs Patrol Disputed Macedonian Border," *Stars and Stripes* 15 Sept. 1996: 1.
4. Ibid.
5. Ibid.
6. Ibid.
7. CPT. Christopher D. Wells, letter to CW2 Saevivat, 14 July 1995.
8. Rutherford, 19 May 1996.
9. Dennis Steele, "Bosnia Update," *Army*. Mar. 1996: 39–42.
10. Staff Sergeant Christopher Stone, interview with Mark Viney, 3 February 2000, Fort Bragg, NC. SSG Stone was the senior cavalryman captured by Serbs in Macedonia in 1999.
11. United States Army, 3rd Squadron, 4th U.S. Cavalry, *Briefing Packet: OH-58D(I) Kiowa Warrior OPD/NCOPD*, Dec. 1995.
12. Ibid.
13. Ibid.
14. United States Army, 1st Squadron, 4th U.S. Cavalry, *Memorandum: Troop History October 95 — April 96; C Troop, 1-4 CAV*, May 1996.
15. Ibid.
16. Ibid.
17. Ibid.
18. CPT. Richard Spiegel, *interview*, Mar. 1996.
19. "Key Dates in Bosnia's Peace Process," *Stars and Stripes*, 15 Sept. 1996.
20. Chester A. Crocker and Fen Osler Hampson, "How to Hold the Peace; Bosnia Can't Afford Any Allied Squabbling, Buck-Passing or Flinching," *Washington Post* 21 Jan. 1996: C2.
21. "Key Dates in Bosnia's Peace Process."
22. "GIs in Bosnia Tackle Tasks," *Washington Post* 14 Apr. 1996.
23. Ibid.
24. Ibid.
25. Dennis Steele, "'A Mission of Peace' in Bosnia," *Army*, Jan. 1996: 19.
26. David Hackworth, "We're the Ones Who Die," *Newsweek*. 11 Dec. 1995: 32.
27. Bill Powell, "Dangers Ahead," *Newsweek*. 11 Dec. 1995: 34.
28. Steele, 19.
29. Ibid, 17.
30. Ibid.
31. Ibid.
32. Ibid, 18.
33. Ibid.
34. Donna Peterson, "Bosnia: A Once-in-a-Lifetime Opportunity," *Army Times* 14 Oct. 1996: 8.
35. Ibid.

36. Ibid.
37. United States Army, 1st Squadron, 4th U.S. Cavalry, *Command Training Guidance, 3rd & 4th QTRs, FY 96.* Apr. 1996.
38. Ibid.
39. Command Sergeant Major John Fortune, interview with Mark Viney, 25 August 2000, Fort Stewart, GA. CSM Fortune was the First Sergeant of Bravo Troop in Bosnia and Macedonia.
40. "Getting Started in Bosnia," *Army Times* 1 Jan. 1996.
41. Ibid.
42. United States Army, 2nd Brigade Combat Team, 1st Armored Division, *Mission Analysis, 2/1 AD, OPORD 96-2.* 11 Oct. 1995. [Unclassified]
43. International Institute for Strategic Studies, "Armed Forces in Bosnia and Its Neighbors," *Washington Post.* 25 Jan. 1996.
44. George Roache, "Vests, Convoy Rules Helping Save Lives; Force Protection Rules are Result of Bloody History Lessons," *Talon* 28 June 1996: 4.
45. LTC. Anthony W. Harriman, *Crosstalk* 2.4 (22 Feb. 1996).
46. Roache.

## Chapter 2

1. LTC. Anthony W. Harriman, *Crosstalk* 1.4 (26 Dec. 1995).
2. Sean D. Naylor, "The Nuts and Bolts of Building Peace," *Army Times* 1 Jan 1996: 6.
3. Harriman, 26 Dec. 1995.
4. First Lieutenant Scott Rutherford, interview with Mark Viney, 17 May 1996, Banovici, Bosnia.
5. United States Army, 1st Squadron, 4th U.S. Cavalry, *Memorandum: Historical Overview of B/1-4 Cavalry in Bosnia,* 23 Jan. 1997.
6. Ibid.
7. Rick Atkinson and Christine Spolar, "Army Opens River Bridge; Tanks Cross, U.S. Armored Forces Begin Occupying Bosnian Sector," *Washington Post* 1 Jan. 1996: A1.
8. Richard C. Gross, "U.S. Takes Care in Deployment to Prevent Casualties," *Washington Times* 1–7 Jan. 1996: 8.
9. Ibid.
10. United States Army, 2nd Brigade Combat Team, 1st Armored Division, *Execution Matrix, OPORD 96-2 (Iron Warrior I),* 11 Oct. 1995. [Unclassified]
11. Ibid.
12. Ibid.
13. Captain Robert Ivy, interview with Mark Viney, August 1996, Kalesija, Bosnia.
14. Doyle Tillman, "American Troops Doing Time at a Very Different Alcatraz," *Stars and Stripes* 9 June 1996: 3.
15. Ibid.
16. Ibid.
17. First Lieutenant Pat Michaelis, interview with Mark Viney, September 1996, Kalesija, Bosnia.
18. Dennis Steele, "Bosnia Update," *Army.* Mar. 1996.
19. Rick Atkinson, "Bosnia Force Testing New Russian-U.S. Ties; Troops Get Along; Americans Wary of General," *Washington Post* 18 Jan. 1996: A15.
20. LTC. Anthony W. Harriman, notes, Nov. 1996.
21. Ibid.
22. Paul Geitner, "Muslim Goes Free at Last; Ex-Suspect Alleges Beating by Serbs," *Stars and Stripes* 16 Aug. 1996: A1.
23. Harriman, Nov. 1996.
24. United States Army, 1st Squadron, 4th U.S. Cavalry, *Memorandum: Historical Overview of B/1-4 Cavalry in Bosnia,* 23 Jan. 1997.
25. United States Army, 1st Squadron, 4th U.S. Cavalry, *Memorandum: Troop History October 95—April 96; C Troop, 1-4 CAV,* May 1996.
26. First Lieutenant Pat Michaelis, interview with Mark Viney, June 1996, Kalesija, Bosnia.
27. Ibid.
28. Kevin Dougherty, "Bosnia Bases Draw Names from Variety of Sources," *Stars and Stripes* 21 Feb. 1996: 19.
29. Bill Gertz, "A Gal Leads the 'Red Horse Guys,'" *Washington Times* Jan. 1996.
30. "Battalion News," *Iron Brigade* 31 July 1996: 3.
31. Rick Atkinson, "Call It Camp Swampy; At Base in Northern Bosnia, First Enemy Is Mud," *Washington Post* 11 Jan. 1996.

32. United States Army, 1st Squadron, 4th U.S. Cavalry, *Memorandum: Historical Overview of B/1-4 Cavalry in Bosnia*, 23 Jan. 1997.

33. Dennis Steele, "Bosnia Update," *Army*, Mar. 1996.

34. Ibid.

35. CPT. Mark A. Viney, letter to 4th Cavalry Association, 7 July 1996.

36. Michaelis, June 1996.

37. Ibid.

38. Ibid.

39. United States Army, 1st Squadron, 4th U.S. Cavalry, *Memorandum: Historical Overview of B/1-4 Cavalry in Bosnia*, 23 Jan. 1997.

40. CPT. Fred W. Johnson, "Establishing a Zone of Separation," *Infantry* May-June 1996: 31.

41. Ibid.

42. Ibid.

43. Ibid.

44. Ibid.

45. Ibid.

46. Ibid.

47. Ibid.

48. United States Army, 1st Squadron, 4th U.S. Cavalry, *Memorandum: Troop History October 95 — April 96; C Troop, 1-4 CAV*, May 1996.

49. Ibid.

50. LTC. Anthony W. Harriman, *Crosstalk* 2.2 (30 Jan. 1996).

51. Johnson.

52. United States Army, 1st Squadron, 4th U.S. Cavalry, *Memorandum: Troop History October 95 — April 96; C Troop, 1-4 CAV*, May 1996.

53. LTC. Anthony W. Harriman, *Crosstalk* 2.4 (22 Feb. 1996).

54. CPT. Mark A. Viney, notes, 13 May 1996.

55. Kevin L. Robinson, "Checkpoint Charlie: Life in Bosnia's Hot Zone," *Talon* 20 Sept. 1996: 4.

56. CPT. Scott Downey, notes, Feb. 1999.

57. United States Army, 1st Squadron, 4th U.S. Cavalry, *Memorandum: Troop History October 95 — April 96; C Troop, 1-4 CAV*, May 1996.

58. Captain Brian McFadden, interview with Mark Viney, 25 September 1996, Banovici, Bosnia.

59. Ibid.

60. Johnson.

61. Captain Brian McFadden, interview with Mark Viney, 30 September 1996, Banovici, Bosnia. Incredibly, LTC Harriman claimed towards the end of Quarterhorse's tour in Bosnia that he had never been made aware of this incident.

62. Ibid.

63. Ibid.

64. Steele, Mar. 1996.

## *Chapter 3*

1. "High-Tech Clothing, Tents to Keep Troops Warm," *Columbus Ledger Enquirer*, Dec. 1995: 5.

2. Soraya S. Nelson, "Dust in the Wind — and on the Troops," *Army Times* 19 Feb. 1996: 10.

3. Bradley Graham, "NATO Commander in Bosnia Concerned About Police Force; Smith Says International Deployment Too Small for Job," *Washington Post* 2 Feb. 1996: A24.

4. CPT. Conor Cusick, notes, Aug. 1996.

5. LTC. Anthony W. Harriman, notes, Nov. 1996.

6. Cusick.

7. Harriman, Nov. 1996.

8. "GIs in Bosnia Welcome Clinton as Commander Visiting Troops," *Washington Post* 12 Jan. 1996: A22.

9. Bill Gertz, "Put on a Happy Face, Troops Told," *Washington Times* 30 Jan. 1996.

10. CPT. Fred W. Johnson, "Establishing a Zone of Separation," *Infantry* May-June 1996: 31.

11. Ibid.

12. Ibid.

13. Ibid.

14. Ibid.

15. Jim Bartlett, "Boots & Saddles; In Bosnia with the 1st Squadron, 4th Cavalry; Keeping the Lid on the Balkan Pressure Cooker," *Pacific Interactive Media Corporation* 1996.

16. Bill Powell, "Weather 1, Grunts 0," *Newsweek*. 8 Jan. 1996: 49.

17. United States Army. 1st Squadron, 4th U.S. Cavalry. *Memorandum: Historical Overview of B/1-4 Cavalry in Bosnia.* 23 Jan. 1997.

18. First Lieutenant Pat Michaelis, interview with Mark Viney, June 1996, Kalesija, Bosnia.

19. Ibid.

20. LTC. Anthony W. Harriman, *Crosstalk* 2.2 (30 Jan. 1996).

21. United States Army, 3rd Squadron, 4th U.S. Cavalry, *Narrative for Award Recommendation for CPL Herbert H. Gadsden*, Feb. 1996.

22. United States Army, 3rd Squadron, 4th U.S. Cavalry, *Narrative for Award Recommendation for CPL Francisco J. Alcantar*, Feb. 1996.

23. Michaelis. Jun. 1996.

24. Ibid.

25. First Lieutenant Scott Rutherford, interview with Mark Viney, 19 May 1996, Banovici, Bosnia.

26. Sergeant First Class John Iacono, interview with Mark Viney, June 1997, Schweinfurt, Germany.

27. United States Army, Center for Army Lessons Learned, *Newsletter No. 98-6, Fighting the Mine War in Bosnia; Techniques, Tactics and Procedures*, Mar. 1998.

28. United States Army, 3rd Squadron, 4th U.S. Cavalry, *Narrative for Award Recommendation for PFC Kyle A. Wren*, Feb. 1996.

29. Private First Class Kyle Wren, interview with Mark Viney, May 1997, Schweinfurt, Germany.

30. LTC. Anthony W. Harriman, *Crosstalk* 2.3 (10 Feb. 1996).

## *Chapter 4*

1. CPT. Fred W. Johnson, "Establishing a Zone of Separation," *Infantry* May-June 1996: 31.

2. CPT. Scott Downey, notes, Feb. 1999.

3. LTC. Anthony W. Harriman, *Crosstalk* 2.4 (22 Feb. 1996).

4. Ibid.

5. Ibid.

6. "Key Dates in Bosnia's Peace Process," *Stars and Stripes*. 15 Sept. 1996.

7. Harriman, 22 Feb. 1996.

8. United States Army, 1st Squadron, 4th U.S. Cavalry, *Memorandum: Historical Overview of B/1-4 Cavalry in Bosnia*, 23 Jan. 1997.

9. Ibid.

10. United States Army, 1st Squadron, 4th U.S. Cavalry, *Unit History: 3rd Platoon, Bravo Troop, 1-4 CAV*, May 1996.

11. United States Army, 1st Squadron, 4th U.S. Cavalry, *Unit History: Mortar Platoon, Bravo Troop, 1-4 CAV*, May 1996.

12. LTC. Anthony W. Harriman, *Crosstalk* 2.3 (10 Feb. 1996).

13. Ibid.

14. Ibid.

15. LTC. Anthony W. Harriman, *Crosstalk* 2.5 (25 Mar. 1996).

16. Ibid.

17. CPT. Mark A. Viney, notes, 28 May 1996.

18. Harriman, 22 Feb. 1996.

19. Viney, 28 May 1996.

20. United States Army, 1st Squadron, 4th U.S. Cavalry, *Memorandum: Historical Overview of B/1-4 Cavalry in Bosnia*, 23 Jan. 1997.

21. Harriman, 25 Mar. 1996.

22. Ibid.

23. Captain Brian McFadden, interview with Mark Viney, 25 September 1996, Banovici, Bosnia.

24. Harriman, 25 Mar. 1996.

25. CPT. Mark A. Viney, letter to 4th Cavalry Association, 7 Jul. 1996.

26. Harriman, 25 Mar. 1996.

27. United States Army, 1st Squadron, 4th U.S. Cavalry, *Command Training Guidance, 3rd & 4th QTRs, FY 96*, Apr. 1996.

28. Ibid.

29. Captain Brian McFadden, interview with Mark Viney, 30 September 1996, Banovici, Bosnia.

30. Ibid.

31. LTC. Anthony W. Harriman, *Crosstalk* 2.6 (3 Apr. 1996).
32. CPT. Mark A. Viney, notes, 13 May 1996.
33. Harriman. 3 Apr. 1996.
34. MAJ. Daniel L. Zajac, "Operations Update." *Iron Brigade* 1996.
35. Harriman, 25 Mar. 1996.
36. Harriman, 3 Apr. 1996.
37. LTC. Anthony W. Harriman, *Crosstalk* 2.7 (20 Apr. 1996).
38. Ibid.
39. LTC. Anthony W. Harriman, *Crosstalk* 2.9 (27 May 1996).

## Chapter 5

1. John M. Goshko, "U.N. Answers Critics of Policing Effort in Bosnia; Spokeswoman Says Countries Broke Promises to Provide Trained Personnel," *Washington Post* 5 Feb. 1996.
2. John Pomfret, "Police Force Slow to Deploy Around Sarajevo; Absence Worries Residents of Serb-Held Suburbs as Troop Pullout Deadline Nears," *Washington Post* 30 Jan. 1996.
3. Bradley Graham, "NATO Commander in Bosnia Concerned About Police Force; Smith Says International Deployment Too Small for Job," *Washington Post* 2 Feb. 1996: A24.
4. John Pomfret, "Perry Says NATO Will Not Serve as 'Police Force' in Bosnia Mission," *Washington Post* 3 Jan. 1996.
5. John Pomfret, "Sarajevo Acts to Boost Party, Silence Dissent; Some Government Steps Violate Dayton Accord," *Washington Post* 31 Jan. 1996.
6. Ibid.
7. United States Army, 1st Squadron, 4th U.S. Cavalry, *Memorandum: Troop History October 95 — April 96; C Troop, 1-4 CAV,* May 1996.
8. CPT. Scott Downey, notes, Feb. 1999.
9. Ibid.
10. Captain Kerry Brunson, interview with Mark Viney, September 1996, Banovici, Bosnia.
11. United States Army, 1st Squadron, 4th U.S. Cavalry, *Memorandum: Troop History October 95 — April 96; C Troop, 1-4 CAV,* May 1996.
12. LTC. Anthony W. Harriman, notes, Nov. 1996.
13. Jim Bartlett, "Boots & Saddles; In Bosnia with the 1st Squadron, 4th Cavalry; Keeping the Lid on the Balkan Pressure Cooker," *Pacific Interactive Media Corporation* 1996.
14. MAJ. Daniel L. Zajac, "Operations Update," *Iron Brigade* 11 May 1996: 4.
15. Gary Younger, "Shalikashvili: America Is Immensely Proud," *Iron Brigade* 11 May 1996: 5.
16. Ibid.
17. Ibid.
18. "Battalion News," *Iron Brigade* 11 May 1996: 3.
19. Zajac, 11 May 1996.
20. LTC. Anthony W. Harriman, *Crosstalk* 2.8 (10 May 1996).
21. Associated Press, "Bosnians Seek Food Among the Scraps from U.S. Troops," *St. Petersburg Times* 27 May 1996: 2A.

## Chapter 6

1. COL. John Batiste, "Commander's Comments," *Iron Brigade* 11 May 1996: 2.
2. Ibid.
3. Ibid.
4. Captain Scott Downey, interview with Mark Viney, September 1996, Kalesija, Bosnia.
5. MAJ. Daniel L. Zajac, "Operations Update." *Iron Brigade* 11 May 1996: 4.
6. United States Army, 1st Squadron, 4th U.S. Cavalry, *Command Training Guidance, 3rd & 4th QTRs, FY 96,* Apr. 1996.
7. United States Army, 1st Squadron, 4th U.S. Cavalry, *Memorandum: Historical Overview of B/1-4 Cavalry in Bosnia,* 23 Jan. 1997.
8. Batiste, 11 May 1996.
9. LTC. Anthony W. Harriman, *Crosstalk* 2.8 (10 May 1996).
10. John Pomfret, "3 Britons, Swede Die in Bosnia Accidents; Apparent Sniper Bullet Grazes U.S. Lieutenant Near Sarajevo," *Washington Post* 28 Jan. 1996.
11. Liam McDowell, "10,000 Troops Quietly Leave Bosnia," *Stars and Stripes* 12 May 1996: 4.
12. Karen Blakeman, "Possible Survivors Turn Up; One Group Causes Problems for IFOR," *Stars and Stripes* 4–5 July 1996: A1.

13. Karen Blakeman, "Armed Men Surrender to Troops," *Stars and Stripes* 12 May 1996: A1.
14. "Battalion News," *Iron Brigade* 30 May 1996: 3.
15. Blakeman, 4–5 July 1996.
16. Ibid.
17. "Muslims Turned in by NATO Tortured," *St. Petersburg Times* 24 May 1996: 10A.
18. Ibid.
19. Blakeman, 12 May 1996.
20. Blakeman, 4–5 July 1996.
21. Ibid.
22. Major Bryan Roberts, interview with Mark Viney, May 1996, Kalesija, Bosnia.
23. "Muslims Turned in by NATO Tortured."
24. Blakeman, 12 May 1996.
25. CPT. Mark A. Viney, notes, 13 May 1996.
26. "Muslims Turned in by NATO Tortured."
27. Blakeman, 4–5 July 1996.
28. "Muslims Turned in by NATO Tortured."
29. Viney, 13 May 1996.
30. Harriman, 10 May 1996.
31. Viney, 13 May 1996.
32. Jerry Merideth, "Troops at Observation Post Understand Their Limitations," *Stars and Stripes* 14 June 1996: 4.
33. Doyle Tillman, "American Troops Doing Time at a Very Different Alcatraz," *Stars and Stripes* 9 June 1996: 3.
34. Ibid.
35. Ibid.
36. Jim Bartlett, "Boots & Saddles; Part 2: The Scouts; Scouts Up! For'ard Yo!" *Pacific Interactive Media Corporation* 1996.
37. Ibid.
38. Merideth,.
39. Jim Bartlett, "Boots & Saddles; In Bosnia with the 1st Squadron, 4th Cavalry; Keeping the Lid on the Balkan Pressure Cooker," *Pacific Interactive Media Corporation* 1996.
40. Ibid.
41. Ibid.
42. Jim Bartlett, "Boots & Saddles; Part 2: The Scouts; Scouts Up! For'ard Yo!" *Pacific Interactive Media Corporation* 1996.
43. Ibid.
44. Ibid.
45. Ibid.
46. Ibid.
47. Jim Bartlett, "Yugoslav Civil War Information Briefing to 1-4 CAV Officers," Kalesija, Bosnia, 21 May 1996.
48. LTC. Anthony W. Harriman, *Crosstalk* 2.9 (27 May 1996).
49. Ibid.
50. Rick Haverinen, "Families Are Well Cared for by Rear Detachment Soldiers," *Marneland Crusader* 22 Mar. 1996: 6.
51. Ibid.
52. Ibid.
53. Ibid.
54. LTC. Anthony W. Harriman, letter to Squadron Family Support Group, Feb. 1996.
55. Haverinen, 22 Mar. 1996.
56. Ibid.
57. Susan M. Carl, "A Little Teamwork, a Taste for Camo Part of Family Day," *Stars and Stripes* 2 June 1996: 3.

## *Chapter 7*

1. John Pomfret, "NATO, Prosecutor Debate Bosnia Aims; Peace Force Commander, S. African Jurist Discuss Troops' Role in War Crimes Probe," *Washington Post* 22 Jan. 1996.
2. Ibid.
3. John Pomfret, "U.S. Official Visits Bosnian Site of 'Sheer Murder,'" *Washington Post* 21 Jan. 1996: A1.

4. Ibid.
5. MAJ. Richard J. Dixon, "Operations Update," *Iron Brigade* 31 July 1996: 4.
6. MAJ. Daniel L. Zajac, "Operations Update," *Iron Brigade* 1996.
7. First Lieutenant Pat Michaelis, interview with Mark Viney, September 1996, Kalesija, Bosnia.
8. Captain Jim Dirisio, interview with Mark Viney, 30 September 1996, Kalesija, Bosnia.
9. CPT. Mark A. Viney, notes, 11 Sep. 1996.
10. Captain Brian McFadden, interview with Mark Viney, 30 September 1996, Banovici, Bosnia.
11. John Pomfret, "Grim Evidence Points to Muslims' Graves," *Washington Post* 18 Jan. 1996.
12. Ibid.
13. John Pomfret, "After 'Ethnic Cleansing,' Srebrenica Is a Wasteland of Garbage," *Washington Post* 16 Jan. 1996: Al.
14. Ibid.
15. Wilbur G. Landrey, "Good Luck, Sarajevo; You'll Need It," *St. Petersburg Times* 20 Sept. 1996: 2A.
16. Ibid.
17. Ibid.
18. Ibid.
19. "GIs in Bosnia Tackle Tasks," *Washington Post* 14 Apr. 1996.
20. Dennis Steele, "'A Mission of Peace' in Bosnia," *Army* Jan. 1996.
21. "GIs in Bosnia Tackle Tasks."
22. Ibid.
23. Ibid.
24. Ibid.
25. Ibid.
26. Ibid.
27. Ibid.
28. CPT. Mark A. Viney, notes, 22 July 1996.
29. *Stars and Stripes*, May 1996.
30. "Key Dates in Bosnia's Peace Process," *Stars and Stripes*, 15 Sept. 1996.
31. "MWR Slate Features Magic, Music, Mind Games," *Talon* 31 May 1996: 12.
32. Bill Sammon, "U.S. Army Medics Rush to Bosnian Boy's Rescue," *Stars and Stripes* 6 June 1996: Al.
33. Ibid.
34. Ibid.
35. LTC. Anthony W. Harriman, *Crosstalk* 2.6 (3 Apr. 1996).
36. Bill Sammon, "Troops in Bosnia Get Rare Taste of Home — Vegas-Style Showgirls," *Stars and Stripes* 6 June 1996: 4.
37. Ibid.
38. Ibid.

## Chapter 8

1. United States Army, 1st Squadron, 4th U.S. Cavalry, *Command Training Guidance, 3rd & 4th QTRs, FY 96*, Apr. 1996.
2. LTC. Anthony W. Harriman, *Crosstalk* 2.10 (2 July 1996).
3. United States Army, 1st Squadron, 4th U.S. Cavalry, *Command Training Guidance, 3rd & 4th QTRs, FY 96*, Apr. 1996.
4. LTC. Anthony W. Harriman, *Crosstalk* 2.5 (25 Mar. 1996).
5. Johnston, Jody. "1-4 Cav Troopers Shoot, Qualify on Hungary Range." *The Iron Brigade* 11 May 1996: 1.
6. Ibid.
7. Ibid.
8. LTC. Anthony W. Harriman, *Crosstalk* 2.7 (20 Apr. 1996).
9. LTC. Anthony W. Harriman, *Crosstalk* 2.10 (2 July 1996).
10. United States Army, 1st Squadron, 4th U.S. Cavalry, *Command Training Guidance, 3rd & 4th QTRs, FY 96*, Apr. 1996.
11. MAJ. Richard J. Dixon, "Operations Update," *Iron Brigade* 31 July 1996: 4.
12. MAJ. Richard J. Dixon, "Operations Update," *Iron Brigade* 10 Aug. 1996: 4.
13. Dixon, 31 July 1996.
14. Kirk Emig, "First JAAT Exercise in Bosnia a Success," *Iron Brigade* 15 June 1996.
15. Dixon, 10 Aug. 1996.

16. Len Butler, "Thunder Rocks Resolute Barbara Range." *Talon* 9 Aug. 1996: 6–7.

17. Ibid.

18. CPT. Conor Cusick, notes, Aug. 1996.

19. Captain Mike Lisowski, interview with Mark Viney, September 1996, Banovici, Bosnia.

20. United States Army, 1st Squadron, 4th U.S. Cavalry, *Command Training Guidance, 3rd & 4th QTRs, FY 96,* Apr. 1996.

21. MAJ. Daniel L. Zajac, "Operations Update," *Iron Brigade* 15 June 1996: 4.

22. "GIs in Bosnia Tackle Tasks," *Washington Post* 14 Apr. 1996.

23. Ibid.

24. Zajac, 15 June 1996.

25. Ibid.

26. MAJ. Daniel L. Zajac, "Operations Update," *Iron Brigade* 29 June 1996: 4.

27. Ibid.

28. Ibid.

29. Joseph Garrison, "Boot Camp Buddies Continue Friendship in Bosnia," *Talon* 17 May 1996: 10.

30. Jeffrey Smith, "High-Tech Cooperation in Bosnia," *Washington Post* 19 Jan. 1996: A30.

31. Ibid.

32. MAJ. Daniel L. Zajac, "Operations Update," *Iron Brigade* 11 May 1996: 4.

33. Captain Jim Dirisio, interview with Mark Viney, 30 September 1996, Kalesija, Bosnia.

34. Ibid.

35. Ibid.

36. Ibid.

37. Ibid.

38. Craig Pickett, "PSYOPS Campaigns for Peace," *Iron Brigade* 28 Sept. 1996: 1.

39. CPT. Mark A. Viney, notes, 9 Aug. 1996.

40. Dirisio, 30 Sep. 1996.

41. MAJ. Richard J. Dixon, "Operations Update," *Iron Brigade* 28 Sept. 1996: 4.

42. Ibid.

43. Ibid.

44. Brian Bowers, "Civil Affairs Is a Real Family Business," *Stars and Stripes* 30 Sept. 1996: 4.

45. Viney, 9 Aug. 1996.

46. Dirisio, 30 Sep. 1996.

47. Ibid.

48. Ibid.

49. CPT. Mark A. Viney, notes, 30 Sept. 1996.

50. CPT. Scott Downey, notes, Feb. 1999.

51. LTC. Anthony W. Harriman, *Crosstalk* 2.13 (15 Sept. 1996).

## *Chapter 9*

1. *Chicago Tribune*, June 1996.

2. Bill Sammon, "The Hate Hangs on in Bosnia; 'Long Way to Go' Before Peace Arrives," *Stars and Stripes* 23 June 1996: A1.

3. Ibid.

4. Ibid.

5. Ibid.

6. Ibid.

7. LTC. Anthony W. Harriman, *Crosstalk* 2.10 (2 Jul. 1996).

8. Jim Bartlett, "Boots & Saddles; In Bosnia with the 1st Squadron, 4th Cavalry; Keeping the Lid on the Balkan Pressure Cooker." *Pacific Interactive Media Corporation* 1996.

9. Harriman, 2 Jul. 1996.

10. CPT. Mark A. Viney, notes, 4 July 1996.

11. Captain Brian McFadden, interview with Mark Viney, 30 September 1996, Banovici, Bosnia.

12. Harriman, 2 July 1996.

13. Ibid.

14. CPT. Mark A. Viney, notes, 19 Aug. 1996.

15. COL. John Batiste, "Commander's Comments," *Iron Brigade* 29 June 1996: 2.

16. United States Army, 1st Squadron, 4th U.S. Cavalry, *Command Training Guidance, 3rd & 4th QTRs, FY 96,* Apr. 1996.

17. Ibid.

18. Brian Bowers, "Troops Healthier by the Numbers; Restrictions Work to Reduce Illness," *Stars and Stripes* 22 Sept.1996: 5.

19. Ibid.

20. Ibid.

21. Ibid.

22. Donna Peterson, "Bosnia: A Once-in-a-Lifetime Opportunity," *Army Times* 14 Oct. 1996: 8.

23. MAJ. Daniel L. Zajac, "Operations Update," *Iron Brigade* 29 June 1996: 4.

24. Harriman, 2 July 1996.

25. Dana Priest, "U.S. May Send $100 Million in Arms, Equipment to Bosnia," *Washington Post* Mar. 1996.

26. Aaron Reed, "Bosnian Federation Army Set to Get Weapons and Training; U.S.-Led Train and Equip Program Not to Involve IFOR Troops," *Talon* 9 Aug. 1996: 1.

27. CPT. Mark A. Viney, notes, 22 July 1996.

28. CPT. Mark A. Viney, notes, 30 July 1996.

29. *Stars and Stripes* Aug. 1996.

30. Reed, 9 Aug. 1996.

31. John Pomfret, "Islamic Fighters Defy Dayton Accord; U.S. Army Views Mujahadeen Who Refuse to Leave Bosnia as 'Passive Threat' to Peacekeepers," *Washington Post* 15 Jan. 1996.

32. "U.S. Aiding Bosnian Force Linked to Iran," *Washington Post* 26 Jan. 1996: A28.

33. Pomfret, 15 Jan. 1996.

34. *Stars and Stripes* 14 Sep. 1996.

35. MAJ. Richard J. Dixon, "Operations Update," *Iron Brigade* 31 July 1996: 4.

36. LTC. Anthony W. Harriman, *Crosstalk* 2.11 (26 July 1996).

## Chapter 10

1. "Again, West Threatens Serbs, Backs Off," *St. Petersburg Times* 2 July 1996: 2A.

2. Ibid.

3. Ibid.

4. Effie Bathen, "Standoff Ends Peacefully; Threats Spawned Tension Near Mladic's Base," *Stars and Stripes* 8 July 1996: A1.

5. Ibid.

6. Ibid.

7. MAJ. Daniel L. Zajac, "Operations Update," *Iron Brigade* 20 July 1996: 4.

8. Captain Scott Downey, interview with Mark Viney, July 1996, Kalesija, Bosnia.

9. Bathen, 8 July 1996.

10. Zajac, 20 July 1996.

11. Ibid.

12. Bathen, 8 July 1996.

13. Zajac, 20 July 1996.

14. Ibid.

15. Ibid.

16. Bathen, 8 July 1996.

17. Zajac, 20 July 1996.

18. Bathen, 8 July 1996.

19. Ibid.

20. Downey, July 1996.

21. COL. John Batiste, "Commander's Comments," *Iron Brigade* 20 July 1996: 2.

22. MAJ. Daniel L. Zajac, "Operations Update," *Iron Brigade* 15 June 1996: 4.

23. LTC. Anthony W. Harriman, *Crosstalk* 2.11 (26 July 1996).

24. "Battalion News," *Iron Brigade* 31 July 1996: 3.

25. "Battalion News," *Iron Brigade* 20 July 1996: 3.

26. Daniel Paschall, "The Force Is with You," *Talon* 26 July 1996: 1.

27. MAJ. Richard J. Dixon, "Operations Update," *Iron Brigade* 31 July 1996: 4.

28. LTC. Anthony W. Harriman, "LTC Harriman's Musings," *Crossed Sabers* Aug. 1996: 3.

29. Ibid.

30. "Standoff Leads to Increased Force Protection Here," *Talon* 16 Aug. 1996: 10.

31. LTC. Anthony W. Harriman, *Crosstalk* 2.11 (26 July 1996).

32. CPT. Mark A. Viney, notes, 9 Aug. 1996.

33. CPT. Mark A. Viney, notes, 30 July 1996.

34. Jim Bartlett, "Boots & Saddles; In Bosnia with the 1st Squadron, 4th Cavalry; Keeping the Lid on the Balkan Pressure Cooker," *Pacific Interactive Media Corporation* 1996.

35. Ibid.

36. United States Army, 1st Squadron, 4th U.S. Cavalry, *Command Training Guidance, 3rd & 4th QTRs, FY 96*, Apr. 1996.

37. Kenyon McAfee, "Lake Balaton Offers Best of Both Worlds," *Talon* 28 June 1996: 8.

38. United States Army, 1st Squadron, 4th U.S. Cavalry, *Command Training Guidance, 3rd & 4th QTRs, FY 96*, Apr. 1996.

39. Keirya Langkamp, "Royal Treatment Awaits in Budapest," *Talon* 10 May 1996: 8.

40. Ibid.

41. Ibid.

42. Ibid.

43. "Battalion News," *Iron Brigade* 15 June 1996: 3.

44. LTC. Anthony W. Harriman, *Crosstalk* 2.2 (30 Jan. 1996).

45. United States Army, 1st Squadron, 4th U.S. Cavalry, *Command Training Guidance, 3rd & 4th QTRs, FY 96*, Apr. 1996.

46. COL. John Batiste, "Commander's Comments," *Iron Brigade* 10 Aug. 1996: 2.

47. United States Army, 1st Squadron, 4th U.S. Cavalry, *Command Training Guidance, 3rd & 4th QTRs, FY 96*, Apr. 1996.

48. Ibid.

49. CPT. Mark A. Viney, notes, 19 Aug. 1996.

50. Ibid.

51. MAJ. Richard J. Dixon, "Operations Update," *Iron Brigade* 10 Aug. 1996: 4.

52. Viney, 19 Aug. 1996.

53. Ron Jensen, "Italian Engineer Unit Making Tracks on Rail Line," *Stars and Stripes* 1 Sept. 1996: 4.

54. Captain Kerry Brunson, interview with Mark Viney, September 1996, Banovici, Bosnia.

55. Dixon, 10 Aug. 1996

56. Craig Pickett, "PSYOPS Campaigns for Peace," *Iron Brigade* 28 Sept. 1996: 1.

57. Rudy Carter, "3 Crashes Later, Marines Settling In; Remote-Controlled Aircraft Do the Job," *Stars and Stripes* 1 Sept. 1996: 4.

58. Captain Scott Downey, interview with Mark Viney, September 1996, Kalesija, Bosnia.

59. CPT. Mark A. Viney, notes, 30 Oct. 1996.

60. CPT. Mark A. Viney, notes, 23 Sept. 1996.

61. Downey, Sept. 1996.

62. Ibid.

63. Ibid.

64. Sergeant First Class John Iacono, interview with Mark Viney, June 1997, Schweinfurt, Germany.

65. LTC. Anthony W. Harriman, *Crosstalk* 2.12 (3 Sept. 1996).

66. CPT. Mark A. Viney, notes, 11 Sept. 1996.

67. Downey, Sept. 1996.

68. Ibid.

69. Harriman, 3 Sept. 1996.

70. United States Army, 1st Squadron, 4th U.S. Cavalry, *Memorandum: Historical Overview of B/1-4 Cavalry in Bosnia*, 23 Jan. 1997.

71. Downey, Sept. 1996.

72. Harriman, 3 Sept. 1996.

73. Downey, Sept. 1996.

74. Harriman, 3 Sept. 1996.

75. Downey, Sept. 1996.

76. Harriman, 3 Sept. 1996.

77. Colleen Barry, "U.S. Tanks Keep Bosnia Town Quiet," *Stars and Stripes* 1 Sept. 1996: 1.

78. Downey, Sept. 1996.

79. MAJ. Richard J. Dixon, "Operations Update," *Iron Brigade* 28 Sept. 1996: 4.

80. Harriman, 3 Sept. 1996.

81. CPT. Mark A. Viney, notes, June 1999.

82. Harriman, 3 Sept. 1996.

83. Ibid.

## Chapter 11

1. LTC. Anthony W. Harriman, *Crosstalk* 2.12 (3 Sept. 1996).
2. United States Army, 1st Squadron, 4th U.S. Cavalry, *BiH Election Day Primer*, Sept. 1996.
3. Ibid.
4. Ron Jensen, "Ready or Not, Bosnia Gets Ready to Vote," *Stars and Stripes* 13 Sept. 1996: A1.
5. Bill Sammon, "The Hate Hangs on in Bosnia; 'Long Way to Go' Before Peace Arrives," *Stars and Stripes* 23 June 1996: A1.
6. Karen Blakeman, "Most Refugees Choose to Side with Their Side," *Stars and Stripes* 14 Sept. 1996: A1.
7. Kevin Dougherty, "Traffic Could Snarl Vote; Displaced Bosnians to Put Freedom of Movement to the Test," *Stars and Stripes* 14 Sept. 1996: A1.
8. Ibid.
9. Ibid.
10. Blakeman, 14 Sept. 1996.
11. *Stars and Stripes* Sept. 1996.
12. Dougherty, 14 Sept. 1996.
13. Ron Jensen, "IFOR Facing Tough Election Choice," *Stars and Stripes* 13 Sept. 1996: 4.
14. United States Army, 1st Squadron, 4th U.S. Cavalry, *BiH Election Day Primer*, Sept. 1996.
15. Ibid.
16. CPT. Mark A. Viney, notes, 12–13 Sep. 1996.
17. Ron Jensen, "NATO Wants No Excuse on Vote; Alliance to Ensure Officials Know Rules," *Stars and Stripes* 20 Aug. 1996: A1.
18. CPT. Mark A. Viney, notes, 9 Aug. 1996.
19. Ibid.
20. Craig Pickett, "PSYOPS Campaigns for Peace," *Iron Brigade* 28 Sept. 1996: 1.
21. LTC. Anthony W. Harriman, *Crosstalk* 2.13 (15 Sept. 1996).
22. CPT. Mark A. Viney, notes, 11 Sept. 1996.
23. Jensen, 13 Sept. 1996.
24. Sue Palumbo, "IFOR Carefully Defines Role in Elections," *Stars and Stripes* 24 Aug. 1996: 4.
25. Ibid.
26. Viney, 9 Aug. 1996.
27. Ibid.
28. Palumbo, 24 Aug. 1996.
29. CPT. Mark A. Viney, notes, 19 Aug. 1996.
30. Palumbo, 24 Aug. 1996.
31. Ibid.
32. Jensen, 13 Sep. 1996.
33. Ibid.
34. "Leader's Election Dozen; TF Eagle Guidelines for Success," *Talon* 13 Sept. 1996: 11.
35. Ibid.
36. Viney, 11 Sept. 1996.
37. CPT. Mark A. Viney, notes, 30 Sept. 1996.
38. CPT. Mark A. Viney, notes, 14 Sept. 1996.
39. Ibid.
40. Jensen, 13 Sept. 1996.
41. Harriman, 15 Sept. 1996.
42. CPT. Mark A. Viney, notes, 12–13 Sept. 1996.
43. Viney, 11 Sept. 1996.
44. Ibid.
45. Harriman, 15 Sept. 1996.
46. Brian Bowers and Kevin Dougherty, "U.S. Gets Its Wish: A Dull Day," *Stars and Stripes* 15 Sept. 1996: A1.
47. Harriman, 15 Sept. 1996.
48. Bowers and Dougherty, 15 Sept. 1996.
49. Harriman, 15 Sept. 1996.
50. Viney, 14 Sept. 1996.
51. Bowers and Dougherty, 15 Sept. 1996.
52. Associated Press, "Turnout Reflects Ethnic Split; Cross-Boundary Traffic Lower Than Hoped For," *Stars and Stripes* 17 Sept. 1996: A1.
53. Harriman, 15 Sept. 1996.

54. Ibid.
55. Ibid.
56. Ibid.
57. Ibid.
58. North Atlantic Treaty Organization, Allied Rapid Reaction Corps, *Memorandum: COMARRC's Message to Commanders and Troops*, 14 Sept. 1996.
59. MG. William L. Nash, "Troops Make History," *Talon* Sept. 1996.
60. Harriman, 15 Sept. 1996.
61. Ibid.
62. Associated Press, 17 Sept. 1996.
63. Ron Jensen, "IFOR Election Watchers 'Beginning to Exhale'; Moderate Turnout Brings Few Problems," *Stars and Stripes* 15 Sept. 1996: A1.
64. Ibid.
65. Ibid.
66. Wilbur G. Landrey, "Bosnian Elections Pass in Relative Calm," *St. Petersburg Times* 15 Sept. 1996: 1A.
67. Karen Blakeman, "Bosnia Tallies Still Fuzzy; But Local Voting to Start Nov. 22," *Stars and Stripes* 22 Sept. 1996: A1.
68. Robert H. Frowick, "Municipal Elections to Proceed," *Talon* 11 Oct. 1996: 1.
69. Ibid.
70. CPT. Mark A. Viney, notes, 23 Sept. 1996.
71. LTC. Anthony W. Harriman, *Crosstalk* 2.14 (2 Oct. 1996).
72. Viney, 30 Sept. 1996.
73. Ibid.
74. CPT. Mark A. Viney, notes, 7 Oct. 1996.
75. Vince Crawley, "Bosnia Vote Delayed; Effect on Pullout of U.S. Unknown," *Stars and Stripes* 23 Oct. 1996: A1.
76. Ibid.
77. Vince Crawley, "NATO Won't Hurry Cutback of IFOR in Wake of Election," *Stars and Stripes* 19 Sept. 1996: A1.
78. Ibid.
79. Kevin Dougherty, "Elections May Delay Troops' Exit," *Stars and Stripes* 22 Sept. 1996: A1.
80. Vince Crawley, "Vote Woes Won't Slow Pullout, Officials Say," *Stars and Stripes* 24 Oct. 1996: A1.
81. Ibid.
82. Ibid.
83. PFC. Christina D. Hampsten, "Teamwork Goes Far," *Stars and Stripes* 6 Oct. 1996: 16.
84. SGT. Michael Long, "Proud of Our Work," *Stars and Stripes* 30 Oct. 1996: 12.
85. CPL. David Hjelm, "Enlisted Overlooked," *Stars and Stripes* 2 Nov. 1996: 12.
86. Ibid.
87. *Stars and Stripes* 1997.

## Chapter 12

1. Captain Scott Downey, interview with Mark Viney, September 1996, Kalesija, Bosnia.
2. LTC. Anthony W. Harriman, *Crosstalk* 2.14 (2 Oct. 1996).
3. Ibid.
4. Brian Bowers, "IFOR Pushes for Muslims to Leave Town," *Stars and Stripes* 25 Sept. 1996: 2.
5. Ibid.
6. Len Butler, "Jusici," *Talon* 11 Oct. 1996: 6–7.
7. Ibid.
8. Karen Blakeman, "Jusici's War Refugees Return Home to Stay," *Stars and Stripes* 8 Oct. 1996: A1.
9. Bowers, 25 Sept.1996.
10. Butler, 11 Oct. 1996.
11. Ibid.
12. Ibid.
13. Brian Bowers, "IFOR Takes Weapons from Muslims," *Stars and Stripes* 23 Sept. 1996: 2.
14. Ibid.
15. Blakeman, 8 Oct. 1996.
16. Ibid.

17. Butler, 11 Oct. 1996.
18. Blakeman, 8 Oct. 1996.
19. Ibid.
20. Ibid.
21. Ibid.
22. "Battalion News," *Iron Brigade* 19 Oct. 1996: 3.
23. Blakeman, 8 Oct. 1996.
24. Ibid.
25. Ibid.
26. Karen Blakeman, "Serbs Back Out of Pact on Joint Police Patrols," *Stars and Stripes* 11 Oct. 1996: A1.
27. CPT. Mark A. Viney, notes, 26 Oct. 1996.
28. Blakeman, 11 Oct. 1996.
29. Ibid.
30. *Stars and Stripes* 13 Oct. 1996.
31. Ibid.
32. Ibid.
33. Ibid.
34. MAJ. Richard J. Dixon, "Operations Update," *Iron Brigade* 19 Oct. 1996: 4.
35. Vince Crawley, "IFOR Raid of Village Fails to Find Weapons," *Stars and Stripes* 1 Nov. 1996: 5.
36. CPT. Mark A. Viney, notes, 7 Oct. 1996.
37. Ibid.
38. Harriman, 2 Oct. 1996.
39. Captain Brian McFadden, interview with Mark Viney, November 1996, Banovici, Bosnia.
40. Ibid.
41. LTC. Anthony W. Harriman, *Crosstalk* 2.15 (3 Nov. 1996).
42. CPT. Mark A. Viney, notes, 23 Sep. 1996.
43. Craig Pickett, "One-Quarter Cav Troopers Reclaim Dutch APCs," *Talon* 1 Nov. 1996: 4.
44. Ibid.
45. Viney, 26 Oct. 1996.
46. Ibid.
47. Ibid.
48. Ibid.
49. Ibid.
50. Ibid.
51. Ibid.

## *Chapter 13*

1. Andrew Compart, "Will We or Won't We? Administration Still Waffling on Bosnia Pullout Date," *Army Times* 14 Oct. 1996: 40.
2. Ibid.
3. Ibid.
4. "Exit," *Stars and Stripes* 29 Oct. 1996: 4.
5. Ibid.
6. MAJ. Richard J. Dixon, "Operations Update," *Iron Brigade* 19 Oct. 1996: 4.
7. CPT. Mark A. Viney, notes, 21 Oct. 1996.
8. CPT. Mark A. Viney, notes, 30 Oct. 1996.
9. Ibid.
10. COL. John Batiste, "Commander's Comments," *Iron Brigade* 19 Oct. 1996: 2.
11. Ibid.
12. Viney, 30 Oct. 1996.
13. LTC. Anthony W. Harriman, *Crosstalk* 2.15 (3 Nov. 1996).
14. CPT. Mark A. Viney, notes, 3 Nov. 1996.
15. Brian Kappmeyer, "Second Brigade Hands-Off Mission," *Talon* 22 Nov. 1996: 3.
16. Ibid.
17. Ibid.
18. Ibid.
19. Vince Crawley, "Bosnian Mission Is Done for 1st and 2nd Brigades," *Stars and Stripes* 4 Nov. 1996: 6.

20. Ibid.

21. Harriman, 3 Nov. 1996.

22. Ibid.

23. Ibid.

24. CPT. Mark A. Viney, notes, 4 Nov. 1996.

25. Jeffrey Smith, "Nash Lauded for Role Leading Peace Force," *Stars and Stripes* 2 Nov. 1996: A1.

26. Tracy Wilkinson, "New Bosnia Forces Get Peacekeeping Initiation; Changing of Guard Tests Soldiers' Resolve," *Stars and Stripes* 27 Nov. 1996: 5.

27. Jeffrey Smith, 2 Nov. 1996.

28. Wilkinson, 27 Nov. 1996.

29. Jeffrey Smith, 2 Nov. 1996.

30. Wilkinson, 27 Nov. 1996.

31. CPT. Mark A. Viney, notes, 14 Nov. 1996.

32. Major Robert Elias, interview with Mark Viney, 15 October 1996, Banovici, Bosnia.

33. CPT. Mark A. Viney, notes, 1 Nov. 1996.

34. United States Army, 1st Squadron, 4th U.S. Cavalry, *Memorandum: Historical Overview of B/1-4 Cavalry in Bosnia*, 23 Jan. 1997.

35. Ibid.

36. Donna Peterson, "Bosnia: A Once-in-a-Lifetime Opportunity," *Army Times* 14 Oct. 1996: 8.

37. CPT. Mark A. Viney, notes, 23 Sept. 1996.

38. Kevin Dougherty, "Elections May Delay Troops' Exit," *Stars and Stripes* 22 Sept. 1996: A1.

39. Dixon, 19 Oct. 1996.

40. Jack Siemienic, "Cavalry Remembers Apache Trooper," *Talon* 1 Nov. 1996: 9.

41. Aaron Reed, *Talon* 18 Oct. 1996.

42. Ibid.

43. Ibid.

44. Department of Defense (Health Affairs), "All U.S. Personnel Redeploying Need Medical Screening," *Talon* 26 July 1996: 9.

45. United States Army, 1st Squadron, 4th U.S. Cavalry, *Memorandum: Historical Overview of B/1-4 Cavalry in Bosnia*, 23 Jan. 1997.

46. CPT. Mark A. Viney, notes, 21 Nov. 1996.

47. Kara Hill, "1/4 Is Not Forgotten," *Stars and Stripes* 3 Dec. 1996: 14.

48. Ibid.

49. J.P. Barham, "Helicopter Scouts, Engineers Return to Germany," *Stars and Stripes* 23 Nov. 1996: 4.

50. Ibid.

51. CPT. Mark A. Viney, notes, 14 Dec. 1996.

52. LTC. Anthony W. Harriman, *Crosstalk* 2.16 (15 Dec. 1996).

53. Ibid.

## *Chapter 14*

1. United States Army, 1st Squadron, 4th U.S. Cavalry, *Memorandum: Annual Historical Report (1997)*, 15 Apr. 1998.

2. LTC. Anthony W. Harriman, *Crosstalk* 3.1 (3 Feb. 1997).

3. Ibid.

4. United States Army, 1st Squadron, 4th U.S. Cavalry, *Brochure: Quarterhorse Welcome Home Ceremony*, 13 Feb. 1997.

5. United States Army, 1st Squadron, 4th U.S. Cavalry, *Memorandum: Annual Historical Report (1997)*, 15 Apr. 1998.

6. Viney, 14 Dec. 1996.

7. MAJ. Robert Elias, notes, 7 Nov. 1996.

8. United States Army, 1st Squadron, 4th U.S. Cavalry, *Memorandum: Annual Historical Report (1997)*, 15 Apr. 1998.

9. Ibid.

10. Ibid.

11. Ibid.

12. Ibid.

13. Ibid.

14. Ibid.

15. Ibid.

16. Ibid.
17. Ibid.
18. Ibid.
19. Ibid.
20. Ibid.
21. Ibid.
22. Ibid.

## Conclusion

1. "The Army as of June 4," *Army Times* 16 June 2008: 7.
2. United States Army, Task Force Eagle, *FRAGO 136, Commander's Intent*, 7 Jan. 1996. [Secret] Information extracted is unclassified.
3. United States Army. *Pamphlet 385-1, Small Unit Safety Officer/NCO Guide*. 21 Nov. 2001.
4. Staff Sergeant Christopher Stone, interview with Mark Viney, 3 February 2000, Fort Bragg, NC.
5. Command Sergeant Major John Fortune, interview with Mark Viney, 25 August 2000, Fort Stewart, GA.
6. Brian Kappmeyer, "Second Brigade Hands-Off Mission," *Talon* 22 Nov. 1996: 3.
7. Robert F. Baumann, George Gawrych, and Walter Kretchik, *Armed Peacekeepers in Bosnia* (Fort Leavenworth, KS: Combat Studies Institute Press, 2004), 76–84.
8. John Pomfret, "Perry Says NATO Will Not Serve as 'Police Force' in Bosnia Mission," *Washington Post* 3 Jan. 1996.
9. John Pomfret, "U.S. Official Visits Bosnian Site of 'Sheer Murder,'" *Washington Post* 21 Jan. 1996: A1.
10. Neil MacDonald, "UK and U.S. Saw Through Karadzic Disguise," *Financial Times* 23 July 2008: 1.
11. Baumann, 196–197.
12. CPT. Mark A. Viney, notes, Sept. 1998.
13. CSM. John Fortune, email to Mark Viney, 21 Aug. 2008.
14. MAJ. John Clearwater, email to Mark Viney, 4 Apr. 2000.
15. GEN. George Casey, conversation with Mark Viney, 16 June 2009.
16. John Batiste, "Commander's Comments," *Iron Brigade* 10 Aug. 1996: 2.

# BIBLIOGRAPHY

## Oral Resources

Bartlett, Jim. "Yugoslav Civil War Information Briefing to 1-4 CAV Officers," Kalesija, Bosnia, 21 May 1996.

Boal, First Lieutenant Matt. Interview with Mark Viney, Oct. 1996, Kalesija, Bosnia.

Brunson, Captain Kerry. Interview with Mark Viney, Sept. 1996, Banovici, Bosnia.

Dirisio, Captain Jim. Interview with Mark Viney, 30 Sept. 1996, Kalesija, Bosnia.

Downey, Captain Scott. Interviews with Mark Viney, Jul. 1996 and Sept. 1996, Kalesija, Bosnia.

Elias, Major Robert. Interview with Mark Viney, 15 Oct. 1996, Banovici, Bosnia.

Erron, Captain Jeff. Interview with Mark Viney, Oct. 1996, Kalesija, Bosnia.

Fortune, Command Sergeant Major John. Interview with Mark Viney, 25 Aug. 2000, Fort Stewart, GA.

Iacono, Sergeant First Class John. Interview with Mark Viney, June 1997, Schweinfurt, Germany.

Ivy, Captain Robert. Interview with Mark Viney, Aug. 1996, Kalesija, Bosnia.

Lisowski, Captain Mike. Interview with Mark Viney, Sept. 1996, Banovici, Bosnia.

McFadden, Captain Brian. Interviews with Mark Viney, 25 Sept. 1996, 30 Sept. 1996, and Nov. 1996, Banovici, Bosnia.

Michaelis, First Lieutenant Pat. Interviews with Mark Viney, June 1996 and Sept. 1996, Kalesija, Bosnia.

Mock, First Lieutenant Matt. Interview with Mark Viney, Sept. 1996, Visca, Bosnia.

Roberts, Major Bryan. Interview with Mark Viney, May 1996, Kalesija, Bosnia.

Rutherford, First Lieutenant Scott. Interviews with Mark Viney, 17 May 1996 and 19 May 1996, Visca, Bosnia.

Shaw, Captain Semuel. Interview with Mark Viney, Oct. 1996, Banovici, Bosnia.

Spiegel, Captain Richard. Interviews with Mark Viney, 8 Feb. 1996 and Mar. 1996, Schweinfurt, Germany.

Stevens, Captain Gary. Interview with Mark Viney, Sept. 1996, Banovici, Bosnia.

Stone, Staff Sergeant Christopher. Interview with Mark Viney, 3 Feb. 2000, Fort Bragg, NC.

Viney, Colonel George C. Discussion with Mark Viney, 30 Apr. 2007, San Antonio, TX.

Viney, Lieutenant Colonel George S. Discussion with Mark Viney, 25 Nov. 2007, Carlisle, PA.

Wren, Private First Class Kyle. Interview with Mark Viney, May 1997, Schweinfurt, Germany.

## *Official Documents*

Department of Defense. *DOD-1540-16-96, Bosnia Country Handbook, Peace Implementation Force (IFOR).* Dec. 1995.

North Atlantic Treaty Organization. Allied Rapid Reaction Corps. *Memorandum: COMARRC's Message to Commanders and Troops.* 14 Sept. 1996. [Unclassified]

United States Army. *Field Manual 1-02, Operational Terms and Symbols.* 21 Sept. 2004.

_____. *Field Manual 3-0, Operations.* Feb. 2008.

_____. *Field Manual 3-07, Stability Operations.* Oct. 2008.

_____. *Pamphlet 385-1, Small Unit Safety Officer/NCO Guide.* 29 Nov. 2001.

United States Army. Center for Army Lessons Learned. *Newsletter No. 98-6, Fighting the Mine War in Bosnia; Techniques, Tactics and Procedures.* Mar. 1998.

United States Army. 1st Squadron, 4th U.S. Cavalry. *BiH Election Day Primer.* Sept. 1996. [Unclassified]

_____. *Brochure: Quarterhorse Welcome Home Ceremony.* 13 Feb. 1997. [Unclassified]

_____. *Command Training Guidance, 3rd & 4th QTRs, FY 96.* Apr. 1996. [Unclassified]

_____. *Draft Narrative for the Superior Unit Award.* Nov. 1996. [Unclassified]

_____. *Memorandum: Annual Historical Report (1997).* 15 Apr. 1998. [Unclassified]

_____. *Memorandum: Historical Overview of B/1-4 Cavalry in Bosnia.* 23 Jan. 1997. [Unclassified]

_____. *Memorandum: Troop History October 95–April 96; C Troop, 1-4 CAV.* May 1996. [Unclassified]

_____. *Squadron Events Calendar (Coordination Draft), 3 NOV 96–12 JUL 97.* 8 Nov. 1996. [Unclassified]

_____. *Unit History: Bravo Troop, 1-4 CAV.* May 1996. [Unclassified]

_____. *Unit History: 1st Platoon, Bravo Troop, 1-4 CAV.* May 1996. [Unclassified]

_____. *Unit History: Mortar Platoon, Bravo Troop, 1-4 CAV.* May 1996. [Unclassified]

_____. *Unit History: 2nd Platoon, Bravo Troop, 1-4 CAV.* May 1996. [Unclassified]

_____. *Unit History: 3rd Platoon, Bravo Troop, 1-4 CAV.* May 1996. [Unclassified]

United States Army. Headquarters, Department of the Army. *Field Manual 101-5-1, Operational Terms and Symbols.* Oct. 1985.

United States Army. Headquarters, USAREUR (Forward). *FRAGO # 430, Redeployment of 1st Bn, 4th CAV.* 5 Nov. 1996. [Unclassified]

United States Army. 2nd Brigade Combat Team, 1st Armored Division. *Execution Matrix, OPORD 96-2 (Iron Warrior I).* 11 Oct. 1995. [Unclassified]

_____. *FRAGO 04 to 2BCT OPORD 96-10 (Tank Endeavor).* 22 Dec. 1995. [Unclassified]

_____. *Mission Analysis, 2/1 AD, OPORD 96-2.* 11 Oct. 1995. [Unclassified]

United States Army. Task Force Eagle. *FRAGO 136, Commander's Intent.* 7 Jan. 1996. [Unclassified]

_____. *Seven Day Redeployment Schedule.* Oct. 1996. [Unclassified]

United States Army. 3rd Squadron, 4th U.S. Cavalry. *Annex Q (Service Support) to 3-4 CAV OPORD 96-21.* Dec. 1995. [Unclassified]

_____. *Briefing Packet: OH-58D(I) Kiowa Warrior OPD/NCOPD.* Dec.1996. [Unclassified]

_____. *Memorandum: Assumption of Command Authority.* 20 Oct. 1995. [Unclassified]

_____. *Memorandum: Planes, Trains, and Automobiles.* 28 Dec. 1995. [Unclassified]

_____. *Memorandum: 3-4 CAV Deployment Departure Schedule.* 28 Dec. 1995. [Unclassified]

_____. *Narrative for Award Recommendation for CPL Francisco J. Alcantar.* Feb. 1996. [Unclassified]

_____. *Narrative for Award Recommendation for CPL Herbert H. Gadsden.* Feb. 1996. [Unclassified]

_____. *Narrative for Award Recommendation for PFC Kyle A. Wren*. Feb. 1996. [Unclassified]

_____. *Narrative for Award Recommendation for SPC Michael D. Grayson*. Feb. 1996. [Unclassified]

_____. *OPORD 95-18, SABER SHOT GTA, 8–21 NOV 95*. 6 Oct. 1995. [Unclassified]

_____. *Proposed Citation for Award Recommendation for CPL Francisco J. Alcantar* . Feb. 1996. [Unclassified]

_____. *Proposed Citation for Award Recommendation for CPL Herbert H. Gadsden*. Feb. 1996. [Unclassified]

_____. *Proposed Citation for Award Recommendation for PFC Kyle A. Wren*. Feb. 1996. [Unclassified]

_____. *Proposed Citation for Award Recommendation for SPC Michael D. Grayson*. Feb. 1996. [Unclassified]

_____. *Stability Operations TACSOP, 3-4 CAV TACSOP Supplement*. Jan. 1996. [Unclassified]

_____. *3-4 CAV OPLAN 95-15 (Ready Sabres)*. 24 Nov. 1995. [Unclassified]

_____. *3-4 CAV OPORD 95-14 (Empty Stables)*. 7 Dec. 1995. [Unclassified]

## Commercial Periodicals

"Again, West Threatens Serbs, Backs Off." *St. Petersburg Times* 2 July 1996: 2A.

"The Army as of 4 June." *Army Times* 16 June 2008: 7.

Associated Press. "Bosnia Elections; Facts About Today's Vote." *Stars and Stripes* 14 Sept. 1996: A1.

_____. "Bosnia Refugees Kept from Homes." *St. Petersburg Times* 19 May 1996.

_____. "Bosnians Seek Food Among the Scraps from U.S. Troops." *St. Petersburg Times* 27 May 1996: 2A.

_____. "NATO Says Ammo, Not Mine, Killed U.S. Sergeant in Bosnia." *Washington Post* 5 Feb. 1996.

_____. "Serbs Offer War Crimes Charges Against Bosnia's Izetbegovic." *Stars and Stripes* 13 Sept. 1996: A1.

_____. "Turnout Reflects Ethnic Split; Cross-Boundary Traffic Lower Than Hoped For." *Stars and Stripes* 17 Sept. 1996: A1.

_____. "U.S. Tells Bosnia to Throw Out Muslim Fighters." *Stars and Stripes* 14 Sept. 1996: 5.

Atkinson, Rick. "'The Big Question Mark' in Bosnia; General: 'Follow-On Organization' Will Need to Replace NATO Force." *Washington Post* 7 Jan. 1996.

_____. "Bosnia Force Testing New Russian-U.S. Ties; Troops Get Along; Americans Wary of General." *Washington Post* 18 Jan. 1996: A15.

_____. "Bosnia Pullback on Time, But Prisoner Release Lags." *Washington Post* 19 Jan. 1996: A1.

_____. "Call It Camp Swampy; At Base in Northern Bosnia, First Enemy Is Mud." *Washington Post* 11 Jan. 1996.

_____. "4 Swedes Injured by Bosnian Mine." *Washington Post* 14 Jan. 1996.

_____. "Serbs Detain Croat Soldiers; Faction Generals Snub Nash." *Washington Post* 12 Jan. 1996: A22.

_____. "U.S. Cautious on Opening Roads to Area of Reported Massacres." *Washington Post* 3 Jan. 1996: A17.

_____. "U.S. Paratroops, Serb Soldiers Make Nice in Bosnian Town." *Washington Post* 5 Jan. 1996.

_____. "Warriors Without a War; U.S. Peacekeepers in Bosnia Adjusting to New Tasks: Arbitration, Bluff, Restraint." *Washington Post* 14 Apr. 1996: A1.

Atkinson, Rick, and Christine Spolar. "Army Opens River Bridge; Tanks Cross, U.S. Armored Forces Begin Occupying Bosnian Sector." *Washington Post* 1 Jan. 1996: A1.

_____. "A Riverbank Too Far: The Sava Stalls Army Again." *Washington Post* 31 Dec. 1995: A24.

Baker, Charles A. "Americans Brought Back to Reality." *St. Petersburg Times* 1 Sept. 1996: 24A.

_____. "Springtime Brings Blooms to Bosnia." *St. Petersburg Times* 19 May 1996: 18A.

Barham, J.P. "Covering-Force Unit Is Ready, General Says." *Stars and Stripes* 11 Oct. 1996: 4.

_____. "Helicopter Scouts, Engineers Return to Germany." *Stars and Stripes* 23 Nov. 1996: 4.

_____. "On the Borderline; GIs Patrol Disputed Macedonian Border." *Stars and Stripes* 15 Sept. 1996: 1.

_____. "Soldiers Help Keep the Peace in Tense Region." *Stars and Stripes* 15 Sept. 1996: 5.

Barry, Colleen. "U.S. Tanks Keep Bosnia Town Quiet." *Stars and Stripes* 1 Sept. 1996: 1.

Bathen, Effie. "Standoff Ends Peacefully; Threats Spawned Tension Near Mladic's Base." *Stars and Stripes* 8 July 1996: A1.

_____. "A Time for Hope; Bosnian Elections Another Step Toward the End of Despair." *Stars and Stripes* 14 Sept. 1996: 17.

Bell Helicopter. "Consider This Warrior Prepared for Anything, Anytime." *Army.* Mar. 1996.

Blakeman, Karen. "Armed Men Surrender to Troops." *Stars and Stripes* 12 May 1996: A1.

_____. "Bosnia Tallies Still Fuzzy; But Local Voting to Start Nov. 22." *Stars and Stripes* 22 Sept. 1996: A1.

_____. "Freed Jusici Prisoners Were Beaten by Captors." *Stars and Stripes* 13 Oct. 1996: A1.

_____. "Izetbegovic Declared Victor; Krajisnik, Zubak Join Muslim on Three-Member Presidency." *Stars and Stripes* 19 Sept. 1996: A1.

_____. "Jusici's War Refugees Return Home to Stay." *Stars and Stripes* 8 Oct. 1996: A1.

_____. "Most Refugees Choose to Side with Their Side." *Stars and Stripes* 14 Sept. 1996: A1.

_____. "Possible Survivors Turn Up; One Group Causes Problems for IFOR." *Stars and Stripes* 4/5 July 1996: A1.

_____. "Serbs Back Out of Pact on Joint Police Patrols." *Stars and Stripes* 11 Oct. 1996: A1.

Bowers, Brian. "Civil Affairs Is a Real Family Business." *Stars and Stripes* 30 Sept. 1996: 4.

_____. "IFOR Pushes For Muslims to Leave Town." *Stars and Stripes* 25 Sept. 1996: 2.

_____. "IFOR Takes Weapons from Muslims." *Stars and Stripes* 23 Sept. 1996: 2.

_____. "Troops Healthier by the Numbers; Restrictions Work to Reduce Illness." *Stars and Stripes* 22 Sept. 1996: 5.

_____. "Troops Work to Organize Polling Sites." *Stars and Stripes* 11 Sept. 1996: A1.

Bowers, Brian, and Kevin Dougherty. "U.S. Gets Its Wish: A Dull Day." *Stars and Stripes* 15 Sept. 1996: A1.

Brown, Tawanna. "Camp's New Name Honors Big Red One Veteran." *Talon* 22 Nov. 1996: 8.

Carl, Susan M. "A Little Teamwork, a Taste for Camo Part of Family Day." *Stars and Stripes* 2 June 1996: 3.

Carter, Rudy. "R&R to Slow as Soldiers Redeploy; Last Trips Likely to Go in October." *Stars and Stripes* 21 Aug. 1996: A1.

_____. "3 Crashes Later, Marines Settling In; Remote-Controlled Aircraft Do the Job." *Stars and Stripes* 1 Sept. 1996: 4.

Compart, Andrew. "Will We or Won't We? Administration Still Waffling on Bosnia Pullout Date." *Army Times* 14 Oct. 1996: 40.

Crawley, Vince. "Bosnia Vote Delayed; Effect on Pullout of U.S. Unknown." *Stars and Stripes* 23 Oct. 1996: A1.

_____. "Bosnian Mission Is Done for 1st and 2nd Brigades." *Stars and Stripes* 4 Nov. 1996: 6.

_____. "House Bombs Echo of Past; Villagers Blaming the Bosnian Serbs." *Stars and Stripes* 14 Oct. 1996: A1.

_____. "IFOR Raid of Village Fails to Find Weapons." *Stars and Stripes* 1 Nov. 1996: 5.

Crawley, Vince. "NATO Won't Hurry Cutback of IFOR in Wake of Election." *Stars and Stripes* 19 Sept. 1996: A1.

_____. "Vote Woes Won't Slow Pullout, Officials Say." *Stars and Stripes* 24 Oct. 1996: A1.

Crocker, Chester A., and Fen Osler Hampson. "How to Hold the Peace; Bosnia Can't Afford Any Allied Squabbling, Buck-Passing or Flinching." *Washington Post* 21 Jan. 1996: C2.

Cumbee, James M. "Spurs Are an Honor." *Stars and Stripes* 3 Dec. 1996: 14.

Dobbs, Michael. "U.S. Threatens to Withhold Aid to Bosnian Government." *Washington Post* 24 Jan. 1996: A24.

Dougherty, Kevin. "Bosnia Bases Draw Names from Variety of Sources." *Stars and Stripes* 21 Feb. 1996: 19.

_____. "Brown Crash Report Nearly Done; AF Board Expects to Release Probe Results by Mid-June." *Stars and Stripes* 22 May 1996: 3.

_____. "A Day of Trust, Anxiety and Destiny." *Stars and Stripes* 14 Sept. 1996: A1.

_____. "Elections May Delay Troops' Exit." *Stars and Stripes* 22 Sept. 1996: A1.

_____. "Traffic Could Snarl Vote; Displaced Bosnians to Put Freedom of Movement to the Test." *Stars and Stripes* 14 Sept. 1996: A1.

_____. "Tuzla Still Counting — and All Is Well." *Stars and Stripes* 17 Sept. 1996: 5.

Geitner, Paul. "A Gal Leads the 'Red Horse Guys.'" *Washington Times* Jan. 1996.

_____. "Muslim Goes Free at Last; Ex-Suspect Alleges Beating by Serbs." *Stars and Stripes* 16 Aug. 1996: A1.

_____. "Put on a Happy Face, Troops Told." *Washington Times* 30 Jan. 1996.

_____. "Serbs Spotted in U.S. Army Garb." *Washington Times* 15–21 Jan. 1996: 12.

"GIs in Bosnia Welcome Clinton as Commander Visiting Troops." *Washington Post* 12 Jan. 1996: A22.

Goshko, John M. "Security Council Presses Croatia to Stop Atrocities Against Serbs; Statement Issued with Little Fanfare During Snowstorm Shutdown." *Washington Post* 9 Jan. 1996: A13.

_____. "Tribunal Wants 2 Serb Military Figures Detained." *Washington Post* 7 Feb. 1996.

_____. "U.N. Answers Critics of Policing Effort in Bosnia; Spokeswoman Says Countries Broke Promises to Provide Trained Personnel." *Washington Post* 5 Feb. 1996.

Graham, Bradley. "Funding Proposal Altered for Bosnia Deployment; Agreement Reached on Revised Defense Bill." *Washington Post* 20 Jan. 1996: A4.

_____. "NATO Commander in Bosnia Concerned About Police Force; Smith Says International Deployment Too Small for Job." *Washington Post* 2 Feb. 1996: A24.

_____. "U.S. Plans to Monitor Alleged Serb Burial Pit; NATO Allies Won't Stop Moving of Remains." *Washington Post* 12 Jan. 1996: A22.

Griffith, Stephanie. "U.S. Asks NATO Allies to Back Bosnian Arms, Training Plan." *Stars and Stripes* 1 Nov. 1996: 5.

Gross, Richard C. "The U.S. Is 'Not Playing,' with Its Show of Force." *Washington Times* 1–7 Jan. 1996: 8.

_____. "U.S. Takes Care in Deployment to Prevent Casualties." *Washington Times* 1–7 Jan. 1996: 8.

Hampsten, Christina D. "Teamwork Goes Far." *Stars and Stripes* 6 Oct. 1996: 16.

Hill, James R. "Been There, Done That." *Stars and Stripes* 29 Oct. 1996: 18.

Hill, Kara. "1/4 Is Not Forgotten." *Stars and Stripes* 3 Dec. 1996: 14.

Hjelm, David. "Enlisted Overlooked." *Stars and Stripes* 2 Nov. 1996: 12.

Hudson, Neff. "Concerns Over Security and Access Limit Use of E-Mail." *Army Times*. 19 Feb. 1996: 10.

Hunter, Duncan. "The Commitment in Bosnia: One Year or Five Years?" Publication unknown. 6 Jan. 1996.

Jensen, Ron. "IFOR Election Watchers 'Beginning to Exhale'; Moderate Turnout Brings Few Problems." *Stars and Stripes* 15 Sept. 1996: A1.

_____. "IFOR Facing Tough Election Choice." *Stars and Stripes* 13 Sept. 1996: 4.

_____. "Italian Engineer Unit Making Tracks on Rail Line." *Stars and Stripes* 1 Sept. 1996: 4.

_____. "NATO Wants No Excuse on Vote; Alliance to Ensure Officials Know Rules." *Stars and Stripes* 20 Aug. 1996: A1.

_____. "Ready or Not, Bosnia Gets Ready to Vote." *Stars and Stripes* 13 Sept. 1996: A1.

Kempster, Norman. "What Clinton Hopes the Voting Will Bring." *Stars and Stripes* 15 Sept. 1996: 5.

Landrey, Wilbur G. "Bosnian Elections Pass in Relative Calm." *St. Petersburg Times* 15 Sept. 1996: 1A.

_____. "Good Luck, Sarajevo; You'll Need It." *St. Petersburg Times* 20 Sept. 1996: 2A.

Long, Michael. "Proud of Our Work." *Stars and Stripes* 30 Oct. 1996: 12.

MacDonald, Neil. "UK and U.S. Saw Through Karadzic Disguise." *Financial Times* 23 July 2008:1.

McDowell, Liam. "10,000 Troops Quietly Leave Bosnia." *Stars and Stripes* 12 May 1996: 4.

"Many Plan on Leaving Freed Town." *Washington Post* 5 Jan. 1996: A24.

Merideth, Jerry. "Troops at Observation Post Understand Their Limitations." *Stars and Stripes* 14 June 1996: 4.

"Muslims Turned in by NATO Tortured." *St. Petersburg Times* 24 May 1996: 10A.

Myers, Steven L. "Group Criticizes War Crimes Progress." *Stars and Stripes* 27 Nov. 1996: 5.

Najarian, Mark. "Fallen Soldier Hailed as 'Unsung Hero.'" *Stars and Stripes* 24 Oct. 1996: A1.

Nash, William L. "NATO, Bosnia, and the Future." *NATO at Fifty.* Date unknown: 137–142.

_____. "The Year of Living Creatively, Reflections on the Army's First Year in Bosnia." *Armed Forces Journal International* Nov. 1997: 38–43.

Naylor, Sean D. "Bosnia Death Is Probed; First Mission Fatality Caused by Explosion, Possibly of a Mine." *Army Times* 19 Feb. 1996: 8.

_____. "Troops to Cover Bosnia Withdrawal." *Army Times* 9 Sept. 1996: 8.

Nelson, Soraya S. "Dust in the Wind — and on the Troops." *Army Times* 19 Feb. 1996: 10.

Palumbo, Sue. "IFOR Carefully Defines Role in Elections." *Stars and Stripes* 24 Aug. 1996: 4.

_____. "Unit Moving on Out — and Heading Home." *Stars and Stripes* 16 Aug. 1996: A1, 6.

Peterson, Donna. "Bosnia: A Once-in-a-Lifetime Opportunity." *Army Times* 14 Oct. 1996: 8.

Pomfret, John. "After 'Ethnic Cleansing,' Srebrenica Is a Wasteland of Garbage." *Washington Post* 16 Jan. 1996: A1.

_____. "Aid to Bosnia Is Hit-and-Miss." *Stars and Stripes* 14 Oct. 1996: A1.

_____. "Arming The Bosnians; U.S. Program Would Aid Force Increasingly Linked to Iran." *Washington Post* 25 Jan. 1996: A1.

_____. "A Bosnian Tale of Love and Death; In Still Divided City of Mostar, Crossing the Line Can Prove Fatal." *Washington Post* 2 Jan. 1996.

_____. "Few Bosnian Refugees Returning; Only 1 of 4 Towns Fulfills Pilot Project for Muslim-Croat Exchanges." *Washington Post* 28 Jan. 1996.

_____. "Grim Evidence Points to Muslims' Graves." *Washington Post* Jan. 1996.

_____. "Islamic Fighters Defy Dayton Accord; U.S. Army Views Mujahadeen Who Refuse to Leave Bosnia as 'Passive Threat' to Peacekeepers." *Washington Post* 15 Jan. 1996.

_____. "NATO, Prosecutor Debate Bosnia Aims; Peace Force Commander, S. African Jurist Discuss Troops' Role in War Crimes Probe." *Washington Post* 22 Jan. 1996.

_____. "NATO Troops in Bosnia Fire at Sniper Who Wounded Italian Soldier." *Washington Post* 6 Jan. 1996: A22.

_____. "Peace Between Friends; Kaffeeklatsch Meetings May Defuse Sarajevo Crisis." *Washington Post* 14 Jan. 1996.

_____. "Perry Says NATO Will Not Serve as 'Police Force' in Bosnia Mission." *Washington Post* 3 Jan. 1996.

_____. "Police Force Slow to Deploy Around Sarajevo; Absence Worries Residents of Serb-Held Suburbs as Troop Pullout Deadline Nears." *Washington Post* 30 Jan. 1996.

_____. "Political, Civilian Efforts Off to Slow Start in Bosnia." *Washington Post* 31 Dec. 1995: A25.

_____. "Sarajevo Acts to Boost Party, Silence Dissent; Some Government Steps Violate Dayton Accord." *Washington Post* 31 Jan. 1996.

_____. "Serbs Release 16 Civilians Held for 10 Days." *Washington Post* 5 Jan. 1996: A24.

_____. "Tensions High in 2 Bosnian Cities; NATO Forces Respond to Shooting Incidents in Mostar, Sanski Most." *Washington Post* 6 Jan. 1996: A24.

_____. "3 Britons, Swede Die in Bosnia Accidents; Apparent Sniper Bullet Grazes U.S. Lieutenant Near Sarajevo." *Washington Post* 28 Jan. 1996.

_____. "U.S. Official Visits Bosnian Site of 'Sheer Murder.'" *Washington Post* 21 Jan. 1996: A1.

_____. "U.S. Planes Help Disarm Bosnian Unit; French NATO Troops Kill a Serb Sniper." *Washington Post* 1 Feb. 1996.

Priest, Dana. "Mladic Orders Serbs to Cut NATO Contacts." *Washington Post* 9 Feb. 1996: A24.

_____. "U.S. May Send $100 Million in Arms, Equipment to Bosnia." *Washington Post* Mar. 1996.

"Reflagging Plan." *Army Times* July 1995.

Sammon, Bill. "The Hate Hangs on in Bosnia; 'Long Way to Go' Before Peace Arrives." *Stars and Stripes* 23 June 1996: A1.

_____. "Troops in Bosnia Get Rare Taste of Home — Vegas-Style Showgirls." *Stars and Stripes* 6 June 1996: 4.

_____. "U.S. Army Medics Rush to Bosnian Boy's Rescue." *Stars and Stripes* 6 June 1996: A1.

Scarborough, Rowan. "GIs Get High-Tech Weather Protection." *Washington Times* 1–7 Jan. 1996: 8.

Smith, Caroline. "Tank Movement Over Bridge to Bosnia Slows; Army Crossings Delayed to Avoid Traffic Jams; Just-Completed Span Needs Repairs." *Washington Post* 1 Jan. 1996.

Smith, Jeffrey. "High-Tech Cooperation in Bosnia." *Washington Post* 19 Jan. 1996: A30.

_____. "Nash Lauded for Role Leading Peace Force." *Stars and Stripes* 2 Nov. 1996: A1.

Smith, Jeffrey, and Sally Roberts. "Bosnian Man Dies in Fight; Serbs, Muslims Battle Along Zone of Separation." *Stars and Stripes* 13 Nov. 1996: A1.

"Some Troops May Stay; U.S. Could be Part of Multinational Force After Current Troops Leave. Some See It as the Only Way to Keep Peace." *St. Petersburg Times* 1 Sept. 1996: 24A.

Steele, Dennis. "Bosnia Update." *Army*. Mar. 1996: 39–42.

Sullivan, Stacy. "Serb Forces Cut Contacts with NATO; General's Order Retaliates for Arrest of 8 Soldiers." *Washington Post* 9 Feb. 1996: A23.

_____. "Serbs Fire on Streetcar in Sarajevo." *Washington Post* 9 Jan. 1996.

Tigner, Brooks. "NATO Plans for Follow-on Force in Bosnia." *Army Times* 14 Oct. 1996: 40.

Tillman, Doyle. "American Troops Doing Time at a Very Different Alcatraz." *Stars and Stripes* 9 June 1996: 3.

"U.S. Aiding Bosnian Force Linked to Iran." *Washington Post* 26 Jan. 1996: A28.

Verberne, Alice. "Troop Strength; 1st Armored Division; 1st Infantry Division." *Stars and Stripes* 24 Oct. 1996: A1.

"Where the Troops Are." *Stars and Stripes* 21 Feb. 1996: 20–21.

"Where the Troops Are." *Stars and Stripes* 13 Mar. 1996: 18–19.

Wilkinson, Tracy. "New Bosnia Forces Get Peacekeeping Initiation; Changing of Guard Tests Soldiers' Resolve." *Stars and Stripes* 27 Nov. 1996: 5.

Zachmeier, Kathy. "New Mission, Fewer Camps." *Stars and Stripes* 22 Dec. 1996: 20–21.

## *Official Periodicals*

Batiste, John. "Commander's Comments." *Iron Brigade* 11 May 1996: 2; 29 June 1996: 2; 20 July 1996: 2; 31 July 1996: 2; 10 Aug. 1996: 2; Sept. 1996: 2; 19 Oct. 1996: 2.

"Battalion News." *Iron Brigade* 11 May 1996: 3; 30 May 1996: 3; 15 June 1996: 3; 29 June 1996: 3; 20 July 1996: 3; 31 July 1996: 3; 10 Aug. 1996: 3; 28 Sept. 1996: 3; 19 Oct. 1996: 3.

Butler, Len. "Jusici." *Talon* 11 Oct. 1996: 6–7.

_____. "Thunder Rocks Resolute Barbara Range." *Talon* 9 Aug. 1996: 6–7.

"Casey Joins Task Force Team." *Talon* 2 Aug. 1996: 3.

Conder, Terry L. "Big Red One Moves Downrange; Redeployment Starts as 1st ID Heads South to Cover Old Ironsides' Withdrawal." *Talon* 11 Oct. 1996: 1.

_____. "Bosnian Serb Threats to be Met with Swift Military Action." *Talon* 26 July 1996: 1.

Department of Defense (Health Affairs). "All U.S. Personnel Redeploying Need Medical Screening." *Talon* 26 July 1996: 9.

Fischer, Kelly C., and William Hall. "Tuzla Railroad Rides Again." *Talon* 10 May 1996: 5.

Frowick, Robert H. "Municipal Elections to Proceed." *Talon* 11 Oct. 1996: 1.

Garamone, Jim. "Elections Key to Troop Departure From Bosnia." *Talon* 17 May 1996: 1.

Garrison, Joseph. "Boot Camp Buddies Continue Friendship in Bosnia." *Talon* 17 May 1996: 10.

Harriman, Anthony W. *Crosstalk* 1.3 (9 Dec. 1995); 1.4 (26 Dec. 1995); 2.2 (30 Jan. 1996); 2.3 (10 Feb. 1996); 2.4 (22 Feb. 1996); 2.5 (25 Mar. 1996); 2.6 (3 Apr. 1996); 2.7 (20 Apr. 1996); 2.8 (10 May 1996); 2.9 (27 May 1996); 2.10 (2 July 1996); 2.11 (26 July 1996); 2.12 (3 Sept. 1996); 2.13 (15 Sept. 1996); 2.14 (2 Oct. 1996); 2.15 (3 Nov. 1996); 2.16 (15 Dec. 1996); 3.1 (3 Feb. 1997); Farewell Edition (10 Oct. 1997).

_____. "LTC Harriman's Musings." *Crossed Sabers* Aug. 1996: 3.

Haverinen, Rick. "Cavalry Soldiers Settle in Balkans." *Marneland Crusader* 22 Mar. 1996: 6.

_____. "Families Are Well Cared for by Rear Detachment Soldiers." *Marneland Crusader* 22 Mar. 1996: 6.

Ivy, Robert G. "Mobs, Refugees, and Armor: Tactics, Techniques, and Procedures." *Armor* Sept.-Oct. 2000: 16–17.

Johnsen, William T. "U.S. Participation in IFOR: A Marathon, Not a Sprint" *Strategic Studies Institute Report* 20 June 1996.

Johnson, Fred W. "Establishing a Zone of Separation." *Infantry* May-June 1996: 31.

Johnston, Jody. "1-4 Cav Troopers Shoot, Qualify on Hungary Range." *Iron Brigade* 11 May 1996: 1.

Kamisugi, Lance M. "Redeployment; Grizzly Tactical Operation Center First Stop on Route Home." *Talon* 18 Oct. 1996: 6–7.

Kappmeyer, Brian. "Second Brigade Hands-Off Mission." *Talon* 22 Nov. 1996: 3.

Kerr, Carol. "Army Unveils New Stability Operations Manual." *Banner* 6 Oct. 2008.

Langkamp, Keirya. "Royal Treatment Awaits in Budapest." *Talon* 10 May 1996: 8.

"Leader's Election Dozen; TF Eagle Guidelines for Success." *Talon* 13 Sept. 1996: 11.

McAfee, Kenyon. "Lake Balaton Offers Best of Both Worlds." *Talon* 28 June 1996: 8.

"MWR Slate Features Magic, Music, Mind Games." *Talon* 31 May 1996: 12.

Nash, William L. "Commanding General Supplements General Order No. 1." *Talon* 18 Oct. 1996: 9.

_____. "Troops Make History." *Talon* Sept. 1996.

Lum, Stephen M. "Army Decides Every Medal Has Its Place." *Talon* 18 Oct. 1996: 3.

Paschall, Daniel. "The Force Is with You." *Talon* 26 July 1996: 1.

Pickett, Craig. "Actor Turned Soldier Scores Biggest Role." *Talon* 1996.

_____. "One-Quarter Cav Troopers Reclaim Dutch APCs." *Talon* 1 Nov.1996: 4.

_____. "PSYOPS Campaigns for Peace." *Iron Brigade* 28 Sept. 1996: 1.

Pinkham, Tim. "Hello Big Red One, Goodbye Old Ironsides." *Talon* 1 Nov. 1996: 4.

Reed, Aaron. "Bosnian Federation Army Set to Get Weapons and Training; U.S.-Led Train and Equip Program Not to Involve IFOR Troops." *Talon* 9 Aug. 1996: 1.

Roache, George. "Vests, Convoy Rules Helping Save Lives; Force Protection Rules Are Result of Bloody History Lessons." *Talon* 28 June 1996: 4.

Robinson, Kevin L. "Checkpoint Charlie: Life in Bosnia's Hot Zone." *Talon* 20 Sept. 1996: 4.

Siemienic, Jack. "Cavalry Remembers Apache Trooper." *Talon* 1 Nov.1996: 9.

Soriano, Cesar G. "Entertainers Give Soldiers a Break." *Talon* 14 June 1996: 6.

_____. "Soldiers from the Kansas and North Caroline Army National Guard Are Hard at Work in Bosnia ... Gathering History." *Soldiers* July 1996: 27.

"Standoff Leads to Increased Force Protection Here." *Talon* 16 Aug. 1996: 10.

Summers, Patrick. "IFOR Explains Policy on Indicted War Criminals." *Talon* 26 July 1996: 6–7.

"Task Force Eagle Takes Steps to Meet Heightened Terrorist Threat." *Talon* 16 Aug. 1996: 3.

Tillson, Bettina E. "Congresssmen Visit Troops; Lawmakers Receive 'Firsthand' Look at Balkan Peace Mission." *Talon* 28 June 1996: 3.

21st Theater Army Area Command Chaplain's Office. "Some DOs and DON'Ts for R&R at Home." *Talon* 28 June 1996: 5.

Ward, Colin. "Popular Game Show Looks for Bosnia Soldier-Players." *Iron Brigade* 15 June 1996: 1.

Younger, Gary. "Shalikashvili: America Is Immensely Proud." *Iron Brigade* 11 May 1996: 5.

Zajac, Daniel L. "Operations Update." *Iron Brigade* 30 May 1996: 4; 11 May 1996: 4; 15 June 1996: 4; 29 June 1996: 4; 20 July 1996: 4; 31 July 1996: 4; 10 Aug. 1996: 4; 28 Sept. 1996: 4; 19 Oct. 1996: 4.

## Online Media

Bartlett, Jim. "Boots & Saddles; In Bosnia with the 1st Squadron, 4th Cavalry; Keeping the Lid on the Balkan Pressure Cooker." *Pacific Interactive Media Corporation* 1996. Available from http://jwbartlett.com/index.htm; accessed 1997.

_____. "Boots & Saddles; Part 2: The Scouts; Scouts Up! For'ard Yo!" *Pacific Interactive Media Corporation* 1996. Available from http://jwbartlett.com/index.htm; accessed 1997.

### Unpublished Documents

Clearwater, John. Email to Mark Viney. 4 Apr. 2000.
Cusick, Conor. Notes. Aug. 1996.
Downey, Scott. Letter to Mark Viney. Sept. 1999.
_____. Email to Mark Viney. 25 Mar. 2009.
Elias, Robert. Notes. 7 Nov. 1996.
Fortune,John. Email to Mark Viney. 21 Aug. 2008.
_____. Letter to Mark Viney. 4 July 2001.
Harriman, Anthony W. Letter to Squadron Family Support Group. Feb. 1996.
_____. Notes. 27 July 1996.
_____. Notes. Nov. 1996.
Nash, William L. Notes for Mark Viney. 18 Dec. 2007.
Viney, Mark A. Letter to 4th Cavalry Association. 7 July 1996.
_____. Letter to Lieutenant Colonel (Retired) John A. Seddon. 9 Aug. 1996.
Wells, Christopher D. Letter to CW2 Saevivat. 14 July 1995.

### Books

Baumann, Robert F., George Gawrych, and Walter Kretchik. *Armed Peacekeepers in Bosnia.* Fort Leavenworth, KS: Combat Studies Institute Press, 2004.
Bourque, Stephen A., and John W. Burdan III. *The Road to Safwan: The 1st Squadron, 4th Cavalry in the 1991 Persian Gulf War.* Denton, TX: University of North Texas Press, 2007.
Center of Military History. *Bosnia-Herzegovina: The U.S. Army's Role in Peace Enforcement Operations 1995–2004,* CMH Pub 70-97-1. Washington, D.C.: U.S. Government Printing Office, 2005.
Central Intelligence Agency. *Balkan Battlegrounds: A Military History of the Yugoslav Conflict, 1990–1995, Volume I.* Washington, D.C.: Office of Russian and European Analysis, 2002.
_____. *Balkan Battlegrounds: A Military History of the Yugoslav Conflict, 1990–1995, Volume II.* Washington, D.C.: Office of Russian and European Analysis, 2003.
Wentz, Larry K., editor. *Lessons from Bosnia: The IFOR Experience.* Washington, D.C.: Command and Control Research Program, 1998.

# INDEX